GunDigest® Guide to
MAINTAINING
& ACCESSORIZING
FIREARMS

KEVIN MURAMATSU

Published by

Gun Digest® Books, an imprint of F+W Media, Inc.
Krause Publications • 700 East State Street • Iola, WI 54990-0001
715-445-2214 • 888-457-2873
www.krausebooks.com

To order books or other products call toll-free 1-800-258-0929
or visit us online at www.gundigeststore.com

ISBN-13: 978-1-4402-3989-2
ISBN-10: 1-4402-3989-4

Cover Design by Dane Royer
Designed by Rachael Wolter
Edited by Corrina Peterson

Printed in China

DEDICATION

There is no greater company in the firearms 'verse that deals with accessories than Brownells. There are other great companies in the same vein, and this is not to lessen them, but the Brownells crew has always been easy to work with, with a great selection of parts and tools, and has been generous to writers and the industry alike. The best part is that I can order stuff standard shipping and the doorbell will still ring two days later. The business has survived several generations and I'm sure will continue on through several more. Thank you for the support, folks.

TABLE OF CONTENTS

ACKNOWLEDGEMENTS

The author would like to thank the following people and businesses for their support in creating this book. I was able to borrow, purchase and beg from several of them; others simply gave me stuff.

Larry Weeks from Brownells who got me stuff at the last minute; Brian and Gary from the Wolf's Den Gun Shop for the loan of some stuff, John Paul of JP Enterprises for the loan of some stuff, Doug and Dan from Your Mom's Basement (restaurant and gaming center) who gladly accepted my presence working instead of playing; Jim, Joel, and Adrian, coworkers who lent me some stuff; Pine Technical College School of Gunsmith-ing, who allowed me to take pictures of a lot of stuff; a couple distributors: RSR and Green Supply who gladly sold me some stuff (too gladly); my wife Rachel, who lovingly kept her mouth shut when seeing the influx of stuff; my editor Corrina, for the extension; my neighbor Bill who didn't get all worked up when I pointed a couple of rifles at his truck for pictures; my other neighbor Eric for not calling the cops when he saw me running around my backyard festooned with weapons; and last but not least, anyone who I might be forgetting about who might have loaned me some of their stuff or authorized the use of some photos.

INTRODUCTION

In the last few years we have seen an explosion in gun ownership in the USA. Much of it is due to a fear of newly restrictive legislation that appeared on the horizon. Many new gun owners have purchased their first firearm in response to a "get in now while it's still legal" mentality. Others, due to the expansion of concealed carry laws, have decided to purchase a handgun and maybe pursue the option of legal pistol carry. These are only a couple of reasons, the most common examples, but there are surely more.

It is to these newly minted gun owners that this book is directed. Many of them (you) have questions. How do I shoot, what's the best way to hold the gun as I shoot? What gun should I get and what bullet should it shoot? Why do I even want a gun in the first place and what do I want to use it for? These are questions for other books, so go to the Gun Digest web store and buy them. No, this book is about maintaining and improving those stock factory firearms that we purchased and now we absolutely have to do something with them. How much more stuff do I have to buy to maintain, clean, and even to make it more personalized to me, or more effective as a tool? What if something breaks? Well, in this book we will attempt to answer as many of those questions as possible.

There is a funny scene from the movie "Remember the Titans." It takes place in the home of one of the two coaches and involves the two adolescent daughters of the respective coaches. One of the girls, the sportier one, played by a very young Hayden Panetierre, expresses some veiled disdain at the other girl's playing with Barbie dolls. The latter girl responds with a statement that is on the order of, "I'm not playing. I'm accessorizing."

This is what we do with our guns. Since the phrase "playing with guns" has a rather negative connotation, and probably for the better, we should use a different phrase that describes our activities when we change how our gun shoots, feels, looks, or whatever. We accessorize our guns. We upgrade them with new accessories, like Tritium powered night sights, lasers, more magazines or other loading devices, prettier stocks, pink grips, a fun DuraCoat paint job, better performing aftermarket trigger upgrade, slings, bipods, flash hiders, recoil compensators, free floating handguard tubes, and the list is just beginning.

The point is to personalize our firearms. I might drive off the car lot with an identical minivan as the guy behind me, but it will take less than five minutes before my minivan is different from that other guy's minivan. It starts with crumbs, French fries, or ATM receipts, but might end with steering wheel covers, fuzzy dice, spinners, and maybe a fuzzbuster. We want our mass produced machine to either look or feel different from the identical mass produced machine that our buddy has. The beauty of the free market is that it tends to address this kind of desire in an energetic manner. If someone wants something, somebody else will make it. Then about fifty other somebody elses will also make it oh so slightly differently, so that the first guy that wanted it has his choice of the different styles or colors of the widget to buy. For example: AR-15 pistol grip.

When one purchases a firearm, he or she is best served by also purchasing a few things along with it. We will address in some detail the items that are most useful and most necessary for maintenance and general care of a number of different firearms. You see, most gun owners, even the least involved, will often not be able to resist the lure of aftermarket accessories and upgrades designed to make the firearm more useful, more ergonomic, and yes, even more cosmetically attractive, but they will often neglect the materials to keep the firearm in good working condition. While this area of gun ownership will quickly take you down a bottomless rabbit hole of goodies (particularly with certain guns), in the pages to come, you can hopefully find the keys to segregate the truly useful and vital from those that are simply nice to have money-makers for the various companies in the firearms industry.

Finally, the attempt will be made to make this tome of knowledge an enjoyable volume to read. This author gets ever so weary of the same old boring "this is the newest, coolest gun and this is why you should buy it" shtick. In the following pages you will find tips from other new gun owners, tips from veteran gun owners (that are actually useful), and therefore maybe even find some of your questions answered and your needs met to your satisfaction.

Kevin Muramatsu

CHAPTER 1

THE GUNS, THE CHOICES, AND THEIR ATTENDANT ACCESSORIES

WHY DO WE WANT CERTAIN FIREARMS, AND WHAT STUFF DO WE GET TO GO WITH THEM?

I'm going to present a few hypothetical stories here. Each situation finds the gun owners, mostly new gun owners, in a different situation, with different circumstances of life. Each gets a firearm to accomplish some task – self-defense, hunting, recreation, or combination thereof. None settles with just the basic gun from the sporting goods store. In fact, that is where they start and then move on from that beginning. They buy more stuff to make the gun easier to use, more effective for the task at hand, for bragging rights and to show off their wealth or their sport. All of these reasons and more are used to spend more money on more stuff, to accessorize.

This was Jesus's starting point. A Glock 22 and one mag. He expanded of course, but still kept the price down by buying used and buying smart.

We will explore along in a slightly different format here. Many published works tend to talk about this stuff by purpose, or by kind of gun only, but we're going to look at it in a sort of hybrid way. The reason for this is that most new gun owners or wannabe gun owners tend to look at the issue not from one of those perspectives, but from both at the same time. So the guns they choose and the stuff they buy for them are getting, at least for now, mashed into the same breath for the sake of storytelling. I'm doing this because stories relay information better than just yapping out the text. Stories offer a situational awareness that makes the whole thing fit together better.

EXAMPLE 1: JESUS

For example, my friend Jesus ("HAY-soos" not "GEE-zus") wanted a gun for protection in the home. He wanted something, but was not entirely sure what. So after I charged him a $20 consulting fee (see sidebar for explanation), I guided him along the path of gun picking serenity. He has multiple children including foster kids. He has had reason to fear forcible entry of his home both when he is home and when he is away. As one should always assume multiple intruders or assailants, the bigger the ammo capacity, the better. I told him to buy a Glock pistol. Believe it or not he actually did what I told him to do and he got a Glock, instead of a shotgun, rifle, or nickel plated sissy pistol. Here's why.

Jesus doesn't have a lot of money, so that immediately ruled out anything expensive and pretty much limited the whole kit-and-kaboodle to well under $1K. Furthermore, this eliminated the best options available from a rifle standpoint because of the cost. We'll get into this in a later chapter, but you've got to get more than just the gun. Ammo, maintenance equipment, safe, etc., all have to be factored in when you are on a budget. Jesus also was pretty clear he wanted a pistol, not a rifle or shotgun.

Next, Jesus had no current intention or desire to legally carry his firearm in a concealed fashion on a daily basis. This would make a long gun a good choice, but that has already been eliminated because of cost and design. Fortunately, it does ideally allow for a full-sized pistol that would otherwise be harder for him to conceal on his person.

Jesus was then introduced to a selection of full sized pistols in the $500 range, including Glocks, Smith & Wesson M&Ps, among others. Since he paid me a consulting fee, I felt it was incumbent upon me to recommend the Glock brand because of its ease of maintenance, ease of use, commonality of parts and parts availability, and extreme record of reliability. Its sheer omnipresence in the law enforcement community suggests that if it's good enough for them, it will probably be good enough for Jesus. The high ammo capacity pretty much was the icing on the cake. Fortunately, he had another friend with a used Glock 22 .40 cal. with night sights on the selling block and Jesus got a pretty good deal on a lightly used pistol.

For security concerns, Jesus got a small biometric pistol safe. See, Jesus knows that little kids are smart and they can be very determined to get at things they shouldn't. This is why I recommended a biometric lock that reads

fingerprints over a key-only or combination lock safe. That sucker will not open without his finger (emergency override key is kept on his work key chain) and it's reasonably unlikely that his kids will cut off his finger to get into the gun safe on the top shelf of the closet. I suppose they could, though I think reasonable precautions have been taken.

All told, Jesus spent on the order of $800 for the gun, safe, three extra magazines, and some starter ammo. The gun came with night sights and an enhanced aftermarket trigger. Since he is unlikely to carry, unlikely to hunt, unlikely to compete, and unlikely to spend any more money, the basic full-sized high capacity pistol is the best choice for him and his family.

EXAMPLE 2: FRIEDRICH

Friedrich lives in the country. He has a small home on a few acres just outside the city limits, with neighbors several hundred feet to either end of his property, and his land backs up to a wooded hill. He feels pretty safe out here, but the state penitentiary is only a mile away and he wants something that he can use for self-defense and light target shooting off his back deck. He is willing to spend more money than Jesus, since he's single and has no children, but he's not rich either.

So Friedrich comes to me and asks "the expert" what he should buy. I told him I'm only an expert at parallel parking but I'd do my best to help him out. Here's what we went with. He was interested, due to some of the issues floating in the ether, in getting an evil "assault rifle" for home defense and recreational shooting. This is actually a pretty good choice for his situation. A carbine with a barrel length of 16 inches with a red dot optic would be a great choice for him. He can have it in his closet or under his futon where it is quickly grabbed if the need arises. He can easily shoot it off his back deck in a little range he wants to set up behind his house, and he can easily carry it around the very large back yard if wants to. If he does have to use it within his home, he has little worry about shooting through the walls and hitting his neighbors because of the distance between houses. Furthermore, there is no one else in the house that he needs to avoid shooting accidentally.

So why not, say, a shotgun? Friedrich shoots trap and skeet and already has a Browning Auto-5 that his grandfather willed to him, with a 28-inch barrel and he just wants something lighter, handier, and more appropriate for the task at hand. So I directed him to a basic entry level AR-

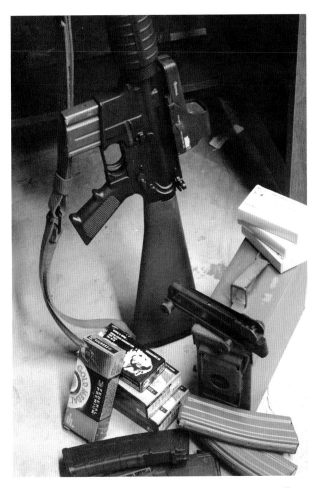

Friedrich landed this stash of goodness. Firearm, ammo, mags. All you need now is alcohol and tobacco and the trifecta is complete.

type rifle available from a number of manufacturers, such as Armalite, Bushmaster, Colt, DPMS, or Rock River Arms. He can get one of these carbines for around $1000 bucks or less, brand new. He also wanted some type of optic, because he knew that a red dot can speed up your aiming. It's easier to simply aim with a single dot than to line up two sights, particularly in low light. Friedrich decided to get a small fire-resistant safe, since when seconds count, the police or fire department are only minutes away. The safe can then be used to store his shotgun and his new rifle (when it's not under the futon), as well as the 500 rounds of ammo and five spare magazines he bought with the gun. Friedrich spent around $1900 bucks for that stuff and a middle level red dot sight. He also decided to start saving up for a night vision scope so he can nail the coyotes if they get too close to his deck. He'll be looking at another $400 for the cheap versions.

EXAMPLE 3: BELLE

Belle has a beast of an ex-boyfried. The kind of guy who says if he can't have her no one can. Beastman is the kind of guy who got a free trip to the clink in a deputy sheriff's cruiser after slapping her around on their last date because she wouldn't get in the back seat with him. Since we can't just feed these kind of guys to piranhas (A very relevant science experiment. I, for one, would very much like to know how fast fifty hungry piranhas could skin a 180-pound Beastman), Beastman makes bail and promptly starts harassing Belle with threatening phone calls and vandalism to her vehicle when she's at work. Belle is justifiably in fear for her life and she files a restraining order. She also convinces the county sheriff the next day to issue her an emergency carry permit, and she goes to the local gun shop to find some protection. Unlike most gun store sales-counter commandoes, the sales person, "Kevin," suggests a subcompact gun would be the most appropriate for her dilemma, a reasonable recommendation. Belle does not want everyone to know what's going on because it's kind of embarrassing, she's pretty new to the area and doesn't know many people, and she doesn't want to involve anyone else that she does know in any potential danger either, so she agrees that a small gun that will fit in her purse or in her pocket/waistband would be good.

Fortunately the store also has a small test range and some test samples which allow Belle to engage in some invaluable test shooting. The clerk rightly tells her that the biggest bullet she can stand to shoot would be best since it will be more likely to hit something vital. But Belle is a petite, small handed young lady and the .40s and .45s simply have more recoil than she is comfortable with, especially from the small guns she's shooting. She narrows it down to a Ruger LC9 9mm, a Smith & Wesson Model 60 Ladysmith revolver in .357 Magnum, and a Smith & Wesson Bodyguard 380 pistol.

Finally, because of cost and size (since revolvers can be pretty wide at the cylinder) she rules out the excellent Ladysmith. Belle settles on the Bodyguard 380 because it has the one thing the others lack: a laser incorporated into the frame. Lasers are useful for point shooting (can be very important when stressed out) and for intimidation. She really doesn't want to shoot Beastman, so the intimidation aspect of a laser might work, since no one is comfortable with a pulsing red dot bouncing around on his chest. But she still has the ability to shoot if necessary. The Bodyguard is also extremely thin and she can conceal it even when she is out jogging after supper. Recoil is stiff, as befits a lightweight pistol, but it's not horrible.

Belle bypasses cleaning and maintenance equipment for now because, like Jesus, she is on a limited budget. After all, she didn't plan ahead for this crap happening to her – I mean, who does? - so she buys the gun for $350, gets some spare batteries for the laser, a small cheap holster she can put in her purse or wear under her belt, and both practice ammo and hollow pointed defensive ammo. She spent less than $450 and she can pay it off in a couple months because she put it on her credit card.

EXAMPLE 4: ELMER

Elmer wants to shoot sporting clays at the local club and shoot ducks at the pond, and he wants a quality shotgun! This one's easy. Elmer should buy a camouflage finished semiautomatic 12 gauge shotgun. Many are available on the market such as a Benelli Super Black Eagle, Browning A5, Beretta Xtrema, or Browning Gold. These range from around $800 to around $2000, all can be purchased with

Belle's Bodyguard 380 is perfect for the Woolstenhume fashion concealed carry purse her aunt bought for her two days after Belle bought the gun. It doesn't scream "there's a gun inside my pocket" like a hip pouch might.

camo, most can shoot magnum shells, and all are readily available. The only thing they would be less ideal for is self-defense in the home, because of their length, but Elmer doesn't really care about that so that isn't a concern. The problem is he doesn't like any of the camouflage patterns he sees. So he asks Kevin if there are any other patterns available. Kevin replies in the negative. However, if Elmer purchases the plain old slightly used Beretta Xtrema, Kevin would be happy to apply a custom, one of a kind, camo pattern in Duracoat for another $350. Kevin shows Elmer a couple of samples and even though Elmer didn't want to spend that much money, it is just what he wanted when he walked in the door. The used shotgun was a good deal, the paint upgrade wasn't horribly expensive, and it's camouflaged to hide him from the ducks before he pumps flak into them. And, the semi-auto nature of the gun is a good choice for the fast shooting that is involved with sporting clays, as long as he doesn't mind cleaning it regularly.

EXAMPLE 5: DICK

Dick is a chiropractor and really wants to show off a little to the other back-wrenchers at the range. His buddies in the skeet club have been pestering him to join in the festivities every Thursday evening, so Dick decides he is going to get an expensive shotgun, figuring that spendier equals better, and that will help him compensate for the things that he lacks, like skill, for instance. He goes to the same store that Belle went to. You know, the one with the counter salesman that actually knew what he was talking about.

Kevin realizes he can sell some serious iron to this guy and convinces Dick to buy a Perazzi MX12 Extra. Dick doesn't even flinch at spending enough money to buy a truck and says he'll take it. Kevin says okay, I'll have to special order it for you. It will take about two years to get here and you need to pay a non-refundable deposit in full. Dick says he can't wait two years, he needs the gun tonight. "Ohhh, sorry," says Kevin, "that's just not going

Elmer's handiwork.

to happen, but I do have a great Benelli SuperSport here that is a passable substitute, and would probably do for what you need until the Perazzi comes in." Dick has to get something or he will be truly embarrassed when he sees Dr. Johnson and Dr. Brown later so he goes ahead and gets the $2100 SuperSport, a red dot sight that fits between the stock and receiver, and a fiberoptic front bead for it, and leaves the non-refundable, full value deposit for the Rolls-Royce, er...I mean the Perazzi. At 7 p.m. Dick can then tell his friends how he will kick their butts when his new mean Perazzi arrives, but until then he will just have to make do with his Benelli. You think I'm completely making this stuff up, but I'm only making up parts of it.

EXAMPLE 6: TYRONE

Tyrone has never fired a rifle in his life. Unfortunately for him, his girlfriend comes from a hunting family. This is a clan that literally made the song "Second Week of Deer Camp" the family anthem. This bunch takes two weeks off from work to go hunting. Every. Year. Tyrone has a good, well-paying job, works hard, and likes to go to movies with

his girlfriend Grace, and he plays Halo with his old college buddies on Tuesday nights. However, Tyrone knows that, if he expects to have a chance with Grace, he needs to quickly assimilate into the Huntington family culture, and the best way to accomplish that is to start smelling whitetail in the air every October. Furthermore, while his potential father-in-law has generously offered him the use of one of the 38 ½ family hunting rifles, Tyrone's not about to fall for that trick. If he's going to be taken seriously he needs to buy his own boomstick. And he certainly is not going to show weakness by asking pops for any advice on this topic. He does what any smart professional does and starts doing some research, reading gun magazines, and watching YouTube videos to get educated on the hunting rifle market.

Having done his research, Tyrone goes down to Billy Bob's House of Guns. This was his only poor decision, because Billy Bob is a 427 pound gorilla on a swivel stool with a sweat stained, too small T-shirt that says "Gun Control means using two hands," food in his beard, and a permanent "What the hell are you doing coming in my shop"

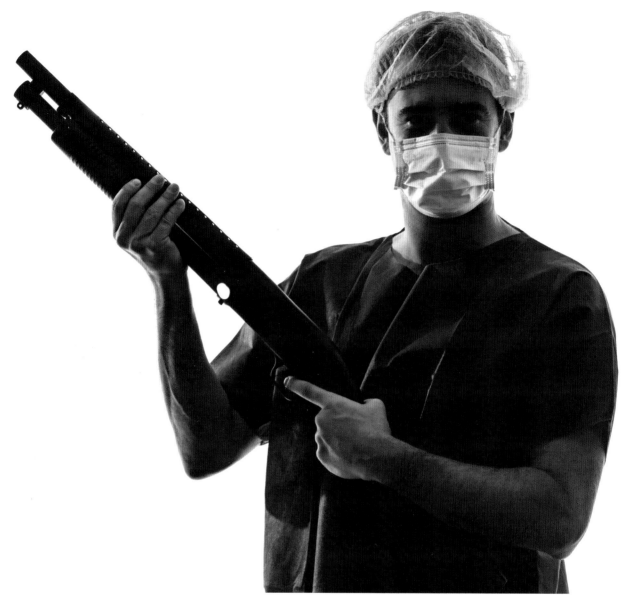

This is not an expensive shotgun and this guy really isn't a doctor. He only plays one on TV. Dick (which really is his name) also has poor trigger finger discipline.

expression on his face. See, Billy Bob only has customers because he happens to know the right distributors and has inherited the oldest shop in town. Customers come in, literally throw their money at Billy Bob, and walk out with their products with little to no conversation involved, because Billy Bob may be a resounding Platinum Grade Class A jerk, but at least he has primers in stock. His prices are ok too.

After being ignored for twenty minutes, despite a complete absence of other customers, Tyrone manages to distract Billy Bob from Judge Judy long enough to shout,

"Hey! Dude! Do you have any Browning A-Bolt IIs with that really cool looking maple stock?" Billy Bob rolls his eyes and without comment goes back to Judge Judy. Tyrone rips off a flap on a box of grossly expensive ammo just out of spite, puts it back on the shelf, then walks out and goes across the street to the store where Kevin works. Kevin greets Tyrone with a smile and asks how he can assist him today. Tyrone tells Kevin what he wants and Kevin just happens to have one in stock because someone ordered it in January and didn't bother to come pick it up. Tyrone buys the rifle, forty rounds of 24 karat, solid gold ammo (the price on the box would suggest that, at least), a rifle case, Walker Game Ear electronic hunting earplugs, an insanely expensive OTIS hunter cleaning kit, and a Nikon Monarch rifle scope with requisite mounting hardware, and yes I'd be happy to mount that scope for you free of charge Tyrone, thank you very much for your purchase. Hey, did you need some boots or anything, 'cause we have that here too? Oh, and here's my card; call me if you need anything. Tyrone just spent in excess of $2500 and will be back for more because he likes Kevin's store a lot more than Billy Bob's.

Tyrone shows up at family deer week with a super set of gear and even manages to impress the p-FIL with his ability to shoot his snazzy new rifle. Grace is so pleased with her boyfriend, she decides to tell the whole family that she's gonna marry Tyrone and they are going to have five beautiful hunting babies together. Tyrone, very subtle-like, face palms and asks for a beer.

All these people purchased extra stuff for their guns. Belle didn't get much but her situation didn't really require it. Dick spent more money than most people make in a year. Friedrich is on the way to going all out on his accessorizing. In the following chapters we will break a lot of this stuff down. We'll examine some of the reasons specifically where certain things bring a benefit to the gun and the shooting. Some things are quite expensive, others not so much. The market is such that the choices are vast for just about any particular item.

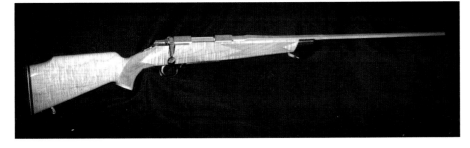

Tyrone saw this rifle and fell in love with it. Maple stocks can be very attractive and highly figured, unlike the birch that is often used for cheap light colored gunstock wood. Photo courtesy of Browning.

CHAPTER 2

TOOLS AND SAFETY STUFF

If you are going to be mucking around on your guns, adding stuff, changing stuff, then there are a few tools that it would be a good idea for you to have on hand. Of course the maintenance of your property will be much easier in the future as well. To be frank, most of the accessorizing that will be covered later in this book can be carried out by anyone with even the smallest amount of mechanical aptitude. Even so, even the best screwdriver turner can get lost when it comes to parts, not necessarily taking them apart, as much as putting them back together again. Which brings us to the first essential tool to have. We'll go over the essentials and then a couple of the convenient and nice-to-have tools later.

MUST-HAVE TOOLS

1. Digital camera. Digital pictures are free. You can take hundreds with even the smallest SanDisk card and you should always have a digital camera when you are taking something apart. Take a picture or two of each assembly before it is removed from the gun. Take a picture of that pin before you punch it out, note the orientation and whether one end is bigger than the other. Take a picture of every spring in assembly before you remove it. Trust me, you will forget how these things go back in, how the assembly looked before you took it apart. Pictures are invaluable. Then, later on, if you need to take the gun apart again, you will have a folder

A small digital camera is sufficient and necessary. As long as you can take a multi megapixel image or fifty you will be fine. Just remember to use it a lot. Digital images are free.

in your computer with all the pics. Most people won't do this kind of thing often enough to memorize it. Even gunsmiths that do it every day only remember fully the most common firearms that they see. Take pictures. Take lots of them.

2. Gunsmithing screwdriver set. This you must have. The Stanleys in your garage are not going to cut it. Gunsmithing screwdrivers have a hollow-ground tip, not the taper tip that conventional screwdrivers sport. Taper tips chew up the fancy delicate screw heads on the gun screws, and hollow ground tips do not. Nobody wants buggered up screws showing on their gun, nor do they want the value loss inherent in having what is now a defective part. Gunsmith screwdriver sets also come with a much wider range of widths and thicknesses to fit the large variety of screws that exist in guntown. There are only two sets that I can recommend without reservation. They handle maybe 99% of the screws that you will find on firearms. They are the Brownells MagnaTip sets and the Wheeler Engineering Professional set. Both have large numbers of replaceable bits. The Brownells have a lifetime warrantee, and the Wheeler set has some fun-to-have specialty bits. These sets are going to cost over $75 but are worth every penny. There are a lot of cheaper sets on the market and I regret to say that I've found that most of the lower end are priced that way for a reason: the metallurgy of the bits is not appropriate to the task. They are too soft and will not stand up to the task.

3. Hammer or mallet. Go to Brownells and buy the ¾-inch or 1-inch Nylon/Brass hammer, or the Wheeler Engineering 12 oz Nylon/Brass hammer from MidwayUSA . These models are heavy enough to dislodge any part you will find on a gun. Yet it's not so big that it is hard to control. The heads are replaceable so when you chew up the nylon end, you can order a replacement head. The usual advice if a pin or part will not move – to hit it harder or get a bigger hammer – should generally be discarded. If it doesn't move from the force of a hammer of this size, then there's something else going on. Often it's a set screw holding the part in place or something similar.

Gunsmithing screwdrivers must be used. You don't have to get these large sets from Brownells or MidwayUSA, but these are the best and most versatile ones. Note that they will get cluttered quickly.

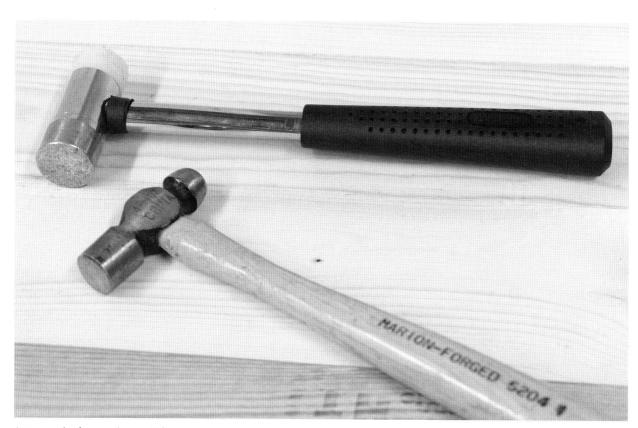

A non-marring hammer is essential.

Make sure you fully examine the part and the assembly before you start whacking away. Sometimes just a little oil or a little heat is all that's needed. A very small steel ball-peen hammer is also sometimes handy.

4. Punches. Good high quality steel punches are necessary for removing pins. Standard punches are basic and really all you need, though you can upgrade to pin holding and roll pin punches as needed.

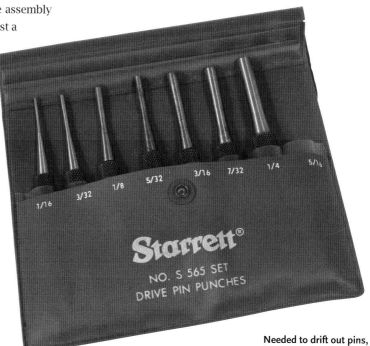

Needed to drift out pins, these punches from Starrett are perfect.

5. Work mat and solid bench. The kitchen table won't cut it. A good heavy garage or workshop bench is needed, for stability and sturdiness. A work mat to help catch parts as they fall out is also a requirement. These nicely inhibit bouncing parts from skipping off the bench onto the floor. Throw in some magnetic trays and you are golden.

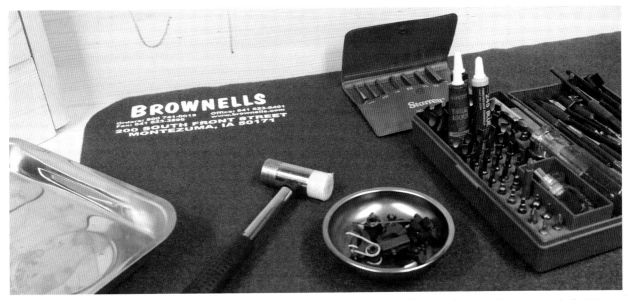

This is a nice work mat from Brownells. It's big enough for elbow room, and has a plasticized back surface to catch solvents and oils. Get your magnetic trays from the local hardware store.

6. Vice. Some sort of vise with padded jaws is a must. Most of us do not have three hands, and a minimum of three hands is needed to work on a gun. The padded semi-soft jaws will cover the hard steel jaws and prevent the vise from damaging the gun. There are a lot of vises made for use in the gun industry, but for starters just a regular bench vise from the hardware store will suffice. As long as you get the jaw pads.

You will need a third hand. Since you cannot grow one, get a bench vise. The AR-15 lower receiver magazine well block is handy to have, too.

7. Hand drill. You will use this for cleaning. If you don't have one, get one. Thirty bucks at the hardware store.

Local hardware store. Corded works well, but can run too fast and be less flexible. Cordless is better.

8. Fire. A plain old propane torch from Ace will be all you need. You are not going to be welding, but you might need heat to help install or disassemble tight parts. The propane flame can slowly heat up the parts to expand them to make them easy to take apart, particularly if there is a lot of dirtiness involved, or if the parts are aluminum.

You may need to heat your muzzle device to get it off, or gently heat a trigger screw to loosen the threadlocker for adjustment.

9. Forceps or tweezers. Small parts are smaller than your fingertips. Get some tweezers, though needle nose pliers can fill the job sometimes.

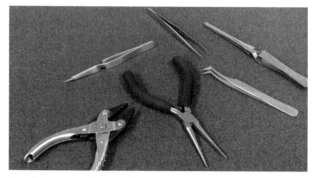

Your fingers are only so small.

10. Hex wrench sets. Increasing numbers of guns are using hex screws, and some torx screws too. Hex (Allen) wrenches, and Torx tips are a must, both standard and metric.

There are a lot more hex bolts and screws than flat-bladed and Phillips anymore. Get standard and metric sets.

11. Bench block. A plastic bench block for pin removal is a must. The holes allow the pins to pass completely out of the gun while maintaining full support for the parts.

Green from Brownells, to match the mat.

NICE-TO-HAVE TOOLS

1. Roll pin punches and pin holding punches. Roll pin punches have a little nubbie on the tip that sits inside the roll pin. These punches reduce (but not eliminate) the damage taken when driving roll and spring pins in and out. The pin holders have shallow hollow tips that hold the pins so you can get them started in the holes. For the non-gunsmith, they are not completely necessary. It should be noted that the more modern the gun, the higher the ratio of spring or roll pins to solid dowel pins.

The little nubbins on the end drive roll pins better, and the ones with holes on the end will hold the pin for you to start the thing in the hole. Reeeeeaaaaallllly nice to have.

2. Specialty/gun-specific tools. AR-15s require a set of tooling all their own. So do revolvers. So do 1911s if you want to build or maintain your own. These tools can get expensive, but if you are doing it a lot for yourself and your buddies, then a few of these tools become quite useful. Example: AR-15 action wrench and stock M4 wrench.

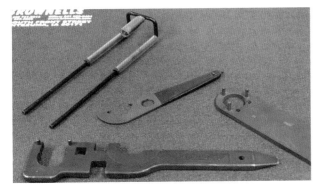

If you get into AR-type rifles (there is a good chance, if you are reading this book) you will need a few essential tools. The action wrench and the stock wrench are the first, followed by receiver blocks and other specialized tools, available at Brownells.

3. Airbrush. If you get into refinishing with DuraCoat or Cerakote or Alumahyde or something like that, you will need an airbrush at a minimum, and an HVLP gun at most.

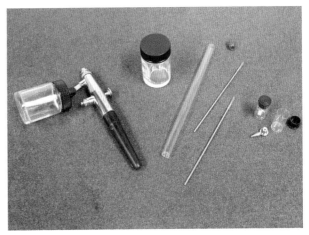

To apply new type spray on finishes requires a sprayer. This Crescendo 175 from Badger is perfect for small jobs, pistols, parts.

4. Gun vises. Several companies make holding equipment for all kinds of guns. The most cost effective are those from Hyskore. There are clamp on vises that can be taken to the range, and mounts that have a magazine insert so that you can set the pistol on the insert instead of in a vise. The grip frame section of pistols can crush easily, so this prevents it by using no clamping.

Hyskore makes some fun, affordable fixturing. This pistol vise with the magazine well inserts can also be used as an anything vise with the included vise head.

5. Bore sighting equipment. Lasers and optical collimators are great tools and are all but necessary for scope mounting. But if you aren't mounting your own scopes then there is no point. Since most rifle owners have attempted to do so, thinking the $35 bucks a gunsmith might charge is a rip off (it so isn't) there are a lot of boresighters in private hands.

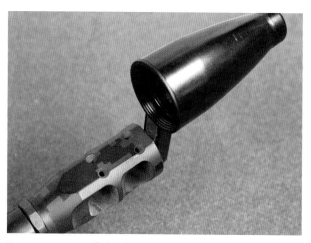

You can save yourself a headache when mounting your own scopes by getting and properly using a boresighter.

6. Headspace gauges. If you are in a position to change out barrels, you will need headspace gauges. Alternatively, they can be rented, as can reamers, from several companies on the net.

If you rebarrel, you will need to use gauges to check headspace. They can be rented from online sources or purchased. Up to you.

7. Bore-scopes. Don't. Nothing good comes from anyone but gunsmiths owning borescopes. Just don't. You will just get torked off and frustrated for no reason.

8. Multi-tool. This can unjam or fix in a jiffy.

9. Pretty much anything else. The possibilities are endless and it's your money.

You can fix a bunch of stuff in the field with one of these. This Leatherman Wave cost $18 on sale at Fleet Farm on Black Friday. Basic tool, great price.

SAFETY EQUIPMENT

There are certain articles of safety equipment that you should have while shooting and playing around with parts. You must have this stuff. I don't care how tough you think you are or how squinty your little beady eyes are.

1. Safety glasses. I have some of the squintiest eyes known to man (just ask my friends and coworkers), but I still get stuff in my eyes if I don't wear safety glasses. You must have glasses when working on guns and you must have them when shooting the guns. No exceptions.

I cannot squint hard enough to keep stuff out of my eyes unless I also am wearing safety glasses. By the way, I can still see perfectly when squinted like this.

2. Hearing protection. This should go without saying when at the range but this is one of the most necessary accessories that is neglected. There are few things more entertaining than shooting a rifle with a muzzle brake right next to the little snot gansta posers at the range who are acting all tough with their gats and got no hearing protection, yo! Furthermore, you might need the earplugs in the shop if it gets loud, or so you can ignore your wife calling you to dinner so you can get more stuff done.

3. Respirator. If you are going to paint or do a bunch of sanding, you should have a respirator. Particulates can mess you up. As I'm writing this, I'm still coughing up DuraCoat that I accidentally inhaled a month ago. Wear a respirator.

Painting, grinding, sanding, and anything requiring the use of hydrocarbon solvents requires lung protection. Get these from your local hardware store.

This isn't just for the range. Grinding, compressor noise, and all kinds of things can damage your hearing.

4. Latex or nitrile gloves. This is to keep the crud and solvents off your tender, supple skin. Solvents that clean guns real well, like acetone and lacquer thinner, will dry the crap out of your hands and really aren't good for you in the long term. Gunk and residue that is coming off the gun also for some reason doesn't come off your fingers nearly as easily as a glove coming off your hand. Get some rags made of tee-shirt material. It works quite goodly.

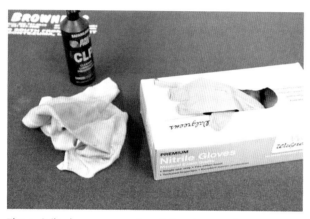

These nitrile gloves were purchased at a pharmacy, but are not very resistant to solvents. You can get some really thick ones from various sources online. If you just want to keep the gunk off your fingers, these are sufficient. You also can't have too many rags.

5. An apron is a good thing to have. I don't particularly like them because they give me headaches (pulls on my neck) but it's still something just about anyone can use. So, no picture. If you don't know what an apron looks like, send me all your guns. I'll pay shipping.

6. Lead wipes. You are going to get lead residue on your hands. Use the lead wipes to get it off before your baby starts chewing on your fingers.

7. First aid kit. If you have a garage shop or something like that, a basic first aid kit in proximity will come in handy when you slam your thumb in your M1 or when you let the slide on your pistol spring forward before you got the meat of your palm out of the way.

Wolverine says, "put together a first aid kit, including a blood clotting agent, Bub, or I'm going to dice you up just to make my point."

You will get lead on your hands. It's not as horrible a thing as some would have you think, but don't go sucking on your fingers until you've de-leaded them with these special wipes. These wipes don't taste very good either, so after you've used them, go wash with soap and water.

CHAPTER 3

CLEANING AND MAINTENANCE

Since you have purchased your new firearm, you are going to need to take special care of it. Most gun owners don't give their gun the love it deserves. This piece of metal and plastic and maybe wood is something that you are going to bet your life on. When it needs to work, you need it to work. When you need it now, it has to be in functional condition. You need to develop some basic skill on how to use it safely and not cause harm to innocent people. When it gets dirty you need to clean it. Yet most gun owners don't do that. They know in their guts that this is a highly-crafted machine and is quite tol-erant of abuse and neglect. Let's look at something else, just as ubiquitous in American life and compare.

When your automobile's service light illuminates like the star on top of your Christmas tree, you go change the dirty lubricant oil for fresh, clean, lubricant oil. When the door light is on, you re-shut the door to make sure it's latched. When the auto gets dirty from nasty grasshop-pers or from the vermin of the sky, Canada geese, pi-geons, and starlings, you take it to the carwash to clean it. Or, if you are guy with misplaced priorities, you might spend an entire day hand washing your Mustang (relax,

Less than 10 bucks. Local sporting goods or department store.

UNIVERSAL KITS

Universal gun cleaning kits are expansive and can be expensive too, or cheap. "Universal" is a loose term, but you can get kits for well under $50 that will clean pretty much anything you want.

dudes). When the upholstery rips you fix it or get new upholstery. If the steering wheel is out of alignment, you get the alignment fixed. Everything I just mentioned on a car, that you rely on to take you from place to place, from home to work, from work to the gym, from the gym home again, has a corollary in a firearm. You change your car oil and clean out the car, and you clean your gun and re-oil it afterwards. If the action doesn't shut you try to find out why, just like how your purse-strap was in the car door preventing it from closing. When you get mud, sweat, Jell-o or some other crap on your gun you clean it off very carefully; just like washing the Mustang by hand, you do so with care to minimize cosmetic damage and maximize sanitation. The upholstery correlates to the furniture of your gun, the grips or stock wood, and when it gets scratched, gouged, or cracked, you fix it or replace it for best performance, just like repairing the fabric on your car seat. If your gun sights are not centered you have them reset so you can hit what you are trying to shoot at.

While it may be a step removed from daily use of a vehicle, your gun is still something that you are going to depend on for your life or livelihood, certainly for law enforcement and self-defense applications. Should you not apply just as much attention to your gun as to your car?

The nice part is that it really doesn't cost a lot of money to do this. Perfectly adequate cleaning kits can be purchased from the big-box stores for under a Hamilton apiece. Really nice "we-got-everything-we'll-ever-need" type of kits can cost over Franklin and you don't really need those, unless you have multiple firearms in multiple calibers. Then those can be very useful. But new gun owners can get by perfectly acceptably by spending under $30, and that is including the consumables like oil, cleaning solvent, and cleaning patches. Frankly, you can make your own patches from a used T-shirt and those will work

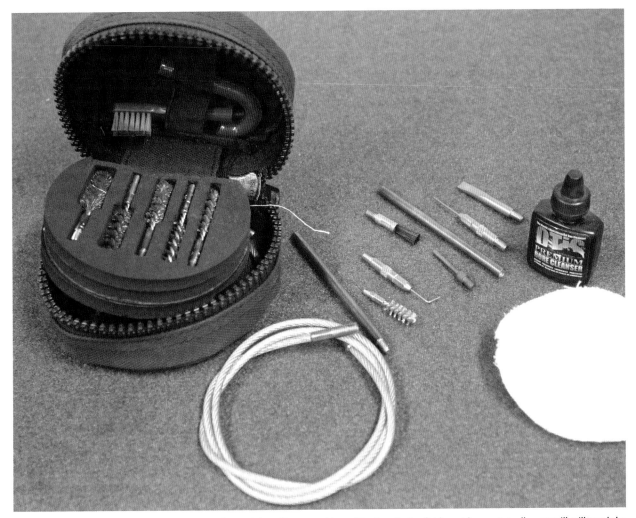

More than 30 bucks, but awesome. Compact and containing all you would need to clean in the field or at home. Actually, you will still need the cheap kit to knock out stuck bullets in the barrel, but the Otis kit cleans quicker and better.

just as well or better than most on the market. Aerosol non-chlorinated brake cleaner from the auto supply store is an excellent cleaner if that's all you can get, but I would stick with the oils fabricated for the gun industry for lubrication. They are cheap and work quite well. There are places for grease and anti-seize products, but we'll get to those later in this chapter.

LET'S CLEAN SOME GUNS! EMPTY GUNS.

What I'd like to do in a minute is pick a few of the guns that have been purchased in numbers in the last few years, things like carry pistols, AR-15-type rifles, SD ("self-defense" – I'm getting tired of typing "self-defense" twelve times a chapter) shotguns. While the information about to be presented is largely gun-specific, most of the info can be transferred to the care of any firearm. Just about

everything boils down to a few specific ideas. The first set is the set that is most important for gun cleaning and gun handling in general. Let's take a look.

RULES OF GUN SAFETY

We are going to use the National Rifle Association's Three Rules of Gun Handling and go over them. Why three? Because three is easy to remember. Some organizations use five, or ten, or even more gun safety rules. This is stupid. The fewer rules there are to remember, the better. All those extra five or ten rules are simply distillations of the three basic rules that the NRA uses, and if you follow those, and use just a little bit of common sense, you will be fine. Let's be serious; do you people writing gun manuals really think the people who buy your guns (and actually read the manual!) are going to remember 10 rules? I bet

Watch where you are pointing your gun. This is called muzzle discipline. It may be elevated, but it's still pointing in the wrong general direction. Note playground equipment.

This is better. Pay attention when you are yapping. If there is no safe direction, there's always "up."

the buyers will remember three a lot easier than 10, and remembering and applying the rules is what's important here. Okay, let's look at the three rules that the NRA uses.

Rule 1: Always keep the gun pointed in a safe direction.

This rules applies whether you are waving it around at the gun store, pointing it downrange at the shooting range, or unloading it to clean it. A safe direction can be defined as: a direction where, if the gun were to be fired, the bullet would not strike something or someone that shouldn't have an extra hole in it. There are too many stories where someone shot their kid or their brother because they had no muzzle discipline, and the press just loves to talk about them. It doesn't happen nearly as much as it used to, since more emphasis on safety has been introduced in recent decades, but it still occurs and there is no excuse for it whatsoever. An adjunct to this issue, like when someone else is shooting nearby, is to make sure you are aware of your surroundings. Don't walk in front of someone who is shooting. Some people don't have good peripheral vision and may not see you walking past because you were too busy boppin' to the hip-hop and not paying attention to where you were going.

Rule 2: Always keep your finger off the trigger until you are ready to shoot.

This builds on Rule 1. If you don't pull the trigger, the gun should not go off. This is probably the hardest rule to follow for new users and old users alike. There is a reason the index finger is called the trigger finger and there is a reason that, phasers notwithstanding, triggers are always placed under the index finger. It is the most functional digit, next to the opposable thumb, that we happen to have on our hands. It is at the top of our hands, thus ideally matching the location for the kill switch, and it can be, with most people, independently operated, unlike the other three fingers of our hands. It is just so easy and normal to set our trigger fingers on the trigger in a totally relaxing way, because that is where that finger is supposed to go. But the first thing you need to know about that trigger is that you should not touch it until you are ready to shoot. You want to get to the point that you are uncomfortable putting your finger on the trigger and it takes some serious training to muscle memory your way into doing this without thinking about it. Frankly, I think this may be the hardest thing to get used to when doing gun training, and it doesn't help that virtually every depiction of gun handling shown in movies and TV shows pays no attention to this discipline whatsoever. Keep that finger completely out of the trigger guard until you are ready to fire that shot.

A gun is inherently safer when the finger does not touch the trigger. Ever.

A gun is inherently less safe when the finger is touching or resting on the trigger. You better be ready to shoot.

Use good light. Stick your finger in there too. I didn't because that would have ruined the photo.

Ditto. This works for shotguns too.

When you are done looking closely at all chambers, DO NOT flick the cylinder closed like the morons on TV. That will damage the crane of the cylinder (arm that connects cylinder to frame).

Rule 3: Always keep the gun unloaded until ready to use.
Again, this rule builds on the first two. If the gun has no cartridges in it, you can accidentally pull the trigger and it will not shoot, and it will not shoot the cat even though you carelessly pointed the gun at it while checking the chamber. However, you should treat this rule as if it resets every time you think about it. Here's another old true snippet of wisdom: "A gun is always loaded." If you treat guns as if they are always loaded, you will adopt a paranoia that they are always loaded, that guns cannot possibly be unloaded, and you will develop the kind of OCD you need to follow these rules religiously. You will automatically and instinctively check each gun you pick up to make sure there are no rounds in the chamber or magazine, and you will do so by pointing the gun in a safe direction, and with your trigger finger completely off the trigger.

"Ready to use" can be a little subjective, but only a little. If your gun is one that you only use periodically at the range or during deer season, then it should always be stored in an unloaded condition, with the action open. It is only ready to use at the firing line or in the deer stand. However if we are speaking of a SD firearm, then "ready for use" is pretty much the standard condition of existence. If you are carrying concealed then that gun needs to be loaded with a round in the chamber at all times. Incidentally, this makes the three rules even more important, because you will be loading and unloading that sucker far more frequently than the buck gun. An HD (again, tired of typing "home-defense" and I also hate hyphens) firearm stored at the ready at home is likewise something that will be needed in short order, but likely not as short order as a carry pistol. A loaded magazine and chamber,

Cheap thin sheet metal, low capacity, but better than nothing.

or even just a loaded magazine with empty chamber is typical with these guns and they can still be considered "ready to use" even when under the futon or in the closet or bedside table drawer.

Furthermore, the oft repeated stricture to keep unauthorized persons away from your guns really falls into this category. If you have kids, then you will need to seriously think about lockable HD gun storage, in order to keep curious little paws away from the guns when not supervised. Similarly, if there might be someone in your home that is either legally prohibited from possessing firearms or is just someone to whom you don't want to grant access, you need to lock up the guns or hide them better than the Nazis hid stolen Rembrandts.

I'm not going to continually repeat these safety instructions. One mention should be enough for one book. Just do me a favor. If you, as a new gun owner, only take away one thing from this book, make it the 3 Rules of Safe Gun Handling. Okay, I guess that's three. Take three things from this book, minimum.

Alright, there's one more thing. Read your gun manual! It will tell you how to clean and maintain your gun and, oh yeah, how to safely operate it. So few people read their manuals that every gun manufacturer has to field some really dumb questions; dumb only because the questions would have been fully answered if the lazy clown of a customer had just taken the ten minutes necessary to read the manual. They also have to stamp information onto the outside of the gun that shouldn't need to be there, because no one reads their manual and then the owner blames the manufacturer when they shoot the round they left in the chamber into their poodle when the magazine

Don't put these on loaded guns or you will be very sorry. Unloaded only.

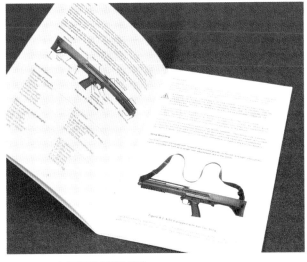

READ THE OWNERS MANUAL!

Lawyer-proofing at its finest. It used to be if you were stupid enough to shoot yourself in the foot, you were just stupid. Now the makers have to resort to this.

was out of the gun. It's not like it has to be accessed online or anything (but it can be if you lose the original), so there is no excuse to not read the manual immediately. That's four things to take away from this book, minimum.

COMPRESSED AIR

Compressed air is your friend. If you have it, use it to blow junk out of your guns, particularly the small cracks and crevices, and to flash evaporate solvents. Just be sure to wear eye protection, blow it away from you, and for heaven's sake don't blow it toward anyone else. That is all.

CLEANING THE BARREL

Most cleaning kits will come with at least one cleaning brush. You will want that brush to have bristles made of bronze or brass, and the shaft that holds the bristles should be made of brass or aluminum. Please don't use steel items in your barrel bore, whether brushes or cleaning rods (a plastic coated steel rod is okay) or you will likely damage either the chamber, rifling, or muzzle crown and the accuracy can degrade. Plastic or nylon brushes are okay, too, but they don't remove gunk as well as brass or bronze. Yes, yes, I realize that there are a bunch of steel brushes and stuff on the market, but there are many more comparable items that are made of more gun-friendly materials.

Most kits will have loops for inserting cleaning patches, and they work but not very well. Rather you should use the cleaning jags that come with many kits and can be purchased independently. Jags are the round solid tips that screw in to the cleaning rod, and have little pointy spears at the business end of them. I like to call them pig stickers because they are really pointy but can't poke anything very far because of the width of the jag body. Use only

MAGAZINE SAFETIES

Many firearms have safeties that prevent you from firing the gun without the magazine seated in its place, but most do not. I'm not going to argue the merits here, but be aware of this issue. Lots of people forget to clear the chamber, and just pull the magazine, absentmindedly thinking the gun is now unloaded. Boom. That's why the magazine safety came to be. Remember to check your chamber.

Use brushes with brass bristles. Even better are brushes that have brass wire cores as well.

Some rods have a plastic, rubberized, or Teflon coating. These are the best to use. Also, one-piece rods are less likely to damage your muzzle than sectional rods.

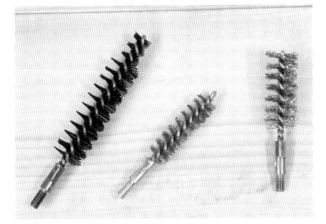

Brushes come in all shapes and sizes for different tasks. They are consumable, so replace them often.

brass jags, the plastic jags are worthless. The reason jags work better than loops is because the jag body is made to be slightly smaller than the bore diameter of the barrel with just enough room to have a patch wrapped around it. The patch will be forced into the rifling and mop up stuff from there, with full, all around, 360-degree coverage. You will not get that with a loop; and the result will be a much quicker bore cleaning with the jag than with the loop.

Barrels have more than the rifled bore itself. Most people neglect to clean a very important part of that barrel – the chamber. This is of particular import to semiautomatic firearms because the cleanliness of the chamber is vital to the proper functioning of the gun. The common thing that happens is that powder fouling and residue, brass shavings

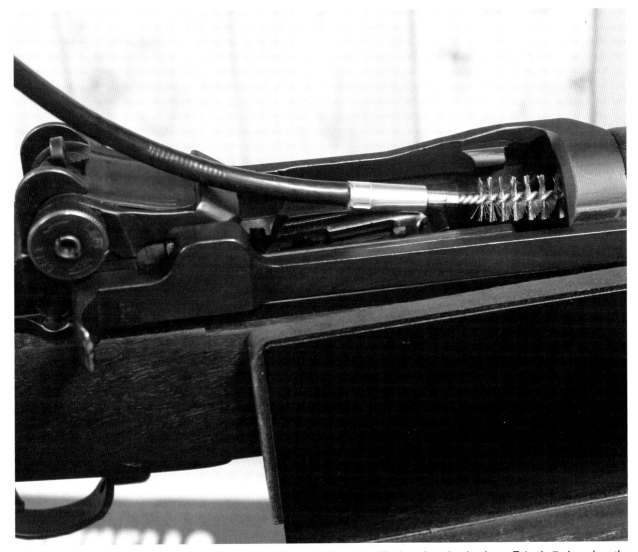

On rifles that do not have the capability to be cleaned from the muzzle, it can be difficult to clean the chamber sufficiently. Tools such as the Chamber Maid from C J Weapons Accessories can be purchased in multiple sizes to clean the chamber. The flexible yet stiff cable works well.

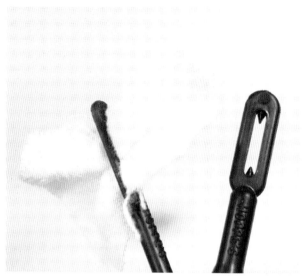

The traditional way to run a patch through the barrel is to stick it in a loop.

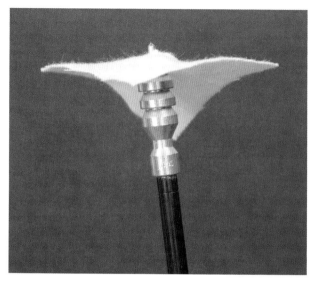

Jags with patches form tightly to the bore, wiping into the grooves of the rifling.

Any cloth patch works. Cut up an old t-shirt. The commercially-made patches will hold a lot of solvent and a lot of oil and a lot of gunk. Barrels should be, whenever possible, cleaned from the chamber end, to prevent damage to the muzzle crown as much as is possible.

A brush on a rod in a hand drill. Good for spinning in chambers.

Chamber brush entering barrel extension.

Closeup of the brush itself. This AR chamber brush has two diameters, some have three. The wide bit at the back is to clean the barrel extention area, the middle and front to clean the chamber itself.

from the case, general unpredictable debris like sand, and even the junk that some companies use to rust-proof steel cartridge cases will make its way into the chamber. This isn't even counting leftover machining issues that came from the factory, such as rings, bulges, and scratches from the manufacturing process. You can't really do anything about that stuff and, until everything else is eliminated from possibility, don't worry about that kind of chamber damage; and if you do, take it to a gunsmith to have them investigate and repair.

The way you clean a chamber can be kind of fun. It is very difficult if you cannot clean from the chamber end. You want to take an appropriately-sized brush, attach it to a segment of cleaning rod, and stick the other end of the cleaning rod into a hand drill. Appropriate means a brush that is only very slightly larger in diameter than the chamber itself. Then spin away, good man, spin away. Most barrels or guns do not have chamber brushes made specifically for this purpose, but

some do. For example, the AR series of rifles, whether in the small frame AR-15 type or large frame AR-10 type, do have chamber brushes made for them. These brushes are really good accessories to get, since they clean the chamber and the bolt locking lug space behind the chamber as well.

SOLVENT

There are a number of "environmentally friendly" cleaning solvents on the market, and honestly the verdict is not quite in on how well these work. I have not had much success with the several I've tried, but to be completely fair, I've been told by others that these cleaners do work pretty well (and don't smell like ammonia), so if you are concerned about the environment to that degree, go ahead and buy the green solvents. Actually, diluted Simple Green can be a pretty good cleaner, but make sure that, after you use it, you re-oil your parts quickly as it

These solvents can clean hard gunk, and fully degrease effectively. They aren't really good for you, so don't breathe the fumes and use gloves when necessary.

(and most traditional cleaners) will completely strip that thin layer of protective oil right off and you will have a very rusty day in short order. Acetone and lacquer thinner are often used in solvent baths to completely and totally degrease parts.

Rather, the standard cleaning solvents work very well on the usual run of the mill dirtiness of both the bore and the rest of the action of the gun. Birchwood Casey has an aerosol product called Gun Scrubber which is much like a brake cleaner designed for the gun industry. It shoots out at high velocity, which blasts a lot of gunk away and quickly evaporates with nary a residue. It is particularly useful when you drop your gun in the mud or the fish tank or something and really need to clean that crap out. Pretty much all of the gun solvents that you would find at Cabelas or Gander Mountain will work well in the bore and action areas. You will often find fluids, like Breakfree CLP

for example, that are formulated to act as solvents and as light lubricating oils.

Sometimes you will need to use a copper solvent to clean the bore. After several thousand shots, copper from the bullet jackets will build up on the rifling and degrade accuracy. Note that I said several thousand. Most new gun owners will not have to worry about copper fouling for some time. Most copper solvents are also primarily made from ammonia, which isn't exactly good for your health, so skip the copper solvents until you've shot that gun for a while.

OILS AND OTHER SUNDRY LUBRICANTS

If you have a gun, you need gun oil. Guns are like any other complex machinery, they need lubrication to work properly. Those of you who have bodies know that the sack of skin and bones that you call yourself doesn't work

All of these solvents work well. The foaming stuff is great for shotgun bores, and the Hoppe's smells really good. I need to have a car freshener made with that emanation.

quite as well as it used to, the older you get. One of the reasons your joints start aching and creaking is that those joints have lubrication in the form of fluids and specialized super smooth cartilage. The older you get, the more worn that cartilage becomes, and the less fluid that the joint produces. Joint replacements are a popular type of surgery because a little over 99.9999% of people have joints that eventually, to some extent more-or-less, start going bad.

The same thing is going to happen to your gun if you don't take care of it. Just like if you pitch a lot of baseballs, don't give your arm down time and you ruin your shoulder joint, sooner or later the finish will wear off your gun, the oil will dry up, and the gun will start to function less ably than it did. The concept is the same with a car engine. Drain the oil and then drive the car around for a little bit and you will see how long that engine continues to work.

Guns are superbly made and most don't undergo the degree of stress you will find in a car engine, or for that matter, a lifetime of use throwing baseballs, particularly since most guns are seldom used. Even so, if you want the best and safest performance from your firearm, it must be lubricated. Most guns will do just fine with a light coat, a small amount of lube on the moving parts, where the parts interact with others. Most guns (in fact let's just say all guns, and go with that default for now) will do even better with ample lubrication, and here's why.

Lubricant in a complex machine has multiple purposes. The first is the most important. It is used to "grease the wheels," so to speak. Lubrication is used to reduce the effect of friction to reduce wear on a part. The more slippery it is, the less wear that will be imparted to the parts that are interacting. Think of walking on ice with super smooth soles on your shoes. Now imagine using shoes with rubber studded soles. They actually work a little better, and it might be possible to traverse the frozen water without butt-planting on the pond. You want your gun parts to be like the smooth soles on ice, and lubrication is the primary way to do that. In combination with some of the high lubricity platings and coatings on the market, like hard chrome and nickel-boron nitride, or Molybdenum Disulphide and powdered graphite, oil can really do

Wrong kind of oil, though it would probably work better than WD-40.

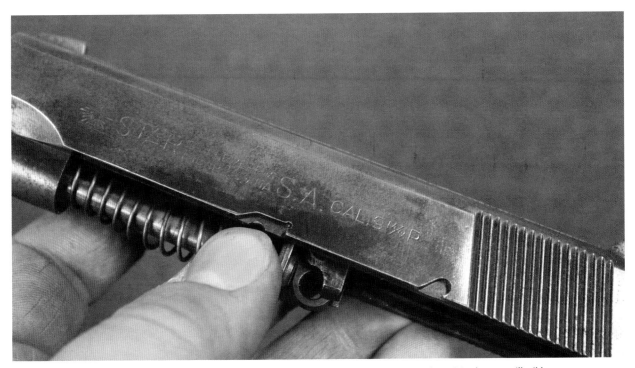

This is what happens when you neglect your gun. First there's rust, then there's pits, pretty soon the writing becomes illegible.

Hold the AR carrier assembly over the garbage and hose it down.

This CNC mill clearly shows the benefit of fluid lubrication and flushing.

wonders. Just don't be tricked into not using lubrication because you have one of those wonder-platings, for the following reason.

Lubrication is also used to flush away debris. Engine oil does this as well and that is why there is an oil filter that must be periodically changed along with the oil. A well designed gun part that moves or interacts with other parts, and bolts are great examples, will have grooves or pockets for debris to be flushed into during the time those parts move. The motion of the part provides the agitation necessary, and the lube is the fluid to carry it away. Insufficient lubrication will still make the parts slippery, but it will not act as a flushing agent. Shoot, even the CNC equipment used to machine all these parts is a self-contained coolant and flushing machine, with sprays used to both cool the tooling and to remove debris from the tool.

The third function of oil and lubrication is a means of removing heat. This is not a major role for guns and truthfully is quite minor. However, in items such as machine guns, it can come into play, but still in only a small way.

We need to mention grease and anti-seize compounds (basically grease with a very fine metallic powder content) and their use on firearms. Anti-seize is very important when mounting barrels and in the use of choke tubes. The former is of no concern to the new gun owner, or veteran gun owner for that matter, but the latter is of extreme importance. If you don't apply choke tube lube (anti-seize), your tube will get stuck sooner rather than later. It can be very difficult to remove a stuck or rusted-in choke tube. Difficult can be translated into "expensive." Gunsmiths charge big money for removing stuck tubes, and for good reason, because at times they can literally not be removed

Belt fed Vickers machinegun, cooled by water in the large jacket surrounding the barrel.

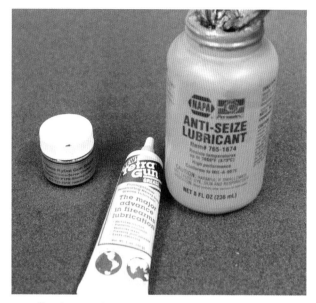

You will at times need to use grease. Use it sparingly.

and then it's time for Howie the Hacksaw to make an appearance. Congratulations, you just turned your goose gun into a turkey gun.

There are some who advocate the use of grease on moving parts rather than oil. With some exceptions which I will cover in a jiffy, I do not recommend this. Grease, if applied thick enough (which is not much), will act as a dirt magnet and collect dust and detritus and stick it to your parts. Furthermore, it does not flush away the gunk like sufficiently-applied oil will. Finally, if you really layer it on, it can form a seal and create a vacuum effect in some systems that will inhibit the function of the gun's action. Grease is good for action springs, such as coiled hammer springs or recoil springs that are contained inside the firearm, again in only light amounts. The choke tube threads are one of the most contained locations in a gun and the choke tube lube anti-seize is perfect for these threads. Grease is well-used on sear/ham-

There are a multitude of oil lubricants. Some are of higher or lower viscosity and some are formulated for lower or higher temperatures. You can afford to be choosy as they are all pretty inexpensive.

mer/trigger interfaces where you really want a smooth interaction, which can really enhance the feel and repeatability of a trigger pull. For the most part, however, you should use oil rather than grease when lubricating your firearms. This applies for situations that are cold and snowy and wet, like the deer hunt, or to dry and dusty environments like the southwestern high deserts. There are differing formulas that work better than others at different temperatures, and a little independent research can steer you in the right direction. Some are thicker in viscosity, others are quite thin. Some freeze at very low temperatures, others freeze or separate in temps that are relatively warm.

Most guns are not sufficiently lubricated by their own-ers. Indeed, many firearms brought in for service to a gun-smith shop are simply victims of insufficient lubrication or insufficient cleaning.

I'm only going to say this once. Industry manufactured gun oil is excellent, it's cheap, and it's available virtually everywhere, like WalMart. Use it. Do not use anything else, no matter what that smartass at the NAPA counter or your buddy with the smarmy look on his face says is his mega unknown uberlube.

Do. Not. Use. WD-40. It works well for a while but then if the conditions are right, like when it's applied to a gun, it will gum up like, well, chewing gum. Removing sticky, nas-ty, crud from your gun is precisely why you clean it. There's no point in voluntarily adding more back into the system.

Check for cartridges and then begin the stripping process.

LET'S CLEAN A SEMI-AUTO PISTOL!

Example: Glock. One of the nice things about Glock handguns is that they don't require a whole lot of maintenance.

As mentioned in chapter two, Glocks are easy to maintain, use, and repair and the result is that they are quite popular. Only three pins hold the frame together and they need never be removed by the owner. The slide needs to be removed, the recoil spring assembly taken out of the slide, and the barrel removed. Compressed air applied to the frame will clean out all the belly lint and dust, and if it doesn't, then use something like Gun Scrubber. The solvent will evaporate in a few minutes. Apply oil drops on the trigger/pin interface, the frame rails, and the connector bar. Likewise, the slide can be cleaned in a similar fashion, but you really only need to apply oil to the rails and the top of the barrel. Glocks are one of the few guns that are designed to operate with little to no lubrication.

A rule can be stated here that should apply to any firearm, and Glock will emphasize this aspect of lubricating their pistols: Do not lubricate the firing pin. Any foreign material in a firing pin channel is a potential danger. Firing pins have been known to stick and cause what are known as slam fires. This is when the bolt closes, and the firing pin is stuck forward and impacts the primer of the cartridge. Boom when you don't want boom. If you are a new gun owner and you think there's a bunch of stuff in any firing pin channel of any gun you have, take it to a gunsmith for cleaning.

The barrel should be cleaned with a brush and/or a jag. Very easy, and very quick. The brush should be pushed straight down the barrel bore and out the muzzle end. Then pull the brush back through and repeat. A jag with a patch soaked in solvent works well, too. Unlike other authorities, I do not recommend dipping your bore brush in the solvent. This just makes a mess and really doesn't work any better than alternating brush and jag-held solvent patches.

When you can look down the bore and no longer see anything but bright shiny barrel, you can stop. Make sure

The GD disassembly manual for automatic pistols is handy if you want to further disassemble your Glock or other pistol.

Remove the recoil spring assembly and the barrel.

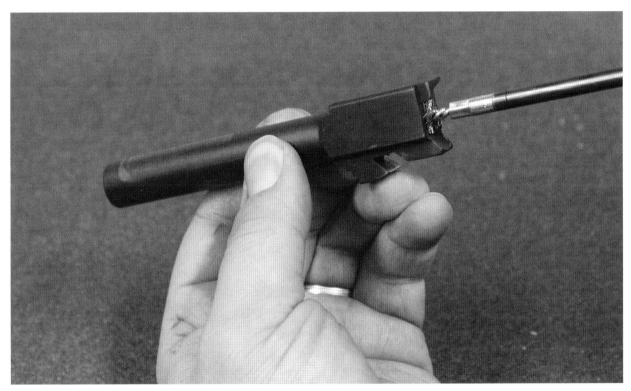

Use a brush to loosen the gunk. Do not dip the brush in solvent.

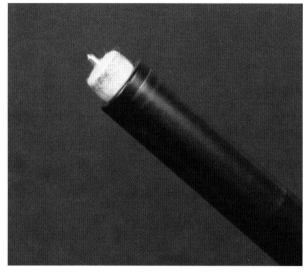

Clean with a jag. Go ahead and use solvent now. Do it until you can look down the barrel and not see any coppery or gunkiness. Clean bright steel only.

The chamber can be cleaned by spinning the jag and patch in the chamber area.

Oil here on the trigger pin. Just a drop or two.

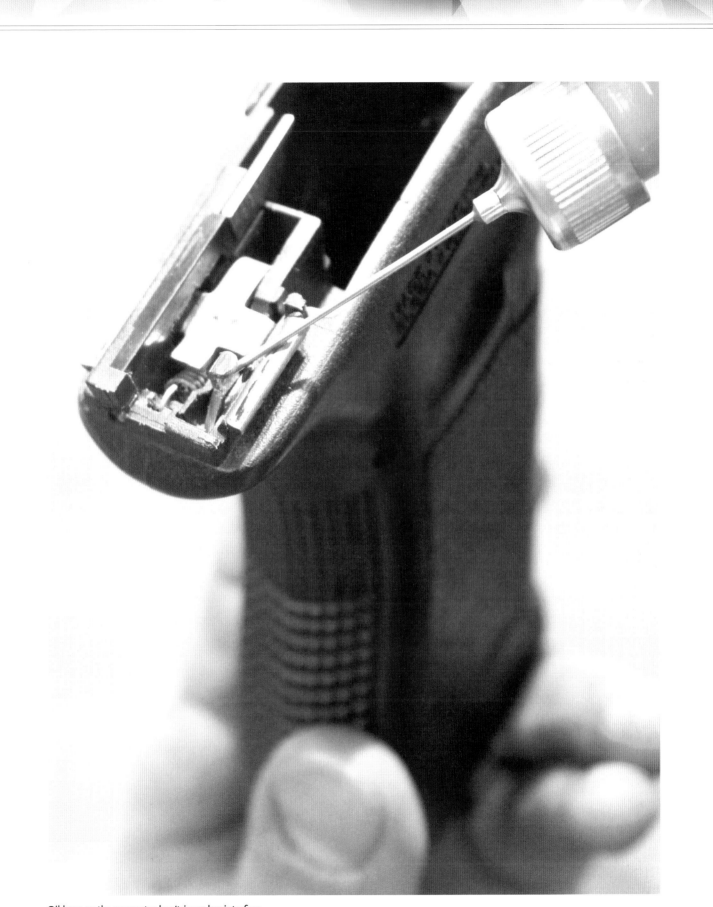

Oil here on the connector bar/trigger bar interface.

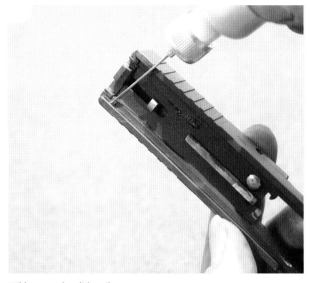

Oil here on the slide rails.

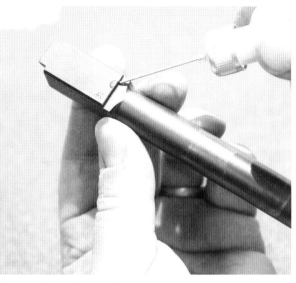

Oil here in front of the barrel hood.

Wipe it down with a lightly oiled rag to regain the shiny black goodness of a well maintained gun.

you clean the chamber, the rearmost area of the barrel. The bore brush, if spun by hand, will work well for this, or a bore mope with some solvent in it.

For the most part, these steps and instructions can be used for any polymer-framed striker-fired pistols like the Glock. Other examples include Smith & Wesson M&P pistols, Taurus 24/7s and similar others from that company, the Springfield Armory XD, any FN pistols, and Kahrs. There are others but these are the most common. It's good practice to wipe down the entire exterior of the gun with a lightly-oiled cloth. The plastic doesn't require an oil coat, nor does the metal on this particular gun, but it won't hurt and will usually make it look just a little bet-

ter. A great supplement to the owner's manual (which you should read), particularly if you want to detail-strip your handgun, is the *Gun Digest Book of Automatic Pistols Assembly/Disassembly*.

LET'S CLEAN A REVOLVER!

Let's say you bought that S&W Model 60 Ladysmith. This is one of those guns that you might want to clean just to keep it pretty, because it is a pretty good looking little handgun. For the most part, revolvers are pretty self-contained and the sideplate that keeps all the guts in order should be left alone. The stuff behind the sideplate is gunsmith material, and some revolvers can be rather difficult to put together,

GD Assembly/Disassembly Revolvers will help if you decide you have to open the revolver frame.

You can't disassemble a revolver as easily as an auto.

so it's best to leave all that alone. With revolvers like the Model 60, and this includes most of the "normal" looking revolvers from places like S&W, Taurus, Rossi, Charter, and Colt, only the barrel and chambers in the cylinder need to be cleaned, and the cracks and crevices can be blown out with compressed air or toothbrush/cleaning brush.

The barrel should be cleaned like the barrel from the Glock. However, except for the rare break-open style of revolver (the barrel itself hinges downward), the revolver barrel must be cleaned from the muzzle end. This is okay as long as care is taken to not damage the crown of the muzzle. A useful tool to prevent damage to the muzzle is a crown protector, and these should always be used when cleaning a firearm from the muzzle.

The chambers in the cylinder can be cleaned by inserting a bore brush and spinning it with a hand drill. This will quickly clean out this super-smooth area and you can then just wipe it out with a mop. You will note that, after even a couple of shots, the front of the cylinder gets dark

You don't need to remove this sideplate. The revolver guts take a very long time to get dirty enough to require cleaning.

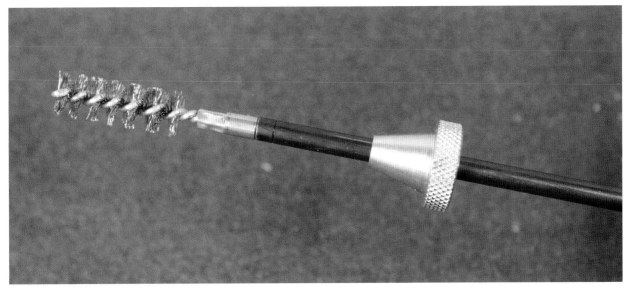

Since you have to clean from the muzzle, the use of a muzzle protector/guide is recommended.

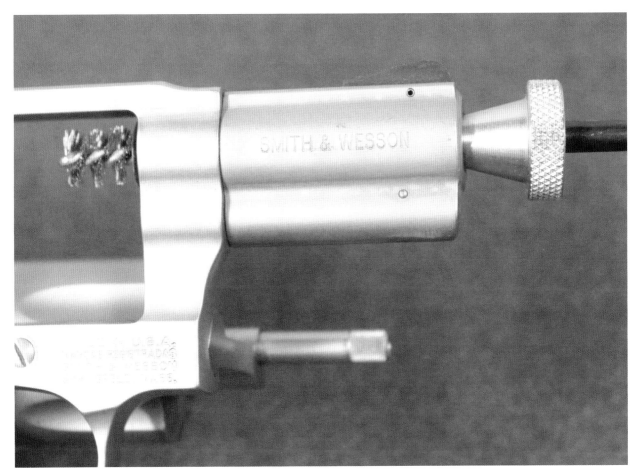

Slowly push the brush through, or you will whack the breech face. Follow the brush with a jag and patch. Make sure you do this thoroughly. If you shoot cast lead bullets and jacketed bullets you should not mix and match. Shoot cast, then clean, then shoot jacketed, then clean, then shoot cast, etc., etc.

Spin a bore brush in each chamber with a drill. You may have to use a slightly larger brush, as the chambers are larger than the bore. Do not spin anything in a rifled bore.

Follow up with a bore mop in the chambers.

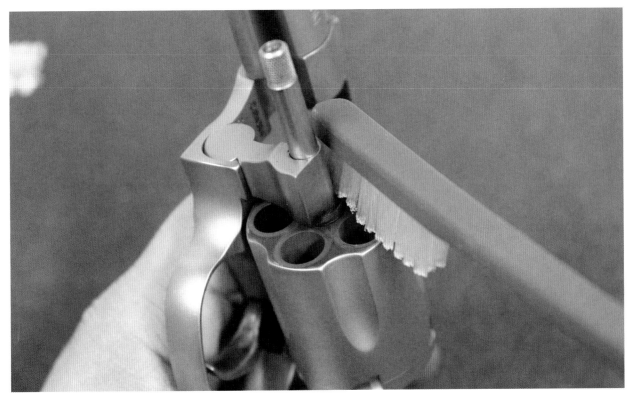

The cylinder front can be cleaned with solvent and brush.

Use the brush to get into the nooks and crannies.

A bore guide will help to keep solvent out of the rest of the gun that isn't the barrel.

with residue. Other than cosmetic appearance, this is not a symptom worth treating. Be aware, if you do decide to remove this residue, that standard gun cleaning solvents will usually do the trick, after a while, but it may not even be possible to remove all indications using a reasonable amount of time and effort. It's my opinion that, unless you are selling the gun and want to clean it up, there is little benefit to super cleaning the front of the cylinder. But if you want to make it look super pretty, like it was in the gun shop, then by all means do so.

A light coat of oil on the exterior of the revolver will make it look snappier and you should be ready to go. If the gun is a safe queen, then a light coat of oil in the barrel wouldn't hurt. When you take it out to shoot it, run a tight patch down the barrel to remove any dust or stuff that may have collected in there while in storage. If you like, buy a copy of the *Gun Digest Book of Revolvers Assembly/Disassembly*. It will give you further disassembly instructions if you want to dig deeper.

LET'S CLEAN A BOLT ACTION RIFLE (OR SHOTGUN)!

Bolt action rifles are usually pretty easy. It's simply a matter of cleaning the bore and chamber, cleaning the bolt,

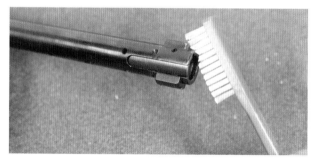

Use a brush to clean off the bolt.

and wiping down the outside of the rifle. Except for using a longer cleaning rod, the principle is the same as with the Glock pistol. Remember to, whenever possible, clean the rifle from the chamber end.

The chamber and the bolt lug recesses in the receiver just behind the rear face of the barrel should also be cleaned on occasion. Get an AR-15 chamber brush to clean this area, as that brush is useful in more guns than just the ARs. You will not likely get much powder residue or stuff like that there, but hunting rifles tend to attract lots of grass, dust, seeds, and ticks, so eventually cleaning there will be a good idea. I'd only worry about it if your rifle got really dirty after

You can use that AR chamber brush to clean other guns too.

Use the *GD book of Centerfire Rifles A/D* for your assistance if you have other rifles you want to clean or poke around in.

Unscrew and remove the magazine tube cap.

you dropped it off the stand or fell in the creek.

Cleaning the bolt may be necessary. Under normal usage, blowing and/or wiping off the bolt is sufficient. Most of the time, taking down the bolt assembly is not indicated. Wipe off the outside, and use your toothbrush to get in the cracks around the extractor and the bolt face. If you dropped the gun in the mud, and you don't exactly feel like bringing the gun to me (or can't afford to, I do so love charging high fees), then it might require disassembly. Remember that firing pins do not like stuff around them, and if there is mud or debris inside the bolt, it could cause problems. Most of the newer, low cost, bolt action rifles on the market have very simple bolts that can be taken apart by the average user. If this is the case, then they will

usually indicate this fact in the owner's manual. An additional resource for the disassembly of these rifles is the *Gun Digest Book of Centerfire Rifles Assembly/Disassembly*, if you want to explore cleaning the rifles any further.

LET'S CLEAN A PUMP SHOTGUN (OR RIFLE)!

Pump action long guns have been around for a long time. They tend to be simply made and robust, and are usually easy to take down for cleaning or storage. Let's use one of the most common pump action shotguns as an example, the Remington 870. This gun tends to get dirty around the bolt, in the trigger group, and on the outside around the forend. The forend area of the barrel and the magazine tube underneath can be cleaned with good old

Disengage the feed latches and pull the forend off the magazine tube. The bolt and carrier will come with it.

You will need to clean and lube the action bars, as they receive the much of the wear when the gun is cycled.

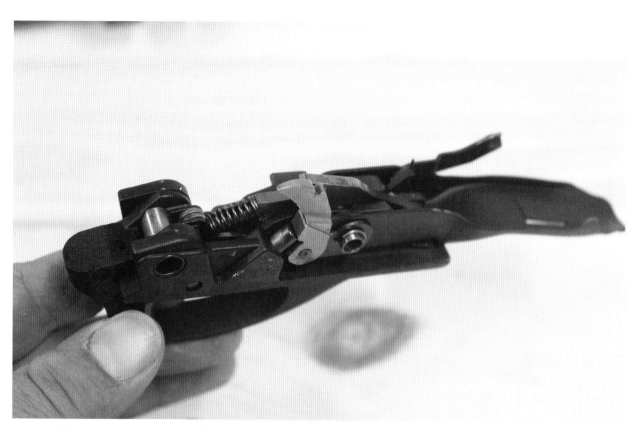

For general cleaning, leave this trigger assembly together. Blow it out and oil the pins. You can even dunk it in solvent or use an aerosol solvent.

Shoot some solvent into the receiver and brush/scrub it. Rinse or wipe it out. There are some sharp edges so watch your fingers.

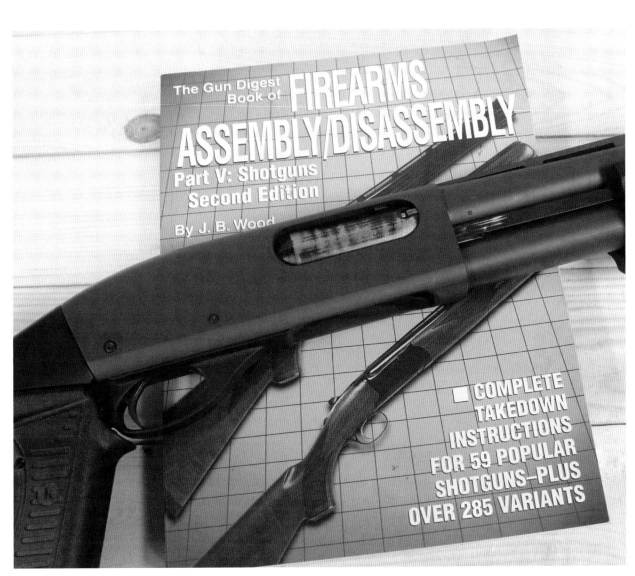

The GD book of shotgun A/D has further input on the 870 and others.

compressed air or aerosol cleaner, then wiped down afterwards with an oily rag.

You have to remove the barrel. In order to do this the magazine tube cap must be taken off. On a lot of used guns the magazine spring retainer that is supposed to retain the magazine spring is missing and the only thing keeping the spring in is the tube cap. So remove that cap carefully, as the spring will flop around and amputate your head if you don't. The forend should be pulled back slightly to unlock the bolt and then the barrel can be removed. You then pull off the forend by depressing the two shell stops inside the receiver and pulling the forend assembly off the front of the magazine tube. This is dif-

ficult to describe, so please refer to the *Gun Digest Book of Shotguns Assembly/Disassembly* for a detailed description and illustration of how this is done. You have to do this step if you want to clean your bolt. The bolt falls off the forend assembly as soon as it clears the receiver. Hose down the bolt and the carrier that it rides on with solvent and then wipe down the action bars that extend backwards from the forend, as well as the inside of the forend tube. It should be easy to clean.

Internally, this gun requires a little more effort. Punching out the two pins in the receiver will allow the entire trigger pack to be removed easily. This assembly should not be disassembled unless you are a gunsmith.

If you insist on doing it, get the *Gun Digest Book of Shotguns Assembly/Disassembly*. Blow it out with air. Be careful with assemblies like this when blowing them out. All the parts, holes, and slots can easily redirect sprays back into your face, so watch how you are blowing. The receiver section can also be effectively cleaned with aerosol cleaners, but should be fully oiled lightly after the solvent evaporates.

There may be a need to clean the magazine tube of dust and tears. Refer to the owner's manual or the assembly/disassembly book on how to remove the magazine spring and follower. Get as big a shotgun bore mop as you can find and run it down the mag tube to remove the debris and stuff that is in there.

When clean, the bolt should be oiled, the magazine tube exterior should receive a light coat of oil, and pins in the trigger assembly should receive a light coat of oil. The rails in the receiver upon which the bolt and action bars ride should also get a couple drops of oil for lubrication.

LET'S CLEAN A SEMI-AUTO RIFLE (OR SHOTGUN)!

Internally, semi-automatic rifles and shotguns are very similar to pump-action guns. The parts are similar or the same, and they operate in the same fashion, except that semis tap some of the energy of the firing of the gun to cycle itself, and pumps use the good old fashioned muscle power of the shooter to cycle the action. A good example for this one, just to ride the coattails of the pump guns, would be a Remington 11-87 shotgun. This is also a very common shotgun, at home on the range, in the field, or in the home. For the 11-87, the cleaning is very much the same as the aforementioned 870, with one big addition. The outside of the magazine tube will become quite dirty, since it is a gas-operated shotgun, and that gas is tapped from the barrel and it wraps around the magazine tube to push a piston that sits around the tube. As a result, this area at the front of the magazine tube gets quite dirty and must be cleaned on a regular basis. Most semi-auto shotguns function in this fashion or a very close approxima-

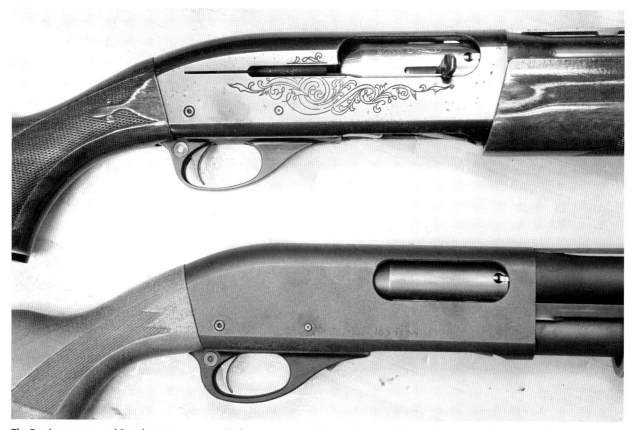

The Remington 1100 and 870 shotguns use many similar or same parts. The receivers are different, for example, but are very alike in appearance and styling. The 1100 is semi-automatic and the 870 is a pump gun.

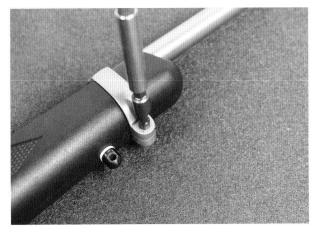

Remove the clamp screw and clamp if they are present.

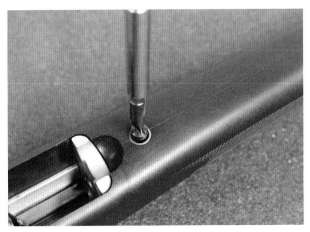

Remove the action screw.

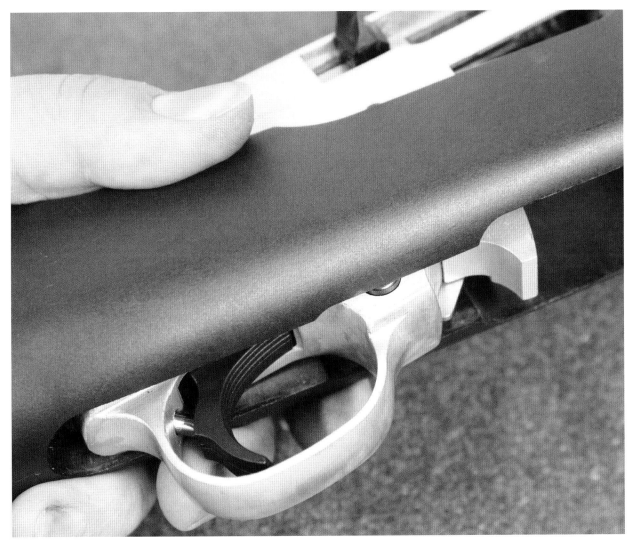

Remove the action from the stock. Make sure the safety button is centered or it will not clear.

Push out this pin and the other, forward of it, to remove the trigger pack. Again, compressed air and maybe a few Q-tips will suffice to clean it out. Lightly oil the pins.

tion of it. Benellis and their Stoeger and Franchi offspring do not, and we should just touch on those inertia-operated models briefly.

If you purchased a Benelli, Franchi, or Stoeger semi-auto, such as a Super Black Eagle II or Vinci, or 48L or Infinity, or M3000, they all operate on the same basic system. These guns tend to be lighter than their contemporaries, and are generally much easier to keep clean. Usually only a small amount of gunk will accumulate around the bolt and a little will get into the trigger assemblies and magazine tubes. Usually the bolts and many of the internals will be chrome plated. Simply wipe them down and reapply some lubrication. Now let's look at a specific and common semi auto rifle, the Ruger 10/22.

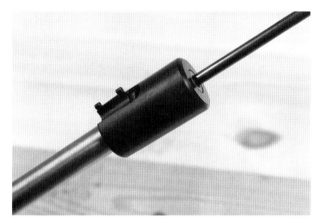

A Dewey muzzle guard is perfect for the 10/22. It aligns perfectly by the slot cut in it.

STORING YOUR GUNS

If your gun is a safe queen (a gun that sits in the safe for long periods of time), then some special care should be taken. Anything made of iron in a safe is subject to rust, and stainless or nickel plated steels are still susceptible.

A periodically replaced desiccant pack or a dehumidifier rod should be used in steel fireproof safes. The desiccant pack will absorb water vapor in the air and make the atmosphere dryer than the moon in the safe. A dehumidifier rod doesn't really dehumidify as much as it causes air circulation in and through the safe to keep the air moving. This helps prevent the surface oxidation that we know and love as rust.

A larger area, such as a safe room or vault, would be better served with a large floor dehumidifier that you might purchase at Menards or other home or office supply store.

While it is useful to run guns well lubricated, a lighter but complete protective coat of lubrication is indicated for storage. Liberal amounts of oil will simply run down to the lowest point in the gun; this is not really a problem but can get messy. In this case I recommend a lube such as Birchwood Casey's Barricade. It comes in an aerosol can and is very easy to get into the cracks as a result. Spray it and then wipe it down and put it in the safe.

If you are considering long term storage, then buy the rust preventative gun bags currently on the market, put the guns in the bags, throw in a couple of desiccant packs, drop it in the PVC tube and bury it, if you are interested in doing that sort of thing, burying a gun and then forgetting where you put it.

The Ruger 10/22 should be cleaned by removing the barreled action from the stock. If the rifle has a barrel band at the front, then this band should be loosened by backing out the screw that is in it, and the action screw just in front of the magazine well should be removed as well. Follow the directions in the owner's manual or the assembly/disassembly manual if you want to clean in detail. Generally, you must remove the trigger housing, followed by the bolt. Don't take any of the stuff in either assembly out. Leave them intact. Take a toothbrush with solvent on it and clean all the powder residue from the bolt, receiver, and trigger guard. Gun Scrubber can be used to clean any gunk in these parts if there is a lot of it. Be careful to spray away from your body so the solvent does not swoosh back at you. Use your compressed air to dry it, or let it sit for a few minutes. The bore must be cleaned from the muzzle unless you want to first remove it by taking off the clamp at the front of the receiver. Put it all back together with an oil squirt in the receiver, on the bolt, and a couple drops on the pins in the trigger housing.

Just about anything needed to clean or upgrade the AR can be found in the AR catalog from Brownells.

LET'S CLEAN AN AR!

As most know, the AR-15 has taken the gun market by storm. Literally millions have been sold over the last thirty years, and the vast majority have been purchased in the last ten. There are well over 100 companies that manufacture the lower receiver (the serial numbered part

Magazines will need to be cleaned on occasion. The box magazines are easy, and brushes like this are used to efficiently do so. Rotary magazines are a pain.

The cleaning toothbrush can be used with great efficacy on the AR upper as well.

The bolt can be wiped and scraped clean. You will occasionally have to remove the extractor and clean that slot out.

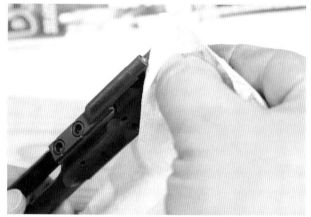

The carrier will need to be wiped and brushed clean. Hard stuff will build up inside and may have to be scraped out. Special tools are available for this.

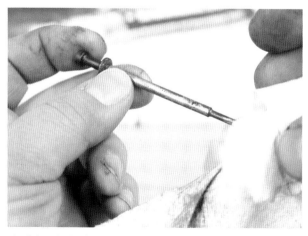

The firing pin is chrome plated and should be wiped clean and reinserted dry. It will get some oil on it from the bolt cycling so you don't need to oil it.

The bolt should look like this when you put it back in before shooting. Before storage, wipe off the excess, but it will function better when wet.

When cleaning, leave the lower parts including the fire control pins alone. Repeated removal and installation for routine cleaning will wear the holes.

Pull the buffer and spring and clean them. Usually it will only require a wipe. A large bore mop can be used to wipe out the tube.

The Tactical A/D manual will help with the AR and other black guns.

AR bolt carrier assembly, wet, properly lubricated.

that is considered the firearm), and not quite that many that build the entire rifle. You can get it as a lower receiver only, a set composed of the upper and lower receivers, an assembled lower receiver with the stock and guts, or the upper receiver assembly with the barrel, handguard, and all. Furthermore, fifty versions of every piece are available at retail for those who want to build a personalized specimen completely by themselves. It is everywhere and for several very good reasons.

The first reason is that the last twenty years have seen an almost constant state of conflict for the U.S. military. Hundreds of thousands of servicemen and women have rotated through the services, learning the M-16 rifle along the way. With their tours completed, they returned home and many of those returned and purchased the civilian model of the gun that was most familiar to them, or was used in combat, for years. The AR-15 is the M-16 minus the full auto capability. The gun is one of the most customizable in existence, it can be made suitable for just about any purpose, and is just plain fun, and generally inexpensive to shoot. Its popularity was improved when the aftermarket arena began producing a truly insane level of parts, accessories, and enhancements. As a result, and not to forget the political statement involved in owning one (cue: middle finger extended in the direction of the gun banners), it has evolved over the years, along with the 1911 pistol, to become the epitome of the American Firearm. There's only one problem. Due to some early difficulties in reliability, directly traceable to the Army trying to save a buck, it has gotten a reputation for unreliability that it has had trouble shaking. This is a reputation that it does not deserve, however it still does require a more intensive maintenance schedule than most other rifles.

The method of gas operation that the AR series of rifles utilizes results in, depending the on ammo used, a significant amount of fouling in the receiver area and bolt assembly. While easily cleaned, it can malfunction in time when it has not been cleaned. Just for the record, the average AR owner that shoots a few dozen or even a couple hundred rounds a month need not worry too much; you can clean it every thousand rounds and probably be fine. A quick wipe down and blow out of the receivers, and disassembly and cleaning of the bolt assembly after every couple hundred rounds is even better.

The AR is a perfect example of a rifle that works better with lots of lubrication. In fact, I personally know the owner of a well-known and respected high end AR manufacturer who doesn't clean his rifles until they stop working. They don't stop working until after many thousands and thousands of rounds have been fired (usually because something broke, like an extractor), because he consistently applies lubrication in generous amounts. His belief is that the lube should splatter on your shooting glasses when you shoot. His rifles just keep working because the gunk, yes there is a lot of gunk, never has a chance to harden into gunk cement. When it does harden, it does so in one of those clearance areas that are machined into the parts, having been oil flushed to those zones, leaving the rifle able to function reliably when other similar rifles have long since failed from lack of cleaning.

The AR bolt carrier assembly must be disassembled, thoroughly cleaned, lubed and reassembled. My suggestion for lubing the bolt carrier assembly is to hold it over a garbage can and hose it down with lube, enough for it to be very shiny and somewhat runny. Put it back in the rifle and start shooting. When you are done shooting, wipe it down, retaining a light coat on it for storage. When you go back out to shoot, hose the carrier down again and have fun. The upper receiver itself should be cleaned as well, but this can be done in conjunction with the barrel, and can be done with a rag or large bore mop. Otherwise the "toothbrushes" that cleaning equipment companies sell, or just new personal toothbrushes, are great for scrubbing out an upper receiver. Use the rigid plastic brushes, not the metal bristled brushes. An AR chamber brush on a stick with a hand drill will quickly and efficiently clean the chamber and bolt lug recesses, and the bore can be scrubbed with the standard rod and brush/jag combination mentioned for previous guns.

The lower receiver should receive or require little attention. Blow out the lower with compressed air and drop a few drops of oil on the trigger and hammer pins. The buffer spring in the stock might get pretty dirty if you get in the habit of using sufficient lube and they should be periodically wiped down to remove the excess oil. Incidentally, little bit of light grease placed on this spring will also quiet down the loud "SPROING" you hear when ARs are fired.

Do not take out the fire control parts from the lower! You don't need to do this unless there is a huge amount of stuff in there or if some of that stuff (like a primer that popped out of a fired case) is interfering with the proper movement of the parts. Repeated removal of these parts will result in damage to the trigger/hammer pin holes in the receiver, which if significant enough can cause the gun to discharge when you don't want it to do so. As with the other mentioned firearms, refer to the *Gun Digest Book of Tactical Weapons Assembly/Disassembly* if you need help disassembling the AR-15 or its clones.

Finally, I want to make an admittedly self-serving plea. Don't feel badly if you can't confidently disassemble or clean your firearms. There are people who went to school to learn how to do that well and quickly and they are called gunsmiths. The cleaning fees are usually pretty nominally priced, and depending on the gun will usually run between $40 and $75. If you don't shoot enough to clean on a regular basis, then take it to the gunsmith once a year to have it done there. I realize, rather acutely, that the average American simply doesn't have time to be good at everything they would like to be. Most gunsmiths have a special catcher's mitt to receive the gobs of money that customers literally throw at them to clean, repair, and upgrade the myriad firearms in existence. The Gun Digest disassembly manuals previously mentioned, and the Gun Digest Book of Exploded Gun Drawings, are designed for gunsmiths and consumers to use in order to disassemble firearms. But my catcher's mitt is still handy, all the same.

CHAPTER 4

GRIPS AND STOCKS

PISTOL GRIPS

Somebody at some point a long time ago decided that the AR-15 A2 style pistol grip really wasn't all that comfortable, what with the finger spacer knobby thingy on the front. People with smaller hands or fingers cannot comfortably use that A2 grip (actually, I have yet to meet someone who admits to liking it) so people started filing the finger bump thingy off. Problem solved and more people were happy. Pretty soon, other variations of grips started appearing, with completely different designs becoming very popular. While there are still quite a few people who are satisfied with the stock A2 grip (usually folks with fatter fingers), many are not and we now have a

generous selection of quite inexpensive pistol grips, such as the models from MagPul, Hogue, Ergo Grips, CAA, and the list continues. Best of all, these grips are mostly under $20 and are plentiful, and come in a variety of colors. All because the A2 grip came with a finger bump (and the A1, incidentally did not).

So let's look at some aspects of the various pistol grips and why one would want to use one. To gain a little perspective, the term "pistol grip" can mean a lot of things. The traditional definition or example would be the wrist area of a standard buttstock, like one would see on most bolt action rifles or hinge-type shotguns. The wrist area is basically the transition from the buttstock to the forend

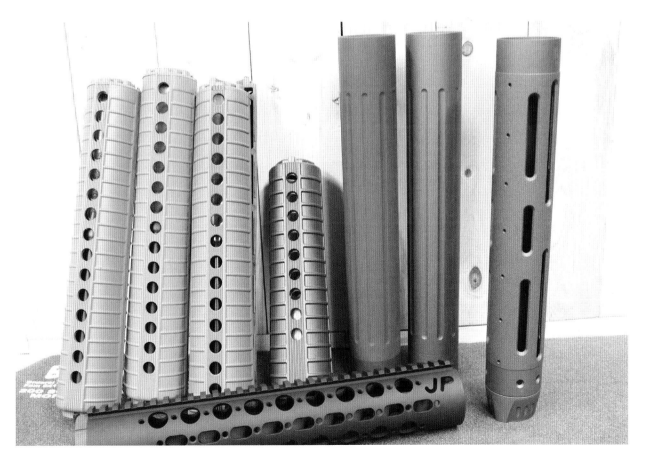

The A2 grip on a lower, the standard.

The A2 grip is not conducive to hands that are not average. It's more comfortable for the author to choke up on it like this than to hold it down using the finger stud.

A two-piece stock where the stock and forend are separate pieces, and the pistol grip is integrated into the stock.

A one piece stock where the stock and forend are the same piece.

The author's son demonstrating proper technique using a stick substituted for a gun. No child needs to be taught this. They figure it out on their own. Good thing he's home schooled, huh? Die Autobot! Die!

area of the entire stock piece. Or if you are looking at a two piece stocked gun, it is the point at which the stock attaches to the receiver.

That section is curved in a fashion that allows the hand to comfortably bend at the wrist. It is integral with the stock but, since it allows the hand to be rather vertical rather than mostly in line with the barrel, it is called a pistol grip and will be described that way whenever someone wants to talk at you about it. Did you ever as a kid play cops and robbers or war on the playground and use a convenient stick to substitute for a gun? I sure did. And I found that sticks with forks on them served as a better gun than just a straight stick because I didn't have to bend my wrist as much to point it. That is why we have integral or non-protruding pistol grips. It's simple ergonomic comfort.

Now you are going to see just the opposite on a lot of guns. You will often find straight wrists on stocks that have no gentle curve or any curve at all. Except on reproduction guns, this type of grip area is no longer commonly used. The first appearance in the US was likely on the early Henry and Winchester lever action guns. The early models of these rifles had straight lever loops that rested flat against the bottom of the gun. It wasn't until a decade or three later that Winchester and Marlin began curving the lever loop and, correspondingly, the wrist area of the stock, to produce a more traditional pistol grip.

To find the earliest examples of straight wristed with the lowered buttstocks that we see today you would have to go back to the early muskets and matchlock guns. The lever action with a falling bolt and straight wrist was used on the Martini-Henry rifles used by the British Empire during its great Imperial days. A great way to see the Martinis is to watch a wonderful little movie called "Zulu," starring Michael Caine and Stanley Baker. This flick is a straight up war movie chronicling the battle of Rourke's Drift during the Zulu wars in southern Africa. Well, I should say that most of the rifles are Martini-Henrys. There are a few inappropriate rifles and pistols present because the film ostensibly ran out of the correct rifles and had to substitute a few incorrect ones in order to film the film. Sorry for the digression, but as you will find, there is nothing really new anymore. You have to go way back in some cases to find stuff that is truly innovative.

The third, but less common pistol grip is the thumbhole stock. In this case what is mostly a traditional stock is left thick in the wrist area and given a curve at the bottom like a traditional pistol grip stock. The big difference is that a cone-like hole is bored through the stock through which to place your big fat thumb. This type of grip is actually very comfortable to use and also allows for a very heavy buttstock, generally used for target applications. We'll talk more about thumbhole stocks and grips when we get to the stock chapter.

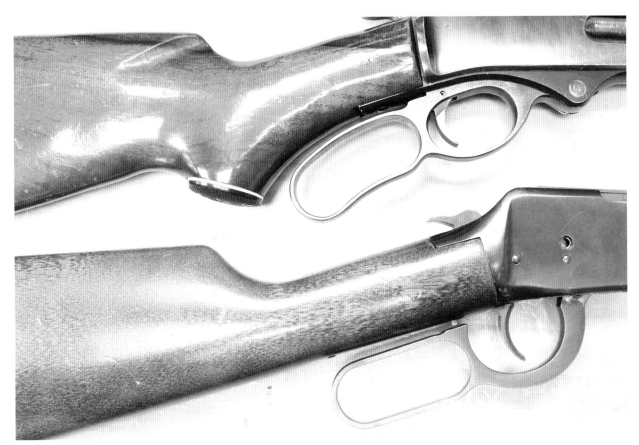

Some guns don't have pistol grips. Most of them are like the Winchester 94 on the bottom.

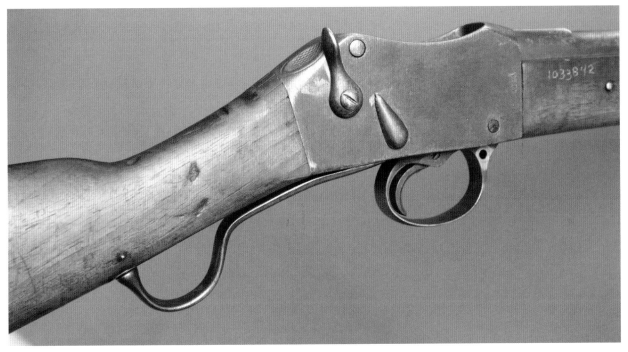

Martini-Henry rifle; the rifle of Victorian British Empire.

The final type of pistol grip is what most think of as a pistol grip. It is a hand-filling section that protrudes from the bottom of the gun, like would be seen on a pistol, and is generally close to vertical. This is what you will see on most Modern Sporting Rifles and increasing numbers of more traditional rifles and shotguns. There are two main reasons to use a protruding pistol grip.

The first relates to the desire to lower the barrel in relation to the shoulder to better control recoil impulse. Most traditional shotguns and rifles' stocks contact the shoulder below the barrel line. This is the primary cause of muzzle rise when firing a gun. You are essentially using a lever that has an off center pivot point. Lowering the barrel so that the recoil force is directed directly into the shoulder minimizes muzzle rise. However, a traditional pistol grip incorporated into the stock is less than comfortable when it is combined with a low bore. So low bore axis guns like ARs, AKs, HKs, basically anything derived from modern military rifles, are equipped with protruding pistol grips so that holding the gun is more comfortable and practical.

The second function is related to the first. Your hand is pretty much perpendicular to the length of your forearm. Keeping your hand nearly vertical also allows your arm to control recoil better. For example, try punching something with your hand closed in a fist, impacting on your knuckles. That's how it's supposed to work. Now try it this way. Punch something really really hard, but instead of impacting on your knuckles, angle your wrist forward so that the impact hits the top of your fist on

A protruding pistol grip typifies the modern sporting rifle. The pistol grip, stock, and forend or handguard are almost always separate pieces.

The protruding pistol grip is designed to facilitate muzzle control. By lowering the bore and moving the recoil impulse straight back into the shoulder, it requires a vertical grip for ergonomic comfort.

the thumb and index finger. Your hand isn't designed to do it that way, is it? It functions the same way with a gun and pistol grip, albeit in a less dramatic fashion.

So you see, there is a reason for putting protruding pistol grips on guns, including guns that don't traditionally have them. And it's not to make it easier to shoot from the hip without aiming, like a certain Senator from California has been known to say. Comfort and recoil reduction are always desirable and the pistol grip in any of its forms contributes to the improvement of those qualities in the action of shooting.

Installing a pistol grip on a rifle

For the most part, the thumbhole and traditional curved and straight styles of grips are not readily removable or replaceable. Since they are integrated in to the buttstock, there is not really the option to remove them from the gun without also removing the stock of which they are a part. Where you can have some fun is with the protruding pistol grip.

So many long guns have protruding pistol grips now that it would be very difficult to name them all. So let's look at a couple of popular options. We've already mentioned a few AR-15 type grips. Let's dig a little deeper into the options. The original Hogue pistol grip is quite popular. It is a plastic grip overmolded with a rubberized coating that makes it very grippy to the touch. The only potential downside is that it has finger grooves in it that don't really fit people with small fingers very well. Hogue has since begun producing a grip that doesn't have finger grooves. A similar item is from MagPul, the MOE+ grip. This grip is also overmolded, but is otherwise just like the standard MOE grip. This overmolding technology is also very common with rifle and shotgun stocks and that will be examined a little later. The rubbery surface increases the grippyness of the grip. Even when wet, the pistol grip is still very solid in the hand, and the overmolding also gives a little, allowing the grip to very slightly adjust to your hand.

Another fun possibility for the rifles is the modular grip, of which there are only currently two prominent in the marketplace. The MagPul MIAD grip is the original and has replaceable backstraps and front straps that slide into the main body. The original models even had a trigger

A small selection of the many pistol grips available for ARs.

AR grips are held by a simple ¼-28 screw.

AK grips are also retained by a single screw.

guard insert, but those are no longer available. The MOE trigger guard has superceded the trigger guard insert. The CAA Universal Pistol Grip is similar, but where the MIAD is a straight grip, the CAA Universal has a slight curve to it. There are folks that like the curved nature of some grips, in fact this grip, and the Ergo grip from Falcon Industries closely approximate the pistol grips from the HK series of rifles. It's all personal preference. I know guys who use only one and no other brand, and others like me that are okay with a bunch of different types of grips, being not too horribly picky.

A unique model is the Stark Industries grip. Very not-AR looking, it is big, increases the trigger length-of-pull, and has a more vertical angle to it. It is rather well suited for big guys with big hands and long fingers.

The really nice thing is that most of these models, regardless of the model of gun that they are designed to fit, are almost always attached by one or maybe two simple screws. Or maybe a screw and nut combination, but either way, it is a very simple matter to take off the old grip and install the new one. Best of all, you rarely need more than a rather large, flat bladed screwdriver.

You will find the largest assortment of grips for a rifle being destined for AR-15s, with the AK type of rifle close behind. However, even those little industries don't hold a candle to the grip market for handguns.

Installing a pistol grip on a pistol

As soon as someone starts building pistols (we're talking modern times here) somebody else starts making grips for them. In fact, sometimes the somebody else makes grips so well that the original pistol maker will use the otherwise aftermarket grips as an OEM product. The best example of this is the wide use of Crimson Trace lasergrips that come on factory pistols. The laser, and possibly the tactical light (addressed more elsewhere), are easily the most purchased accessories for the handgun market. In the case of Crimson Trace, the lasers are incorporated into the grip panels themselves.

The S&W Model 60 Ladysmith was shipped with an attractive cocobolo wood grip.

The Walther-designed P38 pistol of WWII fame was one of the first pistols to be manufactured with plastic grip panels.

I made these grips using a fixture made from a cut-off barrel spud. They look okay and worked great, but I didn't reinforce them. There is a crack at the bottom.

In the case of the 1911 pistols, the Beretta family of pistols, and any other type that uses two side panels on the grip, you will find a glut of products. The original pistol grip panels back in the day consisted of a flat piece of wood on either side of the grip frame, shaped to fit the frame and usually held on by two screws each. You will see this pattern earliest on the Browning designed pistols which include the 1911 and its older brothers, as well as the German Lugers, P-38s, Walthers, and Mausers. Wartime production imperatives often caused the wood to give way to plastic, and it is still quite common that plastic is used in place of wood, but wooden grips still have a place. Revolvers and certain semi-auto pistols still use one-piece slip-on grips on occasion, but they are very much like the two piece grips in style and material.

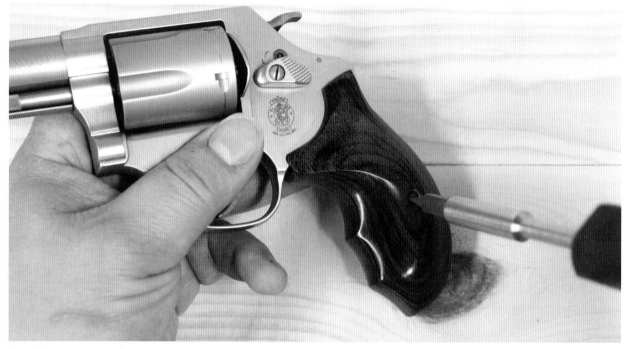

The single grip screw can be removed simply.

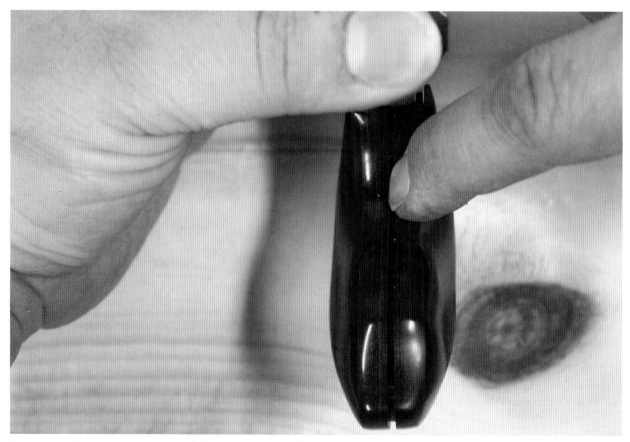

Use a fingernail to gently separate the grip halves. Do not use a tool that will ruin the finish on these sexy grips.

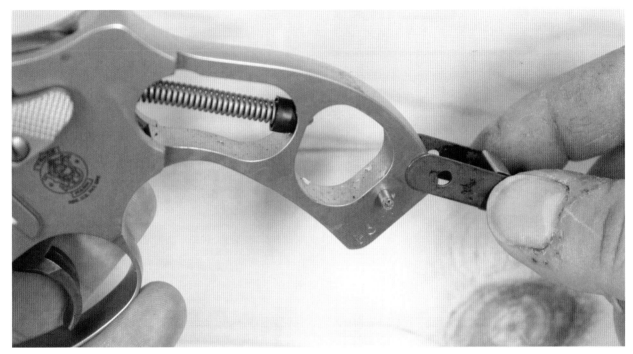

The replacement Hogue grip uses a bracket that is slipped onto the frame around the bottom locater pin.

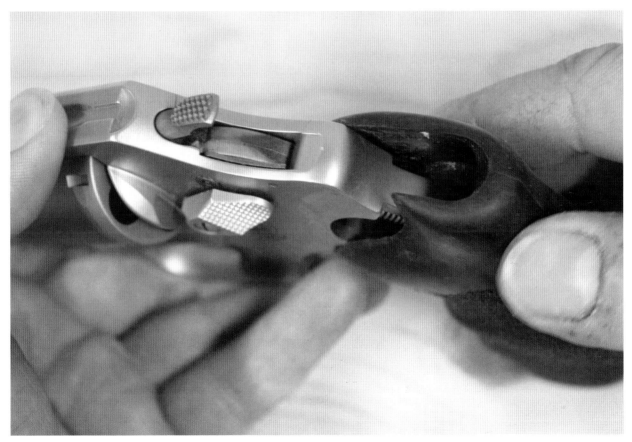

Slide the Hogue grip onto the frame.

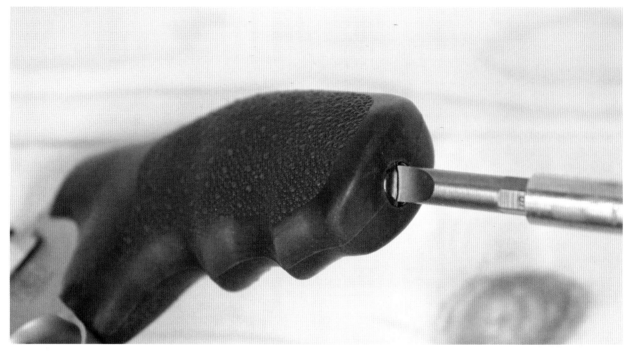

Install the screw through the grip into the bracket.

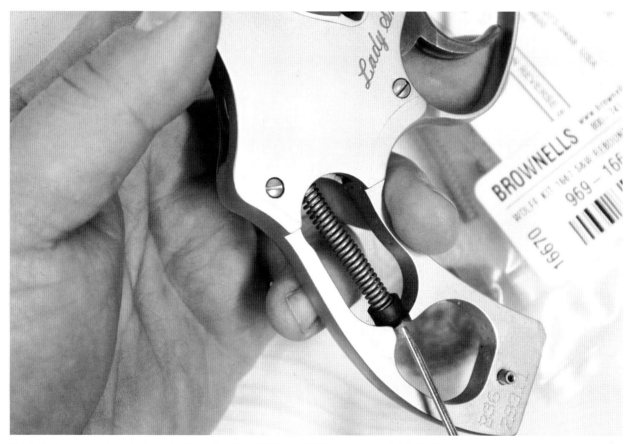

This is the hammer spring which can be changed out for a lighter model. There are upgrade kits for this.

Not as pretty anymore, but the Hogue grip makes the gun more comfortable to shoot.

While rifle stock wood tends to be limited to certain high strength woods such as walnut, birch, and some maples, pistol grips have trended into the exotic. Ebony, rosewood, mahogany, and cocobolo grips are available for just about any pistol that can take them, and you will find some really impressive looking pieces. What's super cool is that some of this exotic wood is actually toxic, so if you want to by a blank set of grips and shape them to your gun, you might want to be choosy on what you get. Inhaling some of the particles or ingesting the oils of some of the exotic woods out there can be damaging to your health. However, the upside for dying early is that you can have, on your carry gun, a set of wooden grips that are nothing like any plain old walnut or other boring domestic wood.

Smooth rosewood grip panel on the left, and checkered cocobolo grip panel on the right. The exotic woods have interesting grain patterns and colors.

The backsides of the two panels show the less finished appearance of the two woods.

Another feature that is shared with long gun stocks is the laminated grip. Just like with the laminated wood panels used for construction, laminated grips are numbers of very thin wood strips that are pressed with adhesive together under high pressure. Usually different woods or differently stained woods are alternated so that, when the grip is shaped and contoured, you see different colors and the contrast really stands out and gives a snappy appearance to the pistol. Gray/black, green/black, red/black, red/white/blue, are just a few of the combinations you will find.

Similar but not identical to the laminated wood grips are the laminated synthetic grips. These are made from fiberglass, micarta, Kevlar, or carbon fiber, among other things. These tend to also be of alternating colors and are often laid in sheets that alternate in fiber direction as well as color. These grips are great for duty and hard core use as they are very atmospherically stable and can take abuse far above what you can expect with traditional wood grips.

Very recently, several companies have made grips with various images on them, from a bald eagle to a zombie or the Punisher skull. While, in my opinion, they are not all that appealing, they allow you to personalize your handgun to the extent that you desire.

Finally, if you want to make your gun heavier, you can use metal grips. Usually checkered and sometimes engraved, metal grips tend to be made of aluminum and I've seen some pewter and other heavier metal grips as well. These are very attractive and will usually set off the gun with a little flash and sparkle, if you are into that kind of bling.

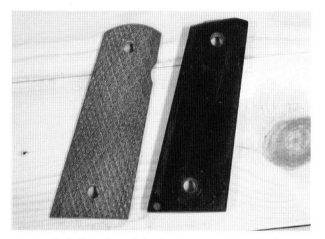

Composed of a fiber-glas resin laminate, G10 is a newer popular material from which to make handles and grip panels. Different colors are a thing to do with G10, and it is impervious to moisture.

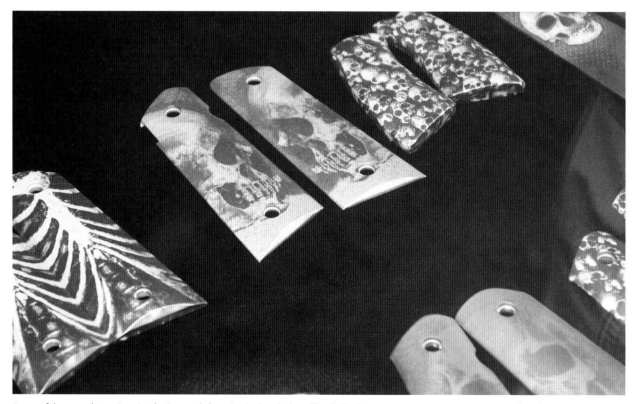

Some of the new alternative pistol grip panels have intriguing designs like skulls, bones, or any pattern you can comprehend.

BUTTSTOCKS AND OTHER "FURNITURE"

Through the history of firearms, particularly in the modern era, buttstocks are probably the most likely thing to be replaced, customized, or otherwise altered or repaired by the owner. Just in types of wood alone used in production, the buttstock stands out. Every kind of walnut has been used, with certain types being highly desirable. Wooden stocks can be plainly figured or highly detailed in grain and cut.

In the last couple decades the use of plastics has become quite common in the production of gun stocks. Fiberglass reinforced stocks and grips, as well as carbon fiber and aluminum have become quite common, and we will analyze each in turn as we proceed.

One thing that should be noted is that some long guns have a one piece stock; that is, a stock that runs the length from the shoulder and recoil pad all the way some distance down the barrel. Others have a two piece stock that separates the buttstock portion from the forend or handguard portion. Typically, in modern common vernacular, the two piece stock is not considered a two piece item anymore. It used to be that both pieces were made from the same piece of wood, thus the two piece description. Generally, they are referred to as the stock and forend nowadays so that is how we will proceed when discussing them. If you want to call the stock, forend, and handguard the gun's furniture, you will be fine, as that is an oft-used term to describe those pieces as a collection.

The stock

Usually, owners forgo changing stocks unless it's on certain firearms, notably MSRs. Most ARs come from the factory with basic A2-style fixed rifle stocks or simple collapsible M4 stocks. Most aftermarket stocks have unique or useful features. Earlier examples, such as the modular stocks made by Vltor started with compartments, often watertight, that allowed the owner to stash useful items like spare batteries for their red dot sight, or a couple last ditch rounds. Later models carried the concept further, or put in a tensioning or locking mechanism to stop the stock from rattling.

The MagPul CTR stock is a direct replacement for the standard M4 stock, but with a twist or two. It has a lock on it that will keep the thing from rattling. It has the added benefit of looking a lot nicer.

MagPul CTR stock with an M4 stock.

Fixed stocks are fewer in number than collapsible stocks and most don't offer much more than extra compartments or a more sexy profile to the gun. A popular alternative is the skeleton stock made by ACE called the ARFX. Very lightweight, it incorporates a foam rubber cheek pad that makes it much more comfortable, particularly in the cold. Most of the Ace stock lineup makes use of the foam pad and it is unique to that brand.

One of the most common things to do is to replace a rifle-length fixed AR stock with a carbine collapsible stock. The advantage to a collapsible stock is not to hide it under a trench coat, as several politicians have intimated. No, it is to adjust the stock's length to the wearer's body, whether because he or she has a thicker coat on while out hunting, or whether it is somebody else's body altogether. Collapsible stocks do not require cutting, sanding, or refinishing to fit to anyone. The AR collapsible stock is so useful and prevalent that adaptors have been made to attach it to just about every other common rifle and shotgun in existence. Shotguns have it, AKs have it, even

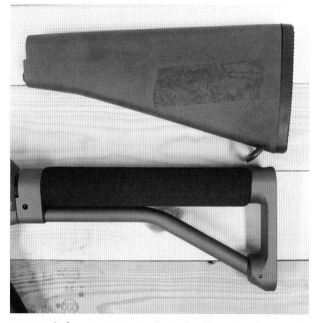

ARFX stocks from Ace are extremely comfortable and very light weight. Much better than the original A2 stock on many rifles.

German guns have it. Going to an adjustable stock loses you little, including expense, and gains you a great deal of flexibility. The same rifle can be comfortably and safely fired by the 6'3" father, the 5'8" wife, and the 4'5" twin sisters, one after the other with just two seconds of easy adjustment in between shooters.

Length of pull adjustments can be added to fixed stock rifles as well. The most recognizable is the model from Graco called the Gracoil adjustable length of pull recoil reducer. This unit can be added on to any shotgun or rifle stock to give a good inch or more of adjustability, combined with recoil reduction on top of that. This Gracoil unit and other similar functioning models can be purchased at Brownells.

Stock composition – Why that and why not?

The material composing a stock can make a real, practical difference. Unfortunately, the atmosphere in which we live can have a significant effect on wood. Wood stock blanks are dried for a year or more to remove as much moisture as possible before work is begun on the shaping and fitting. If it has not been sufficiently dried before the work begins, it will likely change its shape before long. It really stinks when you've put in several hours (hand fitting) the stock only to come back a week later and find that it has warped because of the humidity. The real downside is that humidity, or immersion, can do this even after the rifle has been built and sold to a consumer. This is the deficit inherent in wood stocks. Truthfully, you should have to really try to get this to happen, but it can happen and has done so frequently enough to be mentioned. The benefit of the solid wood stock is the sheer and utter beauty of a traditional stock with high visible figure and color contrast. You will not attain such a thing with synthetic stocks or laminated stocks.

This kind of finish requires many coats of oil and proper buffing at the end.

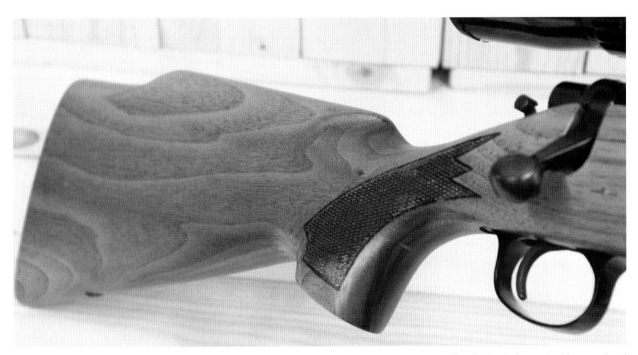

Remington has the annoying habit of covering up nice wood with their detail-hiding lacquer. Clean it off and refinish the stock with tung oil and it is a whole new animal.

Solid wood stocks are also subject to compression. If you make a habit of overtightening some rifles' action screws, the screws that hold the trigger guard and bottom metal to the action by squeezing the stock between the two, you will eventually compress the wood and may end with the result of a loose fitting assembly and negative impacts on accuracy. More on this later.

However, the synthetic stock is impervious to humidity and dang near anything else. You can melt it if you subject it to direct flame or high heat, or you might be able to crack it if you deep freeze it and smack it with a sledgehammer. But humidity and low heat will have no effect. You could hit it with some fun solvent like methyl-ethyl ketone (MEK) and chemically melt it away, but that would nuke a wood stock or laminate stock too. No, the point of a plastic or synthetic stock is that it is cheap to manufacture and purchase, and will take a beating. Not only will it take a beating, but you won't mind that it takes a beating. A well-made, high fig-

The nice thing about synthetic stocks is that some effective antislip surfaces can be molded into them.

ured, solid wood stock is a work of art and you have to have too much money for your own good to want to take it out and risk banging it up. That's what synthetic stocks are for.

The wood laminate stocks are a good compromise between the two extremes of solid wood and synthetic. Laminates are just as expensive as an average solid wood stock, but are not subject to the potential warping and much less susceptible to compression than a solid wood stock. They also are heavier than synthetics but can be much more aesthetically pleasing as well.

The other type of stock is more commonly called a chassis system and we'll forgo talking about that for a little bit, as it's more fitting to discuss when we get into a couple of choice stock modifications.

Stock mods – Fitting

The most common issue with buttstocks is fitting them to the owner. Most owners don't bother, either wanting nothing to do with paying for the modification, or not knowing that such a thing is even necessary. I'll be blunt. At some point in the last hundred and two years, somebody decided that buttstocks should be designed to fit the average white male. This means a stock that has a length of pull (distance from the trigger to the back of the stock) in the 13-14-inch range, and sometimes even longer. This design decision works well for the majority of gun owners, who just happen to be white and just happen to be male. Women and minorities of the Asian persuasion (as you can see by my photo on the back of the book, I am of the latter category), or anyone of smaller or greater stature than the 5'10" average height, can run into issues with off-the-shelf and factory stocks.

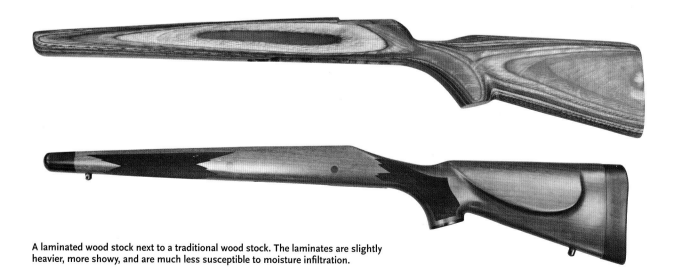

A laminated wood stock next to a traditional wood stock. The laminates are slightly heavier, more showy, and are much less susceptible to moisture infiltration.

Here's an example. If you have access to an Arisaka rifle from WII, stand it up to any modern or even vintage American-made rifle. You will find that the length of pull on the Arisaka is much shorter than on any of our rifles. This is because the Arisaka rifles were made to fit the average Japanese soldier from the early 1940s, whose height rarely exceeded 5'7". Here's another example. The M1 carbine of WWII fame is still plentiful in the shooting community, and it is well loved and well hated, depending who you ask. This rifle was designed to replace a pistol and as such is small profiled, short, and light. The three guns I first deer hunted with when I was a teenager were in this order: M1 Carbine, Type 99 Arisaka, SKS (which also has a short stock). They were all comfortable, because the stocks were short and fit me better than anything else, and coincidentally all had very low recoil. The first rifle I built in gunsmithing school was a Mauser chambered in .270 Win, with a handmade stock. The barrel was 25 inches long because I wanted to be different (most hunting rifle barrels are 22, 24, or 26 inches long) but had a stock length of pull of 12 inches. In fact the gun almost looked disproportionate. I wound up selling it to a young lady with a big chest because she couldn't find anything else that worked for her and fit her as well as that short stock that accommodated her physical contours.

The great part of having a wood stock is the ease of shortening it. Any gunsmith can shorten a gunstock by inches or fractions of an inch for a reasonable fee. The really good ones will fit the gun specifically for you with just the right length and modify the buttpad or plate as necessary. I just bought my six-year-old son his first rifle, a CZ 452 Scout. This is a nice little single shot .22 bolt

The M1 carbine is still a favorite of the author. It's a small Asian sentimental thing.

Poor Jonas is dealing with his birthday present, a CZ 452 Scout, being way too long. Got to shorten that stock for him.

rifle, and I mean it's short. However, my son, also being of the Asian Persuasion, has found that the Scout is still way too long. I need to cut off three full inches before it will fit him properly. But it will fit him, and I'll keep what I cut off to…guess what? Yeah, when he eventually gets bigger I'll put back on what I cut off.

Not only can you shorten the stock, you can lower the comb (the place you rest your oily cheek). If you are more portly than the average white male, your cheek thickness may get in the way. The rule of thumb with scopes is that you want to get it as close to the bore as possible. In that light, a low-mounted scope can often be mounted low enough that you can't see down the center of the scope, no matter how much you press your cheek down on the comb. You have three options. Get higher rings, lose weight, or have the comb dropped a quarter inch. This is a simple task, but is more expensive, since the stock will have to be at least partially refinished. New, higher rings kind of defeats the point of having a low-mounted scope. Losing weight is generally considered the most dif-

ficult and time consuming of the three options, though highly recommended. Dropping the comb will be the most expensive and also the most permanent of the choices. Wood will have to be removed and the stock refinished.

Many trap and skeet shotguns have adjustable combs installed from the factory. The comb section of the stock can be raised and lowered as the shooter sees fit. While somewhat expensive to have an adjustable comb installed in a stock that does not have one, it allows you to use the shotgun to its best effect in multiple disciplines. Most trap-dedicated guns are designed to shoot a little high, while guns designed for skeet or sporting clays are set up normally. You can easily use your adjustable comb to your benefit and your friends' loss by raising the comb slightly when you go the trap range and then dropping it back down when you go to the skeet range. This is an add-on that is much cheaper than buying a second shotgun. The hardware and the labor might run as much as several hundred dollars, but a good target shotgun will run much more than that.

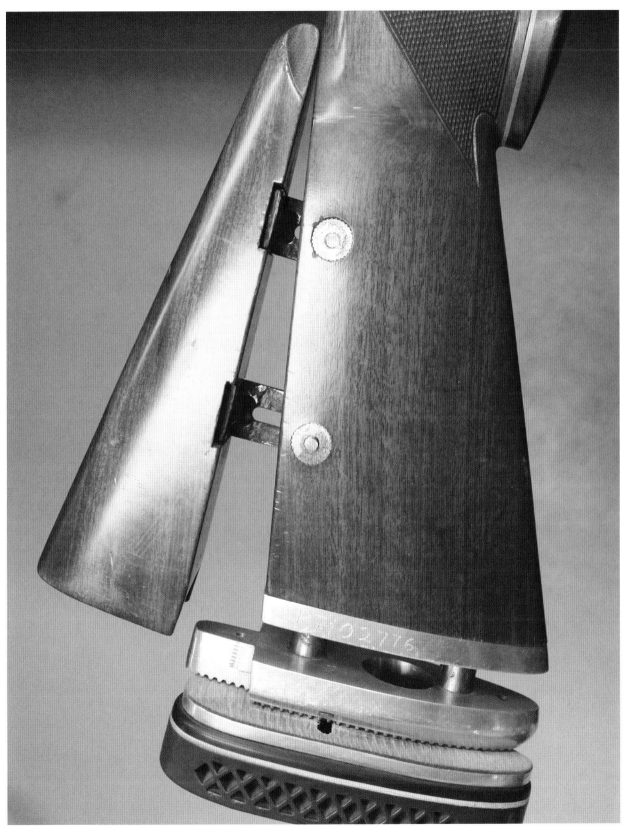

This stock has a fabulously adjustable comb and length of pull.

The inside of a Rem 700 synthetic stock. Compare it to the wooden stock.

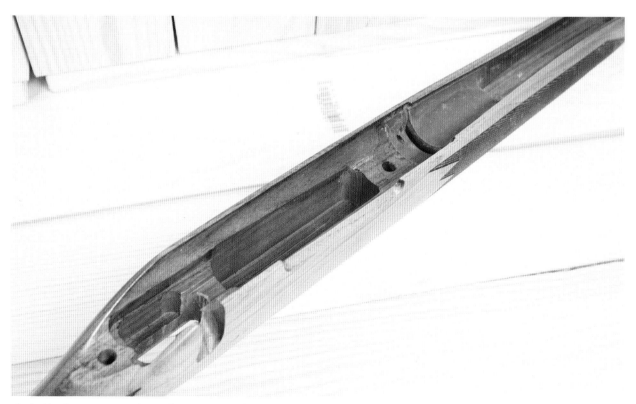

The inside of a Rem 700 wooden stock. Compare it to the synthetic stock.

This Howa stock is unusual in that it has very thick walls and has spines along the top and bottom for affixing pads or sling studs. Unlike most synthetic stocks, this one can be shortened without too much trouble.

Unfortunately, modifying a synthetic stock is a bit more involved, as most of these stocks are as hollow as the average lineman's skullbone. Plastic stocks sometimes have internal pads that run along the top and bottom of the inside of the stock. These pads serve as the anchor points for the screws that retain the butt pad. While certainly possible to successfully shorten, many of these stocks, if you cut them off, will no longer have the pads for the screws to insert into, because you cut them off. Watch out for that. Then you will have to make an insert, or since it's cheaper, just buy a new stock. Comb adjustments on a plastic stock are also not cheaply possible, unless the stock came with an adjustable comb.

If you want your shotgun in particular to fit you perfectly, you will have to have a stock specially made for you and the gun. There are a number of gunsmiths (not me in

this case) that are very skilled in measuring and gauging you and your gun so that the stock is fit to you precisely.

There are several applicable terms here. They involve the direction that the stock takes from its origin point on the receiver. We've already covered length of pull, the distance from the trigger to the back of the stock. Drop is the distance from the sight line of the gun to the top of the stock's cheek comb. The resulting angle caused by the stock drop is called the pitch and the horizontal angle that the stock may be offset to is called cast.

Stock mods – Accurizing

Very few guns come from the factory bearing the best possible accuracy for the platform. That would cost too much. When you are mass producing thousands of rifles, you need to get them out as cheaply as possible and still

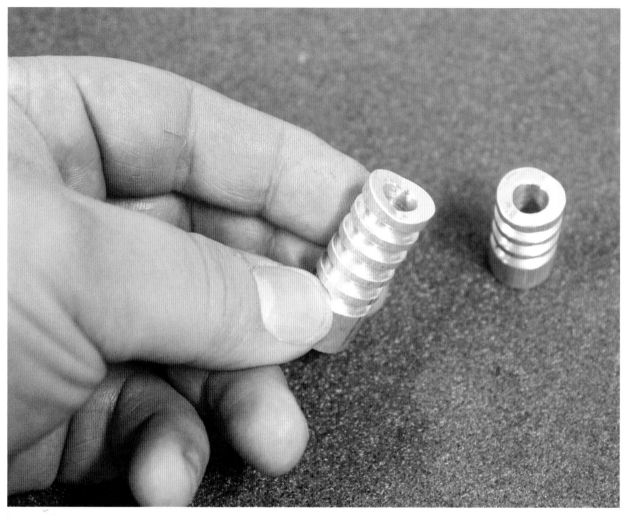

Synthetic or aluminum pillars are often inserted into stocks to help stabilize the rifle and so that the action and trigger guard can be secured tightly to each other without having to be concerned with compression of the wood.

have them work. Hence one major company's habit of shaping a little knobby in the rifle stocks down at the muzzle end to put up tension on the barrel. It has the effect of putting just the amount of repeatable stress on the barrel to make the guns pretty much as consistently precise as any other in the line. But it's not ideal. The most effective single way to make a rifle more accurate is to free float the barrel. A free floated barrel with no outside stresses placed upon it is a better option, but the factory can't really do that reliably and keep the cost down. So one of the common means of customizing Remington bolt rifles, as with any bolt rifle from another company, is to free float the barrel by opening the barrel channel in the forend section of the one piece stock

so that it is sufficiently relieved to not touch the barrel. This is usually performed in conjunction with a process called stock bedding and often with another similar process called pillar bedding.

Pillar bedding is a process where you insert rigid tubes into the stock that surround the stock action screws that hold everything together. These form non-compressible supports that the action and bottom metal is clamped to, with the stock still sandwiched in between. However, the stock is bonded to the pillars and will not be at risk of compression or crushing.

Stock bedding usually takes the form of an epoxy-like filler material that is pushed into sections that are relieved to accept it. The area of the stock that makes contact with

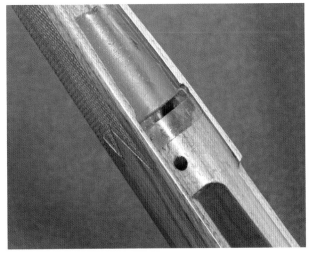

Brownells sells their own bedding formula called AcraGlas. You can mix it with sawdust and pigment, like here, to make it look less like a yellowish epoxy. This stock has been glass bedded to free float the barrel

the receiver front, recoil lug, and the chamber area of the barrel are relieved and filled, and this is sometimes done at the rear and sides of the receiver as well. The most popular products used for this purpose are Acra-Glas, Pro-Bed 2000, and Steel Bed, all of which are available from Brownells. This is not a terribly complicated process and anyone can do it, but it requires some free time and the ability to follow instructions.

Stock mods – Sling swivels

Some long guns do not have swivels or studs for attaching a sling on them from the factory. Many of these however, do have aftermarket kits that are specifically designed for these guns, such as the Rem. 7400, Mossberg 500, and other very commonly used guns. Others require drilling holes, and there is a kit available from Brownells for this that includes the drill bits and everything. Just follow the

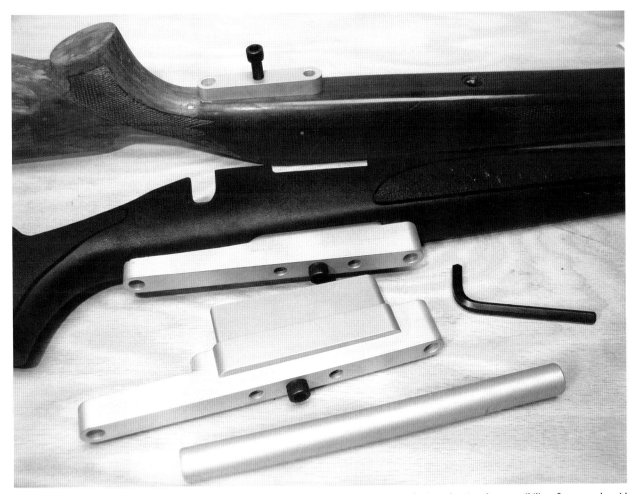

Score-Hi gunsmithing sells a bedding fixture that is a real benefit to stock bedding. It allows for less cleaning, less possibility of error, and rapid easy accomplishment of the task.

You can get inserts that can be glued into a drilled hole that will accept a quick release sling swivel.

instructions, and make sure to tape over the spot to be drilled to prevent splintering.

Another option is installing a small insert into which a quick release swivel is inserted and retained. This allows the sling to be very quickly removed.

Stock mods – Recoil reduction

The desire for recoil reduction is present regardless of the gun. There isn't a whole lot that can be done to a buttstock that will assist with felt recoil reduction. On some newer shotguns, there is a mechanism for changing the drop, cant, and pitch of the stock. Generally this is designed to enhance the fit to shooter for the shotgun, but it can also lower the barrel axis to a small degree so that the felt recoil goes straighter into the shoulder.

Most of these guns, particularly those from Benelli, also have stocks that are designed to absorb recoil, using specially shaped rubber inserts and thick squishy recoil pads. In fact, the stock without the inserts would probably break under recoil, since the top and bottom of

Benelli sells several guns with a Comfortech stock. Here Pete is posing for the camera on a very bright winter day pretending to be engaging descending space alien vermin, also known as Canada geese.

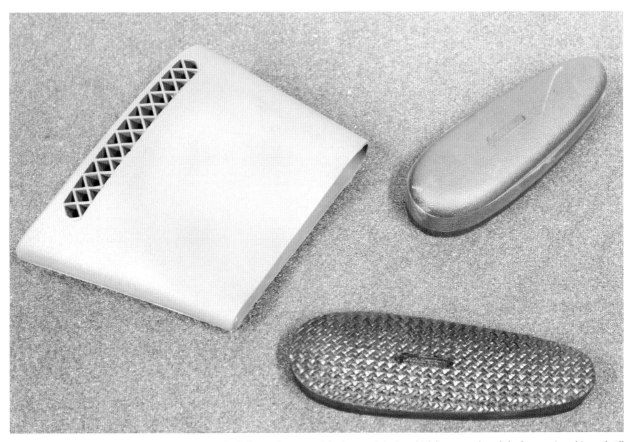

There are options for recoil pads. The big one on the left is a slip-on model. The top right is a thick brown pad, and the bottom is a thin pad. All are made by Pachmayr.

the stock sort of slide across each other, or would if not for the inserts compressing to stop the movement. Basically, some of the energy of the recoil is absorbed, or redirected really, into the expansion of the inserts. As the stock compresses them together, they expand outward. The thick squishy recoil pad works in a similar fashion. It's also called a "gel" pad. Using the word "gel" is like putting the letter "X" in the name of something. Studies have shown that a product with "X" in its name will sell better than the same product without the "X". So a company could sell the crap out of recoil pads if they were to name them the Genesis X-Gel Recoil Stomper. Just you wait and see.

Since we are talking about recoil, let's talk more about recoil pads. This used to be the most common upgrade provided by an average gunsmith shop. Honestly, you can do it at home with a belt sander and hand drill, but to do it really well requires some repetition. Let's say that you want to try this on your 12 gauge. Let's also say that you

Most grindable pads have an aluminum plate inside them. This faint line indicates where the edges of that plate are located.

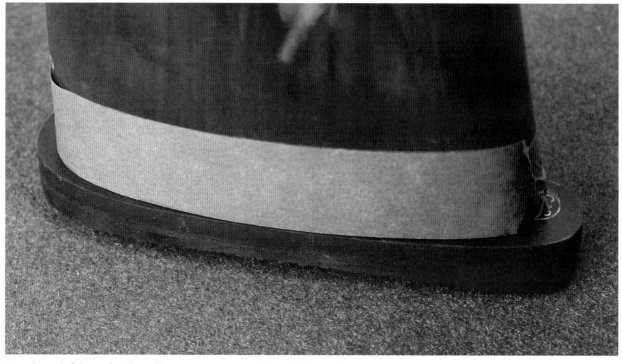

Wrap the end of the stock with masking tape to prevent marring, and then scribe around the edge of the stock to indicate how far to grind. Then go to the grinder or sander and grind it down to the line. Be careful to maintain the angle at the bottom.

want to use a really thick squishy pad that's about an inch thick. You will likely have to shorten your stock by the same amount to keep the length of pull the same.

Pads are sold in different sizes. While some are made to fit certain factory stocks, most are not and must be ground to fit. You want to measure the maximum width and height of your stock at the back edge and find the pad that is sized as close to those measurements as possible, and slightly bigger. You will have to carefully poke holes in the exterior skin of the pad in order to insert screws from the back. You will then have to drill holes at those locations for those screws, and then screw in the screws with a well lubricated screwdriver (to minimize wear to the slot you cut).

At this point you have attached an oversized pad to the stock. You can now try to be a man and do what most gunsmiths do and attempt to grind the pad down to size by hand on the sander. And you will fail, and you will grind a nice flat onto your stock. Turn in your man card immediately. Now you can do the safe thing and try it again this way. You do not need to buy a pad grinding jig from Brownells, though that will certainly help. No, to get an acceptable result, scribe the front of the pad

around the edge of the stock, remove the pad and then grind the outside of the pad to the scribe line. Don't forget the angle at the bottom needs to match the angle of the stock toe.

Now if you failed to that properly, or if you plan on doing a bunch of these recoil pad thingies, then I'd recommend going to Brownells and buying a recoil pad jig. This will help you get the angles right and will allow you to hold the pad to the sander perfectly squarely to get the best results. When you are done grinding you can clean up the edges of the pad with a fine-toothed file and sandpaper. Also be aware that this is a very dirty job that will require a good vacuuming of your hair, neck, and face. And a good sweeping of the floor, followed by a shower.

Recoil-reducing stock inserts are also found on occasion. The simplest is the mercury recoil reducer. This is a hollow cylinder partially filled with mercury. When the gun recoils, it moves rearward but the heavy metal stays because it is fluid. It will still slosh backwards, but not until its additional mass soaks up some of the recoil impulse. Its weight alone compensates for some felt recoil, but the properties of momentum and the liquid nature of

Mercury containing cylinders are used to suppress recoil. They have to have a tight fit (be immobile) to work properly. The screw threads on the end are for getting the thing out again.

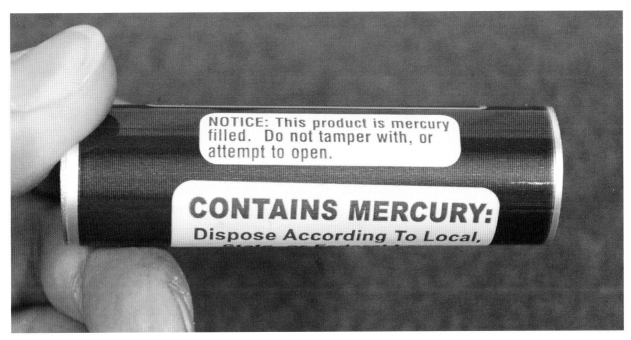

By the way, this product contains Mercury.

Some stocks have plates that are on a spring. The unit compresses under recoil, pulling some of the impulse away.

mercury also add to the felt recoil reduction. These are often placed into the stock bolt hole inside the buttstock and sometimes are contained within or attached externally to the magazine tube or barrel.

There are assemblies that utilize springs to contain recoil as well. The most famous are the assemblies that replace the butt pad, like the previously mentioned Gracoil. Usually these use a large spring or springs that hold the pad out from the stock. The pad is attached to a plate that is inserted into the stock plate with one or two guide rods. Upon recoil, the pad and the plate it is attached to are forced into the buttstock. The spring is then compressed (or stretched, depending on the model), slowing and absorbing some of the recoil impulse into the coils of the spring, which then push the pad back out again. Some models even use hydraulics to reduce the felt recoil

A similar but not identical concept is found on the Blackhawk! Knoxx stocks. A line of collapsible M4-styled stocks are made to fit the most common shotguns, notably the Remington 870 and Mossberg 500. The stock includes a pistol grip with a stock extenstion. The stock piece itself is attached to the extension by means of two powerful springs that extend upon recoil. The effect is the same as with the previously mentioned recoil plate assembly. The difference is that the pistol grip also grants a mechanical advantage to the firing hand for ergonomic relief and recoil control, and you have the length adjustability of the stock as well.

The Howa 1500 is sold in some models with the Axiom stock, which is simply this Blackhawk! stock attached to a chassis system that holds the barreled rifle action. But you can also get the Axiom stock for the Remington 700 models.

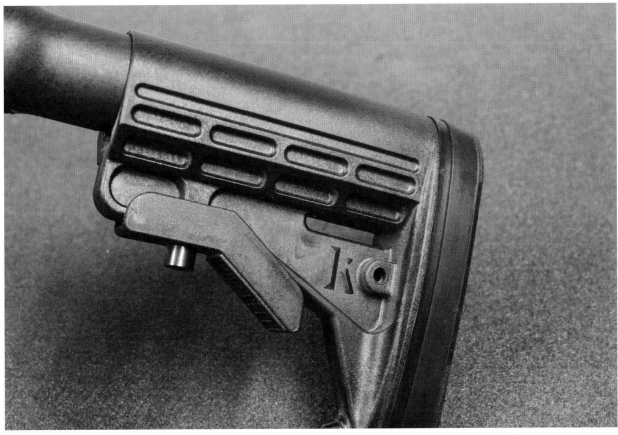

The Knoxx stock from Blackhawk uses a large spring to inhibit recoil, but it is adjustable and modeled after the M4 stock.

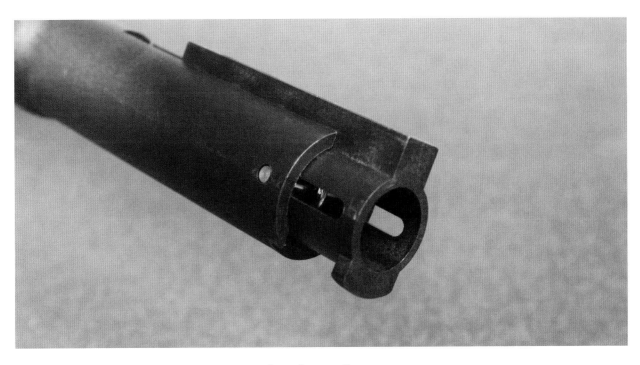

With the stock removed, you can see here the large spring that soaks up recoil energy.

FOREND AND HANDGUARD MODS

Forend and handguard modifications come in two main flavors. The entire assembly can be replaced or stuff can be added or removed to the existing handguard. If you have an AK, AR, or some other variation of the MSR then this category is for you. An endless selection is on the market for the AR series of rifles, both large and small frame, and a significant quantity can also be had for the AK. So we'll look at several excellent examples that also fit in various niches or roles.

Basic replacements

The original two-piece plastic handguards are almost always the subject of distaste to AR owners. This handguard set is almost always the first thing to go on a new AR and, while it is often replaced with a free floating tube, many owners at first go with straight up replacements, albeit of a different design.

The obvious choice for this conversion is the series of MOE handguards made by MagPul. Rather than the round or oval shape of the CAR or M4 style handguards, the MOE type are more suited to being held with the human hand, with a sort of polygonal cross section. They install and remove just as the original M4 set does, but have some enhancements in addition to the shape. You can add accessory rails at different points on the stock if you wish, and they are a little longer, wrapping around the front sight tower a bit to allow the shooter to hold it a little farther forward if desired. These handguards sell for well under $50 and are the best choice if you want a better-feeling handguard but don't want to go with a free floating system.

Several companies also offer handguards with Picatinny rails that also drop into the existing framework and replace the original handguard halves. Daniel Defense and Midwest Industries are the most easy to remember, and

MagPul MOE handguards are good inexpensive replacements for those who do not want to spend bank on a free float tube. They have a more ergonomic design and rails can be added at various spots where needed.

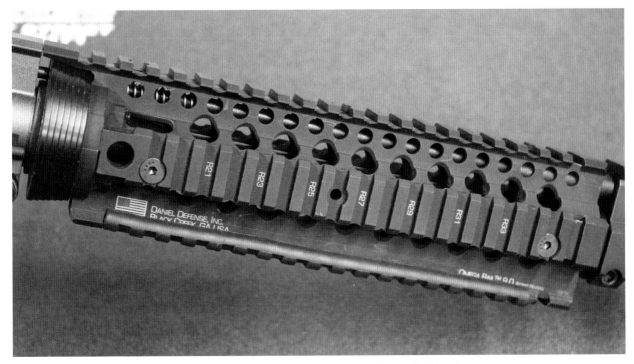

The Daniel Defense Omega rail is thin, yet still has four full length rails. It attaches to the standard barrel nut.

these types of railed handguards are usually around $150, still pretty affordable.

Free floating tubes

As mentioned before, free floating your barrel is the best single way to improve your gun's accuracy, and this is accomplished by removing as many stresses placed on the barrel as possible. With bolt action guns this means relieving the barrel channel. On MSRs like AR-15s it means removing the original handguard and front sight (the front anchor point for the traditional two piece handguards). This requires some simple, inexpensive tools but it is also a very common operation. The barrel is retained to the upper receiver of an AR with a crenellated barrel nut. The wrench engages these crenellations and the nut can be unscrewed from the receiver. There are several free float tubes, one notable example being the Daniel Defense Omega rail that is a two piece unit that clamps to this existing barrel nut.

Basic tubes

Most free float tubes are one-piece extrusions that have the details machined into them. They will have their own barrel nuts that replace the existing nut. The early genera-

This DPMS free float tube utilizes a nut and a tube that is screwed to the nut. And a kickin' Cerakote job.

tions of tubes were and continue to be a simple hollow tube around 1/8-inch thick that is internally threaded at one end. The barrel nut is torqued onto the upper receiver and then the tube is screwed onto the barrel nut and either tightened against a shoulder on the nut or against a lock ring placed between the tube and receiver. These tubes are great as basic tubes, granting the free floating

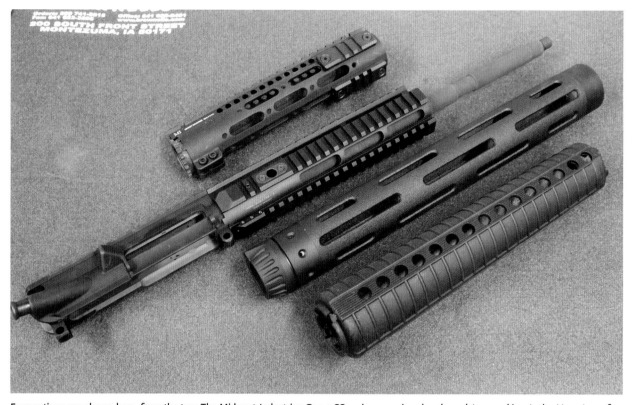

Four options are shown here, from the top: The Midwest Industries Gen-2 SS series one piece handguard (super skinny); the Hera Arms free float tube (heavy but incredibly solid, relatively thin); JP Enterprises Modular XL tube (light, flexible, pretty); and the standard rifle length factory handguard halves.

benefits and a generally good feel, with the downside being a modest increase in weight. Carbon fiber and aluminum are the materials of the day for these tubes, with the carbon fiber being much lighter weight. These solid tubes also trap barrel heat inside the tube, so they are not the best choices for high volume shooting that would be involved in the gaming community and the vermin extermination squads.

Tubes with rails

After the basic tube came a tube-like handguard that had the rails machined into it. These tubes are fairly large in hand and the rails would run from front to back on the top, bottom, and sides. Most of the time these rails are solid with maybe the top rail hollowed out underneath for the gas tube or piston operating rod. Particularly, the tubes meant to be mounted on .308 sized rifles were just huge and you need a really big hand to hold them comfortably.

The current generation of tubes tends to only have a single permanent rail that runs the length of the top of the tube. The original means of attachment with large barrel nut is still common, using a locking ring. On the other hand, people have been complaining that free floating handguards are just too fat, so most companies have gone the other way by making them really skinny. The Omega rail mentioned earlier is not a tube at all, but has a cruciform cross section. This cross section is very thin, and even though it is fully railed it is still pretty comfortable to hold. The other shining examples are those made by Midwest Industries and Troy. They use a proprietary barrel nut and the handguard slides onto this nut. A very simple clamping system is incorporated into the rear end of the tube that has a large linear slot. Two large screws are used to pinch the ears around the slot closed around the barrel nut. Very easy to install, these tubes are incredibly light weight and are covered with holes so that you can add rails wherever you may want them. Tubes have also gotten longer of late and often exceed 15 inches in length.

The reason many handguard tubes are rail-capable but do not have them integrally is that the American public got past the flavor-of-the-month rail-everywhere syn-

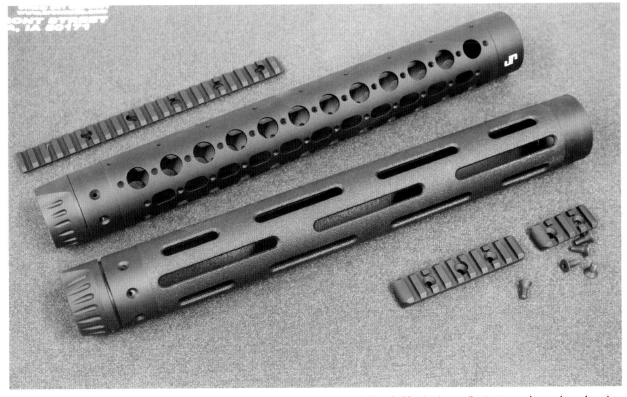

Both JP tubes, the RC above and the original modular below, are configurable with detachable Picatinny rails. Pretty much anywhere there is a hole, you can put a rail.

drome and decided that rails tend to make the handguard too big and uncomfortable to hold without gloves. The rails have a habit of being rather sharp. Rail covers are made to address this but they make the handguard even bigger, and then there are "ladder" covers that actually fill the slots. These are the better choice but are not very attractive.

This brings us to the final type of free float tube. Like other models, they make use of proprietary barrel retaining nuts (or two), but the tubes do not thread or snap on, rather are retained to the nut by separate small machine screws. They are modular in nature with the ability to accept rail-mounted accessories at any point around the outside of the tube. JP Enterprises has had an example on the market since the beginning of free float tubage, and only recently have other companies produced something similar. The original JP modular tube had a number of slots and in a slightly altered version remains the same design. The slots allow a great deal of ventilation to help dissipate the heat generated in the barrel. A new RC handguard is attached in a similar way but removes the slots

and replaces them with a large number of round and ovoid holes. This allows the tube to still have the same amount of ventilation ability but better structural integrity.

Lancer Systems has a similar set up that is octagonal rather than round and uses a ventilated carbon fiber tube rather than aluminum. Both this LWCH and the JP tubes have a following in the 3-gun market, in fact were designed for that competition, but are still very suitable elsewhere in other functions.

The AR tube story is pretty unique, since it's about the only rifle in common use that it works for. AKs and FALs and HKs all use different forms of handguard shapes. This is a good spot to mention that there are some regulations that people with foreign made MSRs need to know. Some dude might want to by an AK. It is a fun gun and cheap to shoot, and is eminently suitable for self-defense. But the crummy, crudely-manufactured stock and handguard wood is, well, just plain crummy and crude. If he wants to put new furniture or other stuff on his AK, he needs to make sure it was made in the US. The applicable regulation is referred to as the 922(r) law. The US gov-

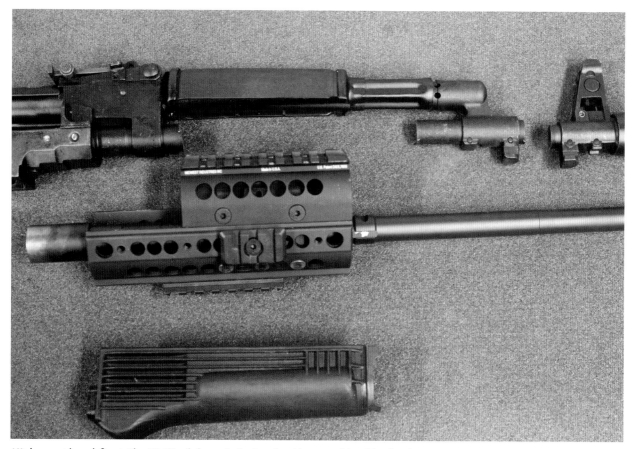

AKs have not been left out. The AK- SS rail clamps to the barrel and is very stable, with rails where you want or need them. You can mount a red dot or something on top.

ernment considers foreign-made semi-automatic rifles to be illegal and evil, so you can't have one unless it has a certain number of US made parts, or to be more precise, doesn't have more than 10 certain foreign made parts. If the number of these parts is less than ten, it is considered a US made gun. If you are going to be swapping around parts on semi-auto rifles, particularly if they are based upon a real assault or military rifle, make sure you adhere to the 922(r) regs.

Appendix 1 has a breakdown of this stuff for your reference.

Railed handguards are very popular for the AKs too. Plastic and aluminum are both represented. However, since the AK has always had only a small handguard/forend, you will quickly run out of smooth space if you use a bunch of rails. The plastic sets are predominantly from TAPCO and the Mako Group and are inexpensive, modular, and easy to install. There are even overmolded models from Hogue. There are not any free floating hand-

guards for AKs, at least on the open market. The design of the barrel and gas piston tube on an AK would generally preclude such an upgrade, though I'm sure somebody has Frankengunned an example together somewhere.

While the free float tube craze and industry is mostly limited to the AR platform, you will find the occasional model for other guns like the FALs, Ruger 10/22s, and. There are a number of lesser known designs that use an AR format for the furniture sets, like the JRC carbine for example. This brings us to the concept of the chassis system.

ONE MORE STOCK MOD – CHASSIS SYSTEMS

I will be brutally honest here. Chassis systems are insanely expensive, but they are superb products. If you want to get into long range shooting with bolt action rifle, not bench rest mind you, but stuff like F-class, sniper matches, and the like, then upgrading or building your own rifle with one of the chassis systems is a great idea, and it's very simple, too. Really all you do is remove your barreled

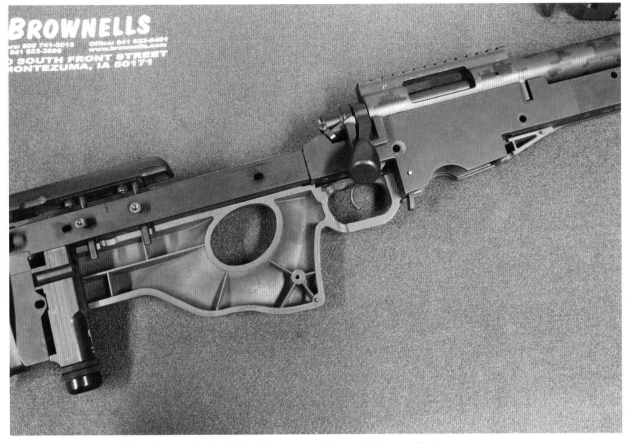

The Accuracy International Chassis System body splits in half to expose the internal aluminum block.

action from the original traditional style stock and drop it into the new chassis.

There are two types. The first is really just a modification or evolution of a traditional stock. The second is a radically different animal, but the interaction with the action is actually very similar to the first. Back in the day a few years ago, stock companies like McMillan, H-S Precision, and Bell & Carlson started making stocks with an aluminum block embedded in the stock. In the place where you would put pillars and stock bedding compound was now just a metal platform into which you bolted your action. This is a better solution and more stable than pillars and bedding because it does not move. At all. These blocks require more space in the stock so these stocks tend to be a bit bulkier and are often of a more radical overall shape, trending to more vertical pistol grips and using fiberglass, and plastic composites. They are all well relieved for a free floated barrel of large diameter. The usual owner drops an accurized bolt rifle with a barrel

that might be an inch or more in diameter into the stock. It will be heavy. This first type is the most common, mostly because it has been around a while, and is quite a bit more affordable than the second type.

The second type dispenses with the traditional stock design and embedded aluminum block entirely and appears to be the culmination of the evolution of the stock pillar. Rather than using an embedded block, why not make the entire stock, or framework for the stock, out of aluminum? The first popular model of this type was the Accuracy International Chassis System or AICS. This is made in England by Accuracy International and is the basis for the British military's sniper rifles. It is composed of a long aluminum block that runs from the back of the stock up to the end of the handguard. Two plastic stock panels then bolt to the outside of the block to form the holding surface. The action sits in the action block section that forms a V-block, with a slot cut out for the recoil lug on the rifle's receiver. The action screws pull the receiver

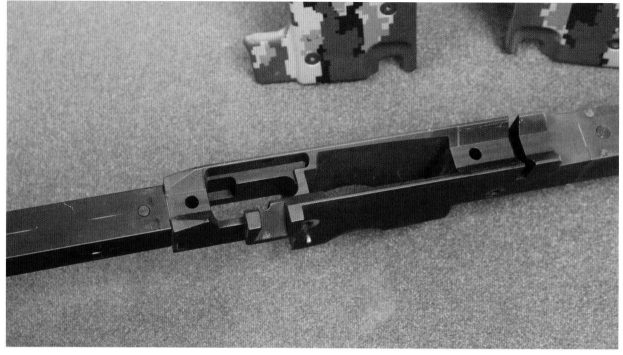

Both sides have been removed and you can see the V-block design of the chassis.

The AICS has an adjustable comb, for height and for left and right motions.

Under the comb are the screws that can be loosened to adjust cheek fit.

down into the V-block tightly holding it into the chassis. This system isolates the barrel from shooter induced stresses and provides the most stable platform for precision accuracy work, without having to have an unwieldy massive stock holding an unwieldy massive barrel, like you will find on some benchrest guns.

There are more chassis systems available now above the AICS. Newer versions dispense with the side panels and simply make the entire thing out of aluminum, stock, action block, and handguard. You will see this style on the Savage 10 BA and JP MR-10 rifles, as well as the aftermarket chassis systems from JP, Modular Driven Technologies, Remington, and Troy. Most are made for Remington 700s and Savage Model 10s, but a few others are designed for rifles like the M-14. Those designed for the bolt rifles pretty much all use AR pistol grips and are designed to

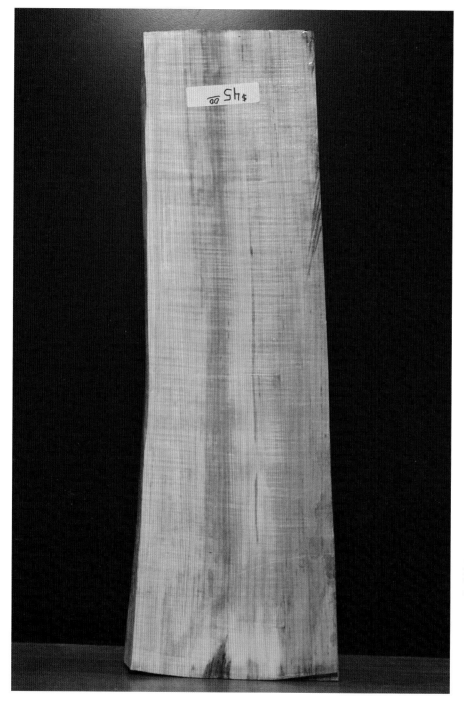

...or you could have some fun and carve your own stock, starting with a blank, like this bit of curly maple.

induce the feel of shooting an AR in the shooter. All are set up so the barrel is fully in line with the shoulder, requiring somewhat higher scope mounting, which incidentally allows for some truly massive optics, and most have fully adjustable stocks and cheek pieces, folding stocks, and some deal of modularity to allow add-ons like lights, lasers, and kitchen sinks. All use some form of detachable box magazine and most of them are interchangeable and based on the original Accuracy International magazine. These types of stock upgrades start in the $600 range and easily surpass $1000. However, if you are looking for an upgrade to enhance accuracy and ergonomics, that price is minor compared to the work you will have to pay for on the rifle.

CHAPTER 5

MAGAZINES

L et's look at the one thing that the vast majority of modern firearms have in common. That is, a detachable magazine. Actually, let's start with some vocabulary. While you can refer to the sidebar for a more detailed explanation, let's at this point just say that a magazine is what a gun uses to hold ammunition, and a clip is a device used to load a magazine. You always want to have extra magazines for whatever gun you have, if such a thing is available. Why? So you can reload quickly. That is the only reason to have extra magazines. If you are hunting and have a four round magazine in the rifle and shoot all four rounds, you will need to reload. It's a lot quicker and easier in the field to reload the gun with another full magazine of four rounds than it is to reload the magazine with cartridges.

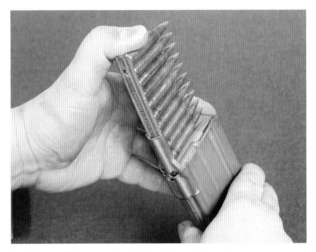

Loading an AR-15 magazine with a stripper clip and spoon.

You can't have too many mags. These SIG551 mags will all link together.

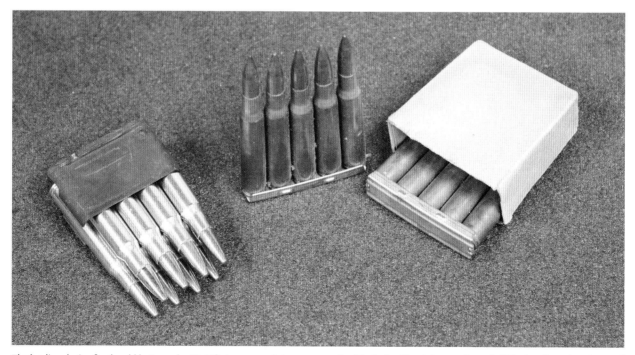

The loading device for the old but popular M1 Rifle is commonly known as an "en bloc" clip. The eight rounds are held in the clip and are inserted into the internal magazine of the rifle. Beside it are two five-round stripper clips from an earlier war, used to load Springfield and Enfield rifles.

Another vocabulary term: the thing that you load into your modern firearm is called a cartridge. A cartridge consists of a bullet, a case, powder, and a primer. Please don't call a cartridge a bullet or I will be very sad and I will track you down. "Shell" is more properly applied to shotguns, and can be used in place of cartridge or interchangeably.

Furthermore, if your gun is being used for CC (concealed carry, hereafter), SD, or HD, it really doesn't hurt to have a few extra magazines. Since most handguns nowadays are shipped with only one magazine, you will have to purchase more of them separately. My personal recommendation is to have four extra magazines for any gun you have as a minimum. That way if one or two do not work reliably, you will still have two extras to carry if you so desire. Ten per gun is a popular number thrown about, and there are larger numbers still. Get as many as you are comfortable with. Please note that magazines are very gun-specific. Get the correct one, since many look very similar. It is the same as with ammunition. Only one type will work, and while there are many different manufacturers, only the magazines designed for your gun will work. Externally the magazines for a 9 mm Glock and a .40 Glock are virtually identical, and they will fit interchangeably in the pistols, but will not function interchangeably. In the end, buy as many magazines as you like. You can use them.

MAGAZINE VERSUS CLIP

This qualifies as a pet peeve. These two words are used interchangeably, but they should not be. Just like the powder magazines in forts, or artillery magazines in battleships, firearms magazines hold ammunition.

Most firearms that are repeaters use box magazines that are detachable, meaning that the shooter can remove the magazine with ease to refill it with cartridges. The magazine is then reinserted into the gun to load it. Some rifles and shotguns use internal magazines that do not detach, such as internal box, or tubular magazines. These cannot be detached but are generally loaded through a loading port or through the ejection port of the gun. Revolver cylinders can also be considered magazines that also happen to be multiple firing chambers as well.

A clip is a device used to load a magazine. Stripper clips are commonly used to load magazines with large capacities, typically for rifles derived from military models such as AKs, ARs, FALs, M1 carbines and the like. These use a "spoon" that fits onto the magazine's top and the stripper clip, usually a sheet metal contraption holding ten rounds linearly, is inserted into the spoon. The ten rounds can then be pushed with the thumb straight down into the magazine. Older guns such Mausers or Springfield 1903s will require the stripper clip to be directly inserted into the rifle itself since the internal box magazines of these rifles do not detach. M1 Garand rifles are very similar, with an non-removable internal box magazine that is loaded with an eight round "en bloc" clip from the top. Revolvers, typically loaded one round at a time into the cylinder, can also use clips. The speed loaders and speed strips used to load several or all rounds at a time are really just fancy clips. And revolvers that use rimless cartridges use "half-moon" or "moon" clips to load two, three, or all rounds into the cylinder (and are not removed until the cylinder is to be reloaded).

In a nutshell, clips load magazines, and magazines load guns.

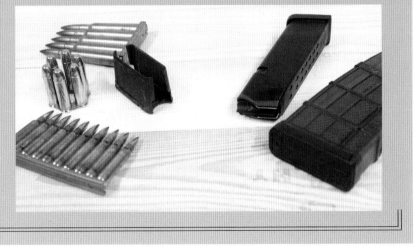

FIRST, A LITTLE BIT OF HISTORY

We will examine some specific firearms and their magazines, the strength and weaknesses of each type, the materials from which they may be manufactured, and some other sundry details of these indispensable devices. But first, let us examine a simple overview of the history of the magazine.

The first firearms were simple and crude. The hand cannons, as they were called, were simply low grade cast or rolled iron tubes attached to a stick. The hand-gunner used a lit match to ignite the powder through a touch hole on the top, in much the same manner as early artillery was fired. He held the stick under his arm and hoped like hell the thing didn't blow up in his face, which they often did.

Soon some smarty pants figured out that they might have a better chance of hitting that barn wall if the gun utilized some sort of stabilization against the body. The buttstock allowed these firearms the chance to direct the projectile in a much more precise pattern. Of course warfare at the time already recognized that the only way guns were going to be effective would be to give entire regiments the same gun and tell them to shoot at that other regiment twenty-five feet away. Even then, the accuracy, if the gun even had sights to aim with, was poor. About all the hand cannon was really good for was scaring horses, but the massed volley fire was finally the ticket to killing large numbers of men in short order. The problem was that the other guy had the same stuff and could do the same to you. Hence began the great arms races. Who could make the gun that could shoot farther, load faster, hit more accurately, and therefore rule the known world.

Pretty soon, somebody decided that you can use a spring mechanism and hammer (called a lock) and a trigger to ignite the powder, rather than having to use your

A reproduction matchlock musket being fired. The trigger is a simple lever that allowed the match to be lowered into the flash pan, igniting the powder. No fun at all.

other hand. After that came improved versions of the same thing, better lock-work, faster ignition, better powder handling and such, but the general design remained the same for a couple hundred years. There were experiments with using multiple barrels so you could shoot two or more shots in short order, but these tended to be complicated, expensive, and unreliable. Furthermore, even though the technology of rifling a barrel by cutting grooves in the bore to spin stabilize the bullet existed, it too was an expensive process and the barrels would be difficult to load because the bullet had to be a tight fit to the bore.

Several valiant attempts to create a breech-loading gun were pursued, notably by the British officer Patrick Ferguson, during the American War of Independence. In an attempt to increase the rate of fire, the Ferguson rifle's breech opened by unscrewing the trigger guard one turn. The soldier then inserted a bullet into the rear of the barrel and then powder; then he closed the breech by screwing the trigger guard back in again, cocked the flintlock hammer and fired the rifle. The small corps of soldiers in Ferguson's unit could fire four or five times the bullets that any similarly sized unit of standard muzzle loading muskets could fire. Fortunately for the American colonists, these rifles were only made in a very small number. Ferguson was wounded in 1777 and later killed in 1780 in the battle of King's Mountain. Ferguson had invented a useful rifle but it had flaws, and the Crown simply couldn't afford to make large numbers of them at the time, no matter how useful they were.

That changed when the percussion cap was invented. Up to this point, loose powder was used to prime the main powder charge, but that loose powder was vulnerable to moisture and loss. The percussion cap allowed a rifle to be loaded and the priming compound (held within the cup of the percussion cap) held in place on the gun, mostly safe from the elements and from jarring loss, and then fired at need. The little issue of having to load from the muzzle and the attendant fouling that a tight fitting bullet would cause in the bore had yet to be licked. The first major improvement was the Minie bullet which had an expandable cone shaped base that was undersized, yet would expand and tightly grip the barrel's rifling when fired.

Being able to shoot the other regiment at two hundred yards instead of twenty-five was definitely an improvement, but having to load from the muzzle while standing was still a super bummer because it was still mighty slow to load and, well, the other guy had a big standing target that was hard to miss. The secret ingredient was the invention of the cartridge. Taking the powder and bullet and making them one entity was key. It was impossible to fire more than one shot from a muzzle loading weapon unless you had more than one barrel. The metal cased cartridge (not the first cartridge, but the most effective, and the one we still use today) allowed the rapid insertion of cartridges at the breach (i.e. near his face), and the use of a loading and firing mechanism that complemented that cartridge allowed the rifleman to shoot ten to twenty aimed shots per minute, but he still had to load one at a time. The metal cased cartridge did finally pave the way for the internal magazine.

The term magazine was used originally to describe a building that held powder and shot for cannons and artillery. It was an obvious usage to then use it for the "housing" on a gun that held the powder and projectiles in a rifle or pistol, regardless of whether the components were separate anymore or not. The early American magazine fed rifles (and European magazines for that matter) used long tubes that were held under the barrel or in the buttstock, that held seven to as many as twenty plus cartridges, and were loaded through the buttstock, the side of the receiver, or muzzle end of the tube. This let the rifleman shoot many times more frequently, and even more accurately since the bullets could now be properly sized to the bore, than the musket-armed soldier. Entire engagements in several wars, including the American Civil War, were determined by smaller numbers of men shooting many more bullets than greater numbers of men shooting many fewer.

The magazine appeared on the pistol with the invention of the revolver cylinder, allowing the pistoleer to fire five to seven shots or more before reloading, but early revolvers took a while to reload, since each chamber had to be "muzzle loaded" and then recapped with a percussion cap. Ooohh, but then around comes that wonderful metal cased cartridge. A cylinder could now be reloaded in a matter of a few seconds; all you had to do was drop out the empty cases one by one and reload them one by one, but a skilled user could do this in less than half a minute.

All of these guns with their cylinders and tubes for magazines had to be manually cycled to shoot them again. You had to thumb cock the hammer, or you had to work the lever, and later the bolt action rifle improved things a bit, but you still had to manually cycle each time to extract the spent case and introduce a fresh unfired cartridge in to the chamber. By this time the old traditional black powder was giving way to smokeless powder that prom-

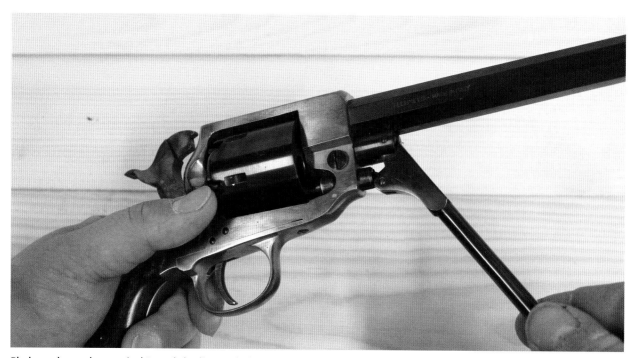

Black powder revolver required "muzzle loading" each chamber in the cylinder. The hammer is partially cocked and powder and ball is inserted and then rammed tight by the lever under the barrel.

ised higher velocities and much superior ballistics. This prompted the creation of bullets that were no longer just lead slugs, but consisted of lead cores surrounded by a harder jacket made of steel or copper. Furthermore, these new bullets were pointed, rather than round or flat nosed, in order to efficiently fly over 2000 feet per second.

Okay, now we have a Big, Big Problem. Tubular magazines and pointed bullets mix about as well as Packers and Vikings fans in a Chicago sports bar. Upon recoil, the bullet tips would impact the cartridge in front of them in the tube and set the primer and therefore the cartridge off, blowing the magazine tube out and potentially setting off a chain reaction in the tube. Not good for your health or the cardiac condition of those around you. This prompted the introduction of the box magazine, which originally was completely internal. The cartridges were stacked horizontally in a side to side fashion, with around four or five rounds in the magazine. A spring and follower pushed the rounds up, and as the bolt cycled it would discard the old empty case and a new round would pop up in front of the bolt to be fed into the chamber. This worked well for those silly Europeans who were always out killing each other over which member or other of whichever inbred dynasty that was popular this year got to rule this or that particular nation state. You could put all five rounds

on a little sheet metal clip, insert the clip in front of the open bolt and push smartly down to instantly load the full magazine with a whopping handful of cartridges.

Enter a man named John M. Browning. (Cue shameless gun designer idol-worship music here, please. I can literally hear Wagner's "The Valkyries" right now. Probably because I'm listening to it on Pandora as I'm writing this.) Browning sat down and said to himself, "Hmm. What if I could make this Winchester cycle on its own without having to swing the loop with my hand after every shot." He MacGyvered up a ramshackle contraption that caught some of the expanding gas as it exited the barrel and used that energy to cycle the lever on the rifle. Ta-da! The semi-automatic rifle was born. Now soon after that he really had some fun and started designing machineguns. Another American brilliant mind-possessor named Hiram Maxim followed shortly thereafter and started making the machinegun that everyone else copied, thus proving the utility and functionality of the design. These firearms were fed by long strips or belts that held hundreds of cartridges. This led to machine guns becoming totally en vogue for all the preppy popular armies to have. Just in time to be used to slaughter millions of men in the bloodletting called WWI.

The desire to more effectively arm soldiers let to an even better innovation, taking the internal box magazine

Internal blind box magazines soon gave way to internal magazines with removable or pivoting floor plates.

Machineguns mostly used belts to feed the guns, like this Browning M1919.

The gun may be a little different, but 210 rounds is the standard load carried by US infantrymen.

of five rounds and giving it the ability to be removed at the touch of a button or flick of a toggle, and incidentally gaining in capacity. Submachine guns and pistols were appearing with quite astounding ammunition capacities for the day, such as twenty or thirty rounds. By the beginning of WWII, every major military was fielding submachine guns, big not-sub-machineguns, and a couple of them, like the US, were using a semi-automatic rifle that held eight rounds and was quickly and easily reloaded. Riflemen could and had to carry a lot more ammo now. The Civil War soldier might have had thirty or forty rounds on him. A WWII soldier might have well over a hundred, and the guys with sub-guns two hundred. This trend has continued on until today, where the standard combat loadout for an American soldier is seven M-16 detachable box magazines of thirty rounds each, a total of over two hundred rounds of much smaller, much higher velocity cartridges.

Here is the point of this history lesson. What you have today are firearms available to the public that are based heavily on the development of ammunition and the ability and capacity to effectively use that ammunition to

the greatest effect on the battlefield. While they are not machineguns, they look like them, and even use much the same parts and ammunition. This makes them scary to those easily scared, and ironically a very appropriate tool for the law abiding. These guns are used for sporting purposes, recreation, and self-defense and virtually all of them use detachable box magazines that hold fifteen, twenty, thirty, fifty, one hundred rounds. I need you to understand that the right of self-preservation as identified in our Second Amendment goes beyond the gun itself. These firearms cannot be utilized if the mechanism of feeding them has been regulated out of existence. This is the point of banning "high capacity" magazines. As we have seen, they haven't stopped at thirty, or twenty, or fifteen rounds. Nor have they stopped at the ten rounds that for years the prohibitionists said was "adequate" for self-defense. Now it's seven in New York. Pretty soon it will be six, then five, then one. It has nothing to do with safety, nothing to do with minimizing the numbers of people shot in a mass shooting (to engage in that argument is pointless); nothing to do with preventing bad people from spraying bullets at school buildings. The point is to pre-

60 rounds man, 60 rounds.

vent you, the lawful gun owner and honest self-sufficient citizen from having the best tool you can obtain for the purpose of self-preservation. The elitist and the oppressor and the criminal cannot ultimately force you to comply if you can direct force back at them. Banning magazines (and insanely taxing ammunition) is simply a means of back door banning the guns that use them. This makes it incumbent upon the owners of firearms that use magazines to purchase a quantity of them, make sure that they function properly, and strenuously object the next time someone says, "No one needs a thirty round magazine for [insert stupid clichéd purpose here] or self-defense."

AR-15 MAGS

Let's take the example of the AR-15 magazine. The original magazine that was used by our military in Vietnam and afterwards was an aluminum sheet that was stamped out and then spot welded to form a tube. A spring and cartridge follower was inserted from the bottom and the bottom was then sealed by a flat aluminum plate that was slid in place and held by a clip that was welded into the magazine tube. It was finished with multiple layers of surface treatments and was very durable. It held twenty rounds, although a common story is that it worked more reliably if something less than twenty rounds were loaded. You can find many of these magazines; they tend to be minus a great deal of the original finish, but still functional. These magazines have been reproduced by several businesses and are very handy. They have an appreciable capacity yet still stick out less than the standard pistol grip, so are good when you are shooting off the bench or shooting prone, where the longer thirty round magazines popular today can get in the way a little.

After the twenty-round magazine came the thirty-round magazine. Again made from stamped and welded aluminum, this is the omnipresent magazine that seems to come with most factory rifles and carbines. The construction is similar, but with a couple major differences. The floorplate is retained slightly differently, but it's a means that is easier to use than on the bottom of the

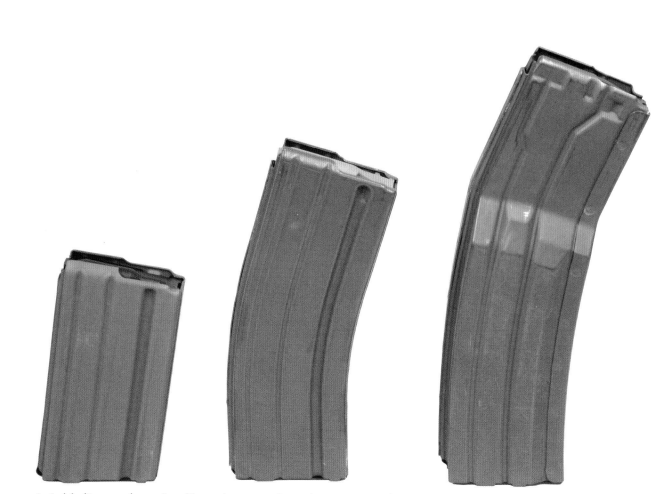

An "original" 20-round magazine with a modern 30-round magazine, next to a Surefire 60-round mag.

twenty mag. The other difference is of course the capacity, which is accomplished by making the magazine body longer and then putting two slight bends in it to allow for the cartridge taper.

Recently, the use of polymer molding tech has allowed several companies, most obviously MagPul, the ability to upgrade the magazine even more. Not only is the entire assembly except the spring made of plastic, but the double bend (which could cause occasional feeding issues) has been made into a constant curve, which is more compatible with a tapered cartridge case than a straight mag with occasional bends. The military noticed that the followers were tipping in the original thirty-round mags and designed a replacement follower that was supposed to address this problem, but did not do so sufficiently. MagPul then also built a non-tipping follower into their magazine that, together with the constant curve, made the feeding go through much more smoothly. They then manufactured replacement followers for the GI magazines that im-

proved the function of those as well. Other manufacturers have gotten into the plastic game, so you will find quality polymer magazines from a number of sources in addition to MagPul, such as Lancer, TAPCO, CAA, Troy, and the list goes on.

Plastic isn't the only alternative material, steel and stainless steel is also heavily used. The use of steel for AR magazines goes back decades, particularly in foreign militaries like those of Singapore and the U.K. who have used steel AR magazines for a long time. We haven't even mentioned the other stuff, like the magazines for alternative calibers like .308, .22 LR, 6.8 SPC, 6.5 Grendel, or 7.62x39 and 5.45x39mm or the bevy of other chamberings that have appeared in the last twenty years, or the trend to having integral windows or outright transparent bodies for round checking, or easy loaders, etc.

Keep in mind that this stuff has been in development for the last 55 years, closely coinciding with the maturation of the rifle system itself. Where the rifle functioned

Magazines are increasingly made of molded plastic. These tend to work very well and are around the same price as the aluminum mags.

Plastic magazines allow the novelty of windows, or transparency, to be used. You can sort of see how many rounds you have left.

in a less than ideal manner when it was adopted by the army, it is to the point where it has become extremely reliable, extremely useful and customizable, and virtually omnipresent. Truly, it has become America's rifle.

AVERAGE PISTOL MAG

Most pistol magazines are going to be made of steel. There are a few exceptions, and we'll get to that in a minute. Ever since the first detachable box magazine for a pistol was made, steel was the way to go, at least for the body itself. You will find other materials for floorplates and followers, most notably aluminum and plastic, but the bodies are mostly made of steel. Even when the Glocks and HK USPs started showing up with plastic magazines, those magazines still had steel liners to provide enhanced rigidity and functional reliability. The plastic simply acted as a durable sheath for the steel liner.

A big difference from rifle magazines that you will find with pistol magazines is the almost universal use of a single-feed magazine. Even the double-stack magazines that hold two cartridge columns will still merge the top rounds into a single column that leaves a single cartridge visible at the top where the magazine feeds. Rifle magazines tend to go with dual feed systems where you will see

Double-stack plastic Glock magazine with single-stack steel magazine. Two magazines from two different universes, Germany and Spain.

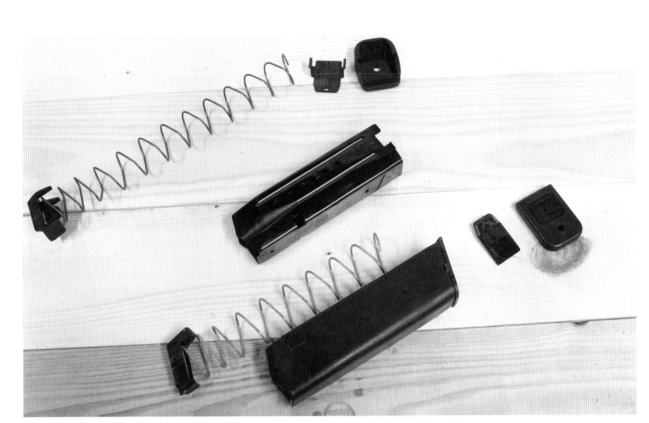

Stick a punch in the hole and pull/slide the floor plate off. Don't let the contents fly away.

Two Austrian magazines. One is plastic with a steel liner, the other is polished steel with an extension.

the two rounds. Let's look at the popular Glock magazine.

Glock mags are black plastic that encapsulates a stainless steel liner. The floor plate is retained by a base plate inside the magazine which also forms the base support for the magazine spring. The floor plate can be easily popped off and the contents removed for cleaning. It is a very strong, well-made piece and is a good accompaniment for the well-designed pistol that it feeds. While they come in different sizes and capacities and calibers, they are all the same basic design. The magazine is affordable, running around thirty dollars, street price, and everyone carries at least a few of them on their shelves. Let's contrast this with a different design.

Steyr M-A1

The Steyr polymer pistol is similar to the Glock in some ways and quite different in others. But the magazine is a much more traditional design. The body is entirely steel with a floorplate and follower made of plastic. Like most pistol magazines, the steel body is highly polished to ensure smooth inserts and ejections and is actually quite attractive. Still, it is a single-feed, double-stack magazine like the Glock. However it and many other magazines like it are a bit more expensive, running over $50 sometimes.

1911 magazine

I've never seen a plastic 1911 magazine. They are always made of steel and often have plastic floorplates, but the followers on good magazines are going to be metal as well. While several companies have built wide-bodied 1911s, the majority follow the original Browning design manufactured by Colt, a single-feed, single-stack magazine. The magazine traditionally held seven rounds and now regularly hold eight rounds of .45 ACP. They will be polished, whether made of carbon steel or stainless steel and the newer models will have witness holes for visual determination of the cartridges present. Mags tend to run cheap for surplus WWII and era mags, around $10, but you

Modern 1911 magazines are superior to the originals. These two are stainless steel (as are most now), one from Kimber, and the other from CMC.

In a twist of irony, .45 is a bigger bullet than 9mm, but magazines that fit .45 tend to be smaller than magazines that fit 9mm. Up till recently anyway. Now more and more .45s are coming with double-stack magazines. They're big.

don't really know what you are getting there. You would be wise to stick to modern made mags such as those from CMC, Novak, or Wilson. These three companies have been refining the 1911 magazine concept for many decades, since back when the only pistol used for competition was the 1911 in its various calibers.

Average .22 LR magazine

There are a number of .22 LR pistols on the market and they are virtually all ten-round sheet steel magazines with plastic floorplates and followers. They are always

relatively expensive as related to the gun they are used in, more so than the centerfire comparisons. This means that buying from the aftermarket is more regular since the guns rarely come with more than one magazine, in order to keep the gun's price down. It should also be noted that since .22 LR is a rimmed case cartridge, it is imperative that the cartridges are inserted properly in the magazine, lest a lower case rim be lodged in front of a higher case rim, as that will cause a jam.

The most popular early model was the Ruger Standard pistol, which was followed upon by the Mark II and

.22 magazines have to be designed to accommodate the case rims, and there are a lot of .22 pistols out there. Most of them have a button on the side to aid in loading.

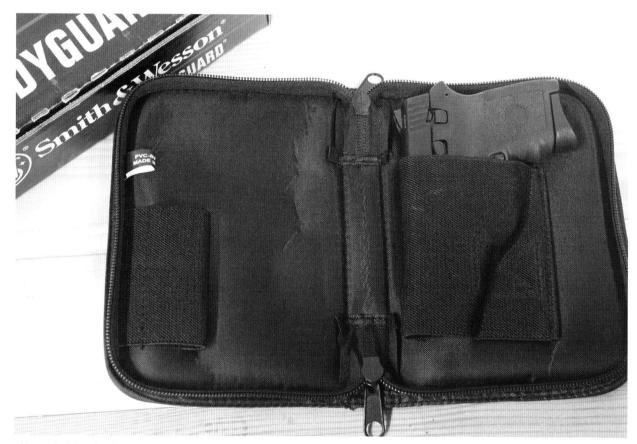

This gun is shipped with one magazine, and in what appears to be a middle finger to the consumer, helpfully comes with an elastic loop in which to insert the second magazine that you have to purchase separately.

Mark III. In its various incarnations it is one of the most popular .22 pistols to date. Other models by Browning, SIG, and Smith & Wesson, among others, all will require additional magazines as most are shipped with only one. There is no point to having only one magazine, since the reason for the existence of the detachable box magazine is to give the ability to rapidly reload. I would happily pay a few more bucks to have a second mag shipped with the gun. I get that you are trying to hit a price point, but not shipping at least two magazines with a gun is just plain stupid. Mini rant over.

GUNS POSSESSING TUBULAR MAGAZINES, LIKE WINCHESTER 94S, MARLIN 60S, AND MOST SHOTGUNS

Tubular magazines are the oldest repeating rifle and pistol magazines, and they are still with us virtually unchanged. The two big things to remember about tube mags are that they are fragile and they cannot use standard pointed tip bullets.

Shotgun tubes are actually pretty thick and resilient. While it is not too difficult to dent one, it can be done, and they are not easily replaced. The dents can be removed relatively easily, but most shotgun tubes are permanently attached to the receiver. The tube magazines on centerfire rifles are relatively strong as well and, ironically because of the smaller inner diameter with roughly the same thickness, they are often stronger than shot-gun tubes. Where you have to concern yourself with tube damage is with the rimfire rifle tubes. These are very thin and are frequently damaged. Fortunately, replacement tubes, both the outer shell and the inner sheath, are commonly available from places like Brownells and the original manufacturers. With these rimfire tubes, you are better off just discarding the damaged tube, as the replacements are relatively inexpensive.

As we've mentioned before, pointed bullets and tube magazines don't mix well. Hornady has recently introduced pointed bullets called LEVERevolution for use in the tube magazines of certain rifles, those using the centerfire rounds common for deer hunting, such as .30-30 Win. and .45-70 Gov. These bullets use very pliable tips that will not sufficiently forcefully impact the primers of the cartridge ahead of them, but will still initiate controlled bullet expansion. There really aren't any pointed bullets that protrude from shells when you are talking about shotgun shells, and pointed rimfire cartridges are not susceptible to the chain reaction, since they are rimfire.

Shotgun magazine tubes are often enhanced with tube extensions. This is extremely common when you are talking about self-defense guns and those used for run-and-gun competitions like tactical shotgun and 3-gun matches. There's nothing like having a few extra rounds, particularly when you only start with three or four rounds from the factory. I want as much ammo as possible in my gun, and I'm sure many readers will agree.

Tubular magazines like this one are easily bent or dented/damaged.

This mag tube extension grants you an extra two rounds.

Here's where the "you don't need "X" shots to do "Y"" horse crap statement comes that you hear all the time. It doesn't matter how much you need. What matters here is how much you want and what makes you comfortable. I am very much a .45 ACP guy. But I really like having a fifteen-round magazine; I like it more than having eight bigger .45 bullets, so I carry a 9mm Glock 19 with the fifteen rounds, which I find to be more comforting. (This is a real personal battle, you see.) I also really like Kel-Tec's KSG shotgun that holds fifteen shotgun shells and is short enough to be a very effective close-quarters gun. I hope I never have to use it, but if I do, I will have a short handy gun with fifteen rounds of 00 buck that I won't bang into the door jambs like I would with a more traditional gun.

BOLT RIFLES

There are a few kits that upgrade internal box magazines for several guns, pretty much only Rem. 700s, Savage 10s, and Howa 1500s. These originally are equipped with opening floorplates that drop the cartridges right out when

Fat magazine with skinny bullet; skinny magazine with fat bullet.

opened. The entire trigger guard and floorplate assembly can be replaced with a new unit that uses a detachable box magazine. These kits are expensive but they do make the rifle much more flexible, as there is no mess of loose cartridges, and these things typically increase the magazine capacity as well.

A QUICK LOOK AT CLIPS

Please understand that the whole clip/magazine thing is a pet peeve for me. They are different things and it doesn't help that some manufacturers refer to their magazines as "clip magazines."

The most obvious rifle that uses a clip to load its internal magazine is the M1 Garand rifle. The eight round "clip" is inserted into the magazine and pops out with the last round ejected. The magazine is completely fixed and internal. The "clip magazines" that Remington and other manufacturers sell are actually just magazines. Other than the M1 clips and the stripper clips that people use

to load their AR magazines and their SKSs, you don't see clips much anymore. They used to be very common in militaries because all those five-round internal box magazine Mausers and such all used stripper clips. In a way, the clip was halfway up the evolutionary ladder to the detachable magazine, as it was a means of quickly reloading the internal magazine.

Revolvers can sometimes use what are called moon or half-moon clips. I won't go into the thousand word origin of moon clips but most revolvers accept only loose rounds when reloading. A moon clip is a simple piece of sheet metal that accepts all six rounds by grabbing them around the ejector groove in front of the rim. Revolvers that use moon clips usually have cylinders that are rebated in the back, allowing the room for the clip, but single loaded rounds will still work as well. A great example of this is the Chiappa Rhino, which has a rebated cylinder, comes with several moon clips, but can be single loaded at will if you wish.

These moon clips allow the loading of all six rounds in a revolver cylinder. AT THE SAME TIME!

Here's a beautiful pile of magazine goodness to whet your appetite.

All in all, true clips are cheap, only a few bucks a piece, and are a good investment. Moon clips make reloading a revolver a much faster circumstance that does not require fine motor skills. Just drop the entire thing into the cylinder, rather than inserting six cartridges one by one.

MAGAZINE CONCLUSION

A magazine is essential to a modern firearm. A properly functioning magazine is critical. If your gun uses a detachable magazine, then you need to get a bunch of them. Test them or a good percentage of them to make sure they work. If you buy five, test them all. If you buy fifty, then just test the ones you will carry or use regularly and replace broken or worn mags from the stash as you need them. Your gun is useless without sufficient and properly functioning magazines and it is imperative that you get them as soon as is practicable, or you won't have them when you actually want or need them. Magazines are the first thing to disappear in a panic rush, such as the two precipitated by recent elections and mass shootings. It will happen again, so get your stuff together while you have the chance.

CHAPTER 6

S ighting systems pretty much boil down to three types: iron sights, optics, and projections. Guns may have one, some, or all, but rarely do any come with more than one from the factory. Even then, except on many pistols, they tend to be cheap and basic. Most hunting rifles found in retail stores have no aiming apparatus whatsoever, which then necessitates the purchase of an optic and mounting equipment. Generally, the cost of rifles and to some extent shotguns is kept down in part by removing nice-to-have-things like sights, scopes, sling swivels, nice recoil pads, extra mags, etc., and you get the picture. This chapter discusses the various iron or open

sights that you are going to find on factory guns, the other kinds to which you can upgrade, and the means necessary to do so.

"Iron sights" is the term used to describe the traditional front and rear type of mechanical sight seen on most rifles and pistols. Some use the term "open sights," but that refers to a type of iron sight, as does ghost ring, or aperture (peep), express, etc. This is the traditional way to aim a gun and is still the most common thing to use on a pistol or shotgun. Basically, you line up the front sight and the rear sight onto the target and fire. Generally speaking, good eyesight is a must, but some types, like

ghost rings sights which use a very large aperture in the rear sight unit, can be used effectively by less than perfect vision. Shotguns tend to always have something, such as tactical ghost ring sights, open notch iron sights, or beads. Pistols will always have iron sights.

OPEN SIGHTS

If a gun comes with sights, they will likely be of the open variety. For pretty much ever, since the means to accurately shoot a gun was invented, guns have been manufactured with open sights. There has to be at least a semi-precise means of hitting what you want to hit. Really anyone can hit something at arm's length with just about anything, sights or not, but then you might as well use a stick with a nail stuck in it. The point of a firearm is to have a weapon that you do not have to get within arm's length to use. There are going to be some people that can point shoot with laser-like skill, but that takes a great deal of practice. Point shooting means not even using sights, but using muscle memory to "remember"

where to point the gun and shoot on feel. It's like putting on your glasses in the morning without even having your eyes open, or putting on your seatbelt the same way every time you get in your car (without even thinking about it). It's pretty impressive to see someone drop a series of steel plates at 25 yards without aiming. While it would behoove the gun owner to learn some rudiments of point shooting, since you can't be guaranteed a well-lit self-defense shooting, most gun owners will not have the time or resources to get really good at it. So we use sights on our guns so that we can reliably and repeatably hit what we want to hit.

Rifles

Until relatively recently, every gun, whether it was a pistol, rifle, or shotgun had some sort of iron sight mounted on it from the factory. That is still the case on pistols and shotguns, but now it's pretty rare to find iron sights on centerfire rifles. Why is that? Optics have become so prevalent and affordable that virtually everyone that purchases a

The Model 1917 Enfield had extremely rugged, well-guarded aperture sights.

Iron sights are often retained as back up or emergency use tools.

rifle will sooner or later mount a scope to it. Generally, if you have a scope, you do not need iron sights on the same gun. You can't use them both at the same time, after all. (We'll discuss multiple sighing systems on the same gun later on). The second reason is that, with things getting more expensive, the guns need to be manufactured and

This 700 ADL had front and rear sights, but the rear sight was removed to accommodate a low mounted scope.

sold as cheaply as possible. This is why there are so many discount rifles available from all the major manufacturers, even though those same manufacturers have and still sell higher end, higher priced, well known models. For example, you can get a Remington 700 BDL with iron sights, but the 770 has none. The 700 will run upwards of $600 and the 770 is less than $350, and it even includes a scope. Savage has been selling the 110-based rifles for

decades and the current price exceeds $500, but the Axis sells for close to $300. Since traditional hunting rifle sales have dipped, these and other companies have had to come up with lower priced models to have something to sell, when what everyone really wants is an AR or a carry pistol. There's nothing wrong with these guns either; some of them are downright exceptional designs, but modern manufacturing technology enables the low cost. Point of the story: none of these guns have sights but are all designed to be shot with a riflescope only.

Where you still regularly find sights on rifles is on rimfire designs. Where most centerfire rifles are scoped anyway, the opposite is true for most rimfire rifles. You will generally find basic stamped, sheet metal open notch sights on these rifles. Increasingly, fiberoptic (FO) examples will be found. The fiberoptics are kind of nice because they light up. Instead of placing black on black, you can place green on red, or red on yellow, or green on green. These sights are very helpful for people with poor or declining eyesight. Fiberoptics are very popular with the more aged population, who tend to like the green and yellow FO pipes, as do a lot of color-blind people.

The down side to the FO sights is that the little colored light pipes are fragile and will break upon any impact. This is partially offset by the fact that most of the sets, particularly when purchased aftermarket, come with replacement light pipes that are easy to replace.

When one breaks you remove the pieces from the loops on the sight and insert a new pipe that is slightly longer than it needs to be. Using an open flame from a lighter or propane torch and just barely touching the flame to either end will expand the ends. The expanded ends will then keep the entire thing in the sight. It works quite well. The loops that hold the light pipe are generally quite thin as well and can be dented or collapsed with not much effort.

Most factory rifle sights consist of a front ramp that is soldered and/or screwed to the barrel that holds a replaceable insert. This has been the practice for generations. The rear sight is also usually a ramp with a two piece adjustable insert, adjustable for elevation and windage. These sights are frequently folding as well, to get them out of the way of a low mounted scope. Anyway, these inserts generally have analogous aftermarket articles that are acceptable for absolutely appreciable accuracy. Yes, I threw in that tongue twister just for the heck of it. Examples

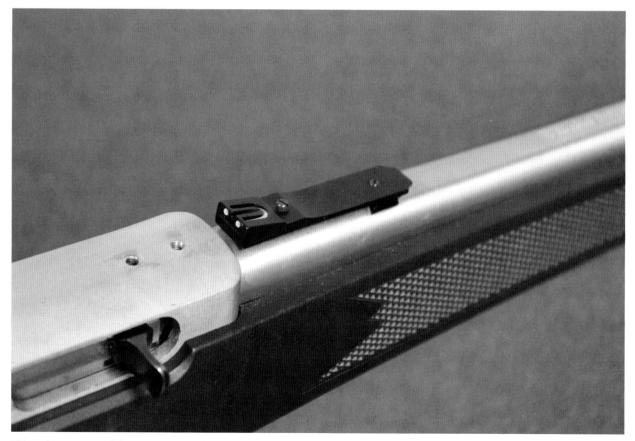

This replacement rear sight on a 10/22 uses fiber optic light pipe inserts to illuminate the dots.

In this front sight of the fiber optic combo, the light pipe has been smashed away leaving damage to the hoops that hold it. FO sights are easily damaged.

Some rear sights fold down to make more space for optics.

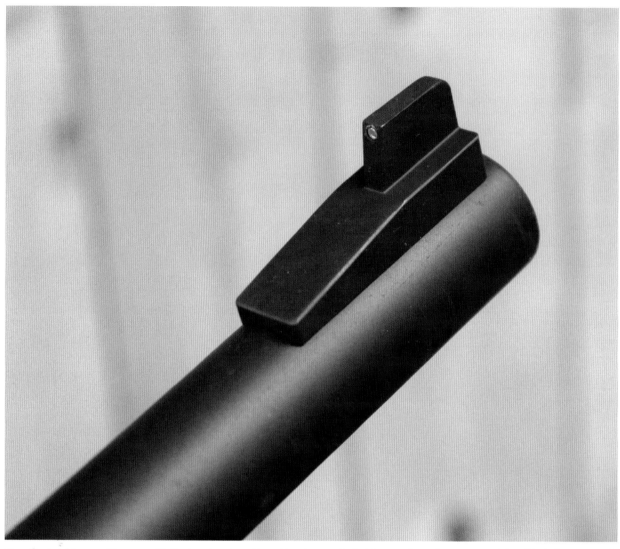

Many front sights cannot be screwed to the barrel, and must be soldered or attached with epoxy. Epoxy is a consumer job, solder is for a gunsmith, since the barrel would have to be refinished as well. This is a Scattergun Technologies ghost ring front sight.

include fiberoptics, increased height or decreased height, apertures that replace the notched open sight, and a number of other options.

Shotguns

The vast majority of shotguns sold in this country are used or intended to be used for bird hunting or clay pigeon shooting. For these purposes you will only find a bead sighting system. This is the most open of open sight systems and is composed of a simple brass or steel ball that sits on top of the muzzle. There is usually a vented rib that is perched atop the top barrel or between the side by side barrels and the bead is screwed into that. That rib is there to help line up your eye with the bead, with your eye functioning as the rear sight itself. You will also often find a very small mid rib bead to assist. Since this kind of shooting requires as much field of view as possible, since you are shooting fast moving, often flying side to side targets, there are no sight housings or scope rings getting in the way. There are some nifty fiberoptic units for wing shooting as well, and many of them just drop on top of the existing bead and are glued or are magnetically held to the rib, or replace the existing dot entirely.

On the other hand, shotguns used and optimized for self-defense tend to be equipped with very large peep sights called ghost rings. Most rifle peep sight apertures are quite small, but the ghost rings are significantly larger. Meant to be used at close range, a large aperture with thin

Typical 21st-century front bead. Steel housing with white plastic easy-see insert.

Brass is still the most common component for mid-rib beads. As the name suggests, they are placed halfway down the barrel.

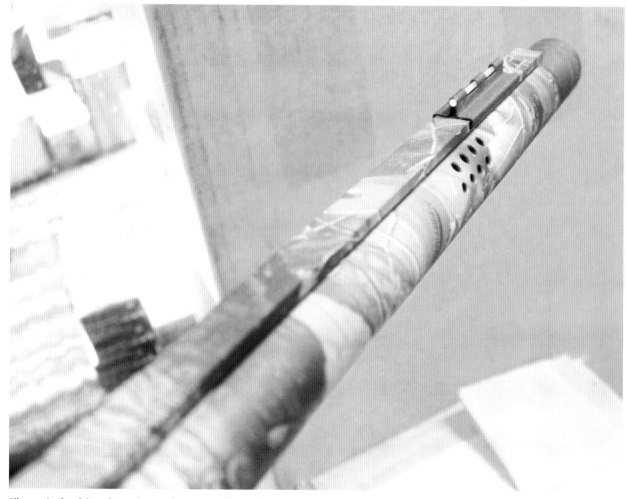

Fiber optic "beads" are becoming much more popular on shotguns, particularly on turkey guns.

housing is desired in order to minimize the blockage of the field of view. For a while these had to be installed on your own or by a gunsmith, but now many shotguns are available with these sights from the factory.

Slug shotguns, often used for big game, are usually blessed with standard rifle sights. You simply shoot those like you would on a rifle. The other option is a cantilevered scope mount. A cantilever mount is screwed or brazed to the barrel just in front of the receiver, and then extends back over the receiver so that the shooter can mount an optic in the traditional position. The scope mount is attached to the barrel because shotgun barrels are designed to be easily removed. This makes a less than rigid fit between the barrel and receiver. A scope mounted on the receiver would not promote consistent shooting. It used to be that gunsmiths could do a good business in the fall by tightening barrel/receiver fit, but then that mostly got ru-

ined when the cantilevers showed up. This doesn't really apply to guns like the Savage 220, which is basically a bolt action rifle chambered for a shotgun shell. That shotgun has receiver-mounted scope mounts like any rifle would.

Handguns

Probably the place where Americans have the most intense sight replacement habit is in handguns, and for a very good reason. While scopes and other optics are regularly added to long guns, the space and utility has traditionally been limited for optics when it comes to handguns. Sure, you will see optics all the time on game guns, like those for open class USPSA or IPSC matches, sometimes 3-Gun, and a few other disciplines. For the most part, however, the average pistol owner will not invest in the optic for his handgun. Carry pistols are rarely seen with optics because the optic makes the gun's profile much different,

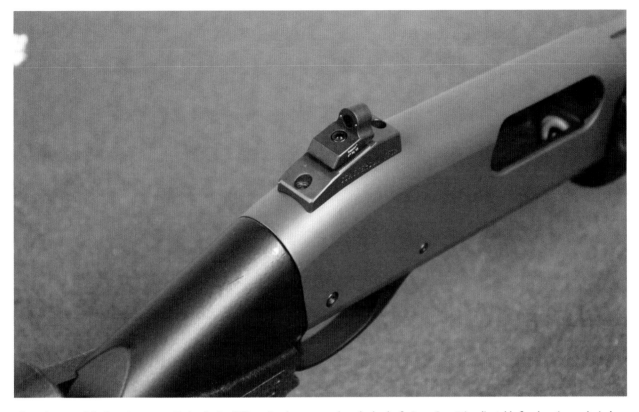

Ghost ring rear sight from Scattergun Technologies/Wilson Combat mounted on the back of a Rem. 870. It is adjustable for elevation and windage and includes Tritium vials, as does the epoxy front sight.

usually bigger. Added to that, most holsters are not made to accommodate an optic. So, better sights are very commonly mounted on the pistols that come with plain old basic sights.

The average handgun site is a simple square notch with a post/ramp front sight. Black rear sight, black front sight, very vanilla, in a photo negative kind of way. Other common factory offerings (and we are talking the basic options here) will come with white dots on the black sight, in a very salt-and-pepper kind of way. Basically you will find that factory sights on pistols are either all black or black with white or some other color of paint as a contrast. There are "variations of the three dots" sights. Rather than three dots, you might find a dot on the front sight with a white outline on the notch, like the sights that come on Glocks. Another example is the diamond that replaces the dots, like on the Speed Sights brand. Regardless of specific style, the idea is to input into the basic black surfaces easily seen reference points that can be more quickly aligned with a similar insert on the front sight. The most radical is probably the triangle/trapezoid type of pairing that is seen on the Steyr pistols.

For a lot of people, those upgrades are not good enough, and for a pretty good reason. When it gets dark, you can't see your sights, unless of course, you possess infrared-detecting eyes. Since most people don't have infra-vision, a different option is called for. Those heat blinded members of society, like myself, then shoot for the tritium sights.

Of particular interest to those who purchase HD or SD guns is the existence of these "glow-in-the-dark" sights. While there are phosphorescent painted sights available (you shine a light on it for a few seconds and it glows), this is not the style of which I speak. No, I mean the radioactivity glow-in-the-dark kind. I mean putting nuclear physics to work for little ole you. If the light is so subdued that you can't see your sights, then you really can't shoot effectively. Sights that are powered by Tritium are the solution. In the dark, these sights produce a low-power eerie glow that is easily seen in the dark and will not destroy your night vision.

It is difficult to overestimate the availability of tritium sights. There are tritium sights made for just about every handgun ever made. The commonality of 1911 pistols

Sight picture with a traditional black notch rear sight, dot in front.

Glock sight picture with factory white line notch in rear.

Steyr pistol sights with pyramid front sight and angled line rear.

Very common three dot type of sight used on most handguns.

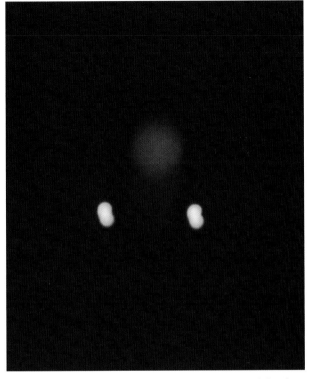

You can't really see anything here except the self-illuminated dots from the Tritium vials.

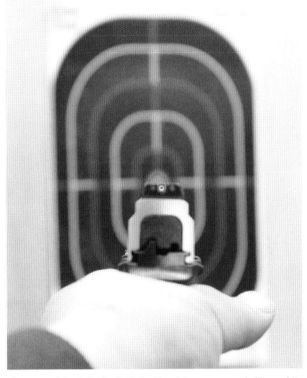

The same night sights in the light. The vials are surrounded by a white circle.

NIGHT SIGHTS

Tritium is a radioactive isotope of hydrogen, consisting of three bonded hydrogen atoms, and is found in nature (in water mostly), but is not at all common. In fact, it is one of the most expensive products of all time to procure, and when it is used, as in the gun industry, it is used in minute amounts. A small vial containing a ridiculously small amount of tritium gas is placed into a sight housing that is lined with phosphor. Early tritium powered sights had significantly more tritium in them and they were so bright it was crazy. If rumors are to be believed, they actually produced measureable clicks on the Geiger counter. So manufacturers realized that only a teensie-weensie amount was really necessary if used in conjunction with run of the mill phosphorescence technology. The small amount of emissions from the tritium now would hit the phosphor in the sight and light it up as

if a light had been shining on it all day. Constantly. It also drastically reduced the cost associated with this type of sight, since the amount of actual tritium used was now miniscule. The result is a wide selection of replacement (and some factory original) glow-in-the-dark sights on the market, most of which can be purchased for around $100 or a little more, and installed inexpensively by your local gunsmith. Best news is that these sights are warranted to work for 10 years or more, and they are quite robust.

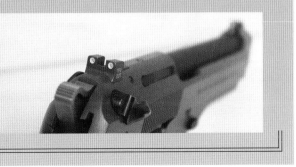

Most full-sized revolvers, like this S&W model 29, have fully adjustable sights.

has generated a market all of its own, with no less than ten manufacturers offering tritium sights for that pistol. For the most part you are looking at simple dots that illuminate in the dark and they are surrounded by a white ring for day usage. Actually the dots are constantly illuminated, but that illumination is washed out by daylight or by the intensity of the artificial lighting that most non-cavemen have come to appreciate, to the point that the enhancement can't be seen except in very low light conditions. You don't want them to be too bright or your own night vision will be ruined as well.

Occasionally pistols will be provided with adjustable sights from the factory. It should be noted that by their very nature adjustable sights are somewhat less resistant to damage than the average non-adjustable sight. Things can break. There are very rugged models on the market but if you are minimalist, paranoid type of dude or dudette, you may want to stick to fixed sights for carry or other self-defense guns.

That said, adjustable sights are a nice thing to have. Even nicer is when they are also fitted with the Tritium vials. The thing that really stinks about standard pistol sights is that you need tools to adjust them. The factories do a really good job of zeroing the sights for windage before shipping them, but sometimes you might want to adjust them left or right within their dovetail slots. You

Some rear sights are secured not by tension in the dovetail, but by a set screw to provide tension against the bottom of the slot.

might find a sight slot that is loose fitting and the sight is held in by a set screw tensioned against the bottom of the slot. These sights are easy-peasy movable, but if that set screw walks your sight will just fall off. The large majority of sights are press fit into the sight slot and you will then have two not-so-great options for moving them, or for that matter installing them at all.

Let's say that you want to do it yourself. The first option is to take a hammer and a punch (brass or plastic,

No longer in production, the JP Enterprises Doublring sights used a double ghost ring, big one in back, small one in front.

Sight movers, like this Glock model from MGW, are the best way to shift sights around or remove them.

Most sights will need to be tapped with a brass or plastic punch to one side or the other. This should not be done with Tritium sights, as the shock may break the vials.

The large screw pulls the sight to the side and out of the slide. In this case, it will not be needed to insert the new sight. Normally you would then leave the screw in this position, insert the new sight and then reverse the screw, pushing the sight into the dovetail slot until it reaches its central position.

NOT steel) and tap the sight out of its slot. Then you tap the new sight back in, preferably with the correct side with the dots facing the rear. Ahhh, crrraaaap!!! You went too far! Now you have to beat it back the other way, at which point you will go too far again. You do this a couple more times then take it to the range, shoot it, it's still two inches to the right at ten yards, and you go back home and adjust it again. Pain in the old caboose, that is.

The second option is to purchase a sight pusher tool. There are some high-quality examples but the hitch is that they are easily as expensive as your new tritium sights, and with few exceptions, they are made unique to each gun. The Glock sight tool that I have works very well. But it

This Aro-Tek rear sight from Brownells is tensioned with set screws but is a close fit to the slot. It can with effort be pushed into position with the thumb. It is centered and the two set screws are tightened.

is only made to use Glock factory sights and their unique shape, and Glock slides. You can insert other sights but not as smoothly, since the contours on the sight engagement interface don't match anyone else's sights. Theoretically, other slides could be stuck on the tool, but again, not perfectly, and perfectly is the whole point to having a gun-specific sight pusher. These tools mitigate or eliminate damage caused by the switching process by exactly fitting the parts to be joined or separated.

The front sight on most pistols is inserted in a dovetail slot and should be drifted out gently to one side, according to the directions in the new sight package. Others need to be staked, like some 1911 front sights. Glock front sights are retained by a screw in the bottom of the slide roof that goes up into the sight body. Most replacement Glock front sights will come with a tool for installing this. You can also get one in the Wheeler Engineering screwdriver kit or from Brownells.

BACK-UP SIGHTS

This is a very interesting concept. In one guise or another, the concept of back-up iron sights has been around ever since magnifying optics have existed in decent numbers. Certainly it can be traced at least to the tip-off mounts from the middle of the last century, although the application of the concept has evolved significantly.

Here is the basic and easily understandable concept in a nutshell. How do you shoot your scoped rifle accurately if you do not want to use, or for whatever reason cannot use, the riflescope that is mounted on the rifle? For example. You are out on a snowy opening day of deer season. It's 6:18 a.m. and you have the opportunity to drop a Bambi at 36.3 yards. You have mounted a typical deer hunter riflescope on your boomstick, a Nibushzeisska "Adamantium Buckshredder" scope. A 3-9x40mm fully multicoated variable power piece of crystal perfection, and you have it set for maximum super power at the 9x setting. You could count the zits on the Bambi's nose with that thing; that is if you can find it on the max power at 6:18 a.m. at 36.3, oops...39.6 yards now. Plus, Bambi is a little jumpy. At that range, a scope is more of a hindrance than an asset. There is a good chance that Bambi will forget that he is out of breath when he sees you crank that glass back down to 3x so you can actually find him in the scope, and he'll frantically bound gracefully out of sight.

This situation is rather common. You buy a scope for precision and convenience and then the deer, coyote, triceratops, or whatever it is you are hunting just kind of sneaks up on you and you only have a split second to shoot. Or, the other problem is that "my scope fogged up" or "my scope was all wet from the snow (or rain, or sleet, or sweat, drool, or mud, whatever, pick one) and I couldn't see through it." Well for the latter excuse, grandpa's generation came up with the pivot mount. This at first glance looked like a standard Weaver type scope base, but it had these funny hinges on one side of the rings where they

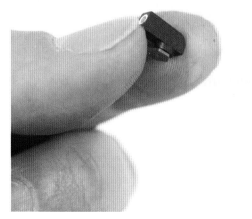

The Glock front sight is composed of a plastic sight with steel screw that enters from the bottom.

A small tool is included for removal of the old sight and installation of the new one.

Old school pivot mount. The scope is installed in the rings and can then be pivoted out of the way, like the one ring is in the photo. Despite the manufacturer's and retailers' protests of denial, accuracy did suffer somewhat.

attached to the base. Whoa! You could just pop that temporarily unusable scope up and it would roll over on its side, out of the field of view and clear the way to use the iron sights that all the guns back then still had. BANG! Plop! Then you roll the scope back over and click it back into place. They worked pretty well, but were a little less rigid than the standard scope base and you would theoretically sacrifice a little accuracy for the convenience. These things aren't made anymore, but they do complement older rifles well if you can find them on Ebay or someplace similar.

Of course, many older rifles could not easily mount scopes at all. Surplus military bolt actions were notorious for this, such as Arisakas, some Mausers, and other WWII bring backs, and even the old Winchester 94s could not mount a scope directly over the receiver and had to have mounts that held the scope off to the left side somewhat. This was not so very good, as the ballistic calcula-

tions became more complex. It was even worse since now you were not able to maintain an ideal cheek weld on the buttstock when you were looking through the scopes. Certainly, it was not the same cheekweld that you would feel when using the iron sights. Keeping a consistent contact between the cheek and the stock is essential to accuracy when shoulder-firing a rifle, if for no other reason than stability. While less than ideal, these mounts still allowed the owner to mount a scope onto an otherwise not scopeable rifle. In effect, this type of scope mount relegated the fixed iron sights to back up sight status. You might still be able to find these, but I wouldn't start drilling holes in old collectible rifles. Just buy a new rifle that is more optimized for optics if you can afford to do so. As I've already mentioned, you can get some good ones for under $400. If you start drilling holes in a collectible $1500 Winchester 94, you quickly create a not so much collectible $500 Winchester 94.

Another option, the see through mounts, mounted the scope high above the receiver so that the shooter could look beneath them.

Old-tech, but still used today, is the see-through mount. Unlike the pivot mount or the side-mounted scopes, the see-through mounts make use of extremely high scope rings, attached to standard Weaver style bases, to mount the riflescope. The rings form a figure eight of sorts with the scope mounted on top of two rings which allow the shooter to always be able to view his iron sights. With your face mounted on the stock in a traditional solid cheek weld, you can use your iron sights as normal. Raise your head and you can use the scope. However, this sort of defeats the purpose of the scope as the primary sighting system on the gun. You are literally resting your chin, or nothing at all, on the gun stock, which removes a great deal of the stability of the whole setup, and the repeatable precision of a good cheek weld. The huge upside to this idea however is the instant availability of both sighting systems, without the need to fiddle with anything. In practice, this results in an iron sight primary and optic secondary arrangement, but it still is worth mentioning in

this chapter, particularly since a great many hunters still prefer this arrangement.

We now move to the folding sights that are all the rage. Recall the see-through scope mounting rings from just a minute ago. The idea was that if the scope was mounted high enough above the line of sight, that line of sight could be permanently accessible in addition to the permanently accessible line of sight through the riflescope. The rather major side effect was the loss of a stable and repeatable cheek weld.

A new approach is to simply plop the red dot sight down between the fixed front and rear sights (usually a little high to put the sights low in the scope) and ignore them unless they are needed. This is really only a partial solution, since you still have to change your face position, albeit much less, and if your scope gets cracked, clouded, or is otherwise disabled that you can't see through it, you still can't use the back-up sights, since they are in line with the optic in the first place. This is why increasing numbers of scope mounts and integrated base/mounts have quick release clamps – so the shooter can remove the optic assembly in short order, without requiring tools to do so. This then obviates the need to replace the optic, since the back-up sights are already there. Furthermore, these scope mounts are rigid and will repeatedly remount to the original zero.

However, a lot of people don't like having the fixed sights stuck in the optic's field of view, so they go another direction, which is having back-up sights that fold to keep them out of the way when they aren't needed. Hence the "flip up" sight. We see here the use of an optic, as often a magnifying optic as a non-magnifying optic like a red dot that is placed in the traditional place on the receiver, or toward the forward end of the receiver. Behind the optic is a back-up flip up sight that is only deployed when the main optic is disabled or when the target is too close to be quickly engaged. This does a fabulous job of clearing clutter from the optic, but also means that after you take a chunk of puke to the lenses and you can't see through them anymore, you still have to remove the optic to use the sights, and then add in a second inconvenience by having to flip them both up for use. These things take time, and they really aren't much of an improvement, if any, to the see-through rings, since the see-through rings were instant transition, and these previous methods of back-up sight use require a number of actions and several seconds to carry out, in addition to the loss of the cheek weld.

As we have found throughout history, it takes competitive shooters to come up with some crazy unconventional things. Often times, these crazy things were invented to better take advantage of, or outright circumvent, some rules of the games. That isn't always the case. Sometimes some of the weird looking stuff is crazy and unconventional simply because it's new, but it serves a purpose in the gaming field and then transitions well to the real world, too. Here's a good example. A long time ago, 3-gun shooters figured out that back-up close range sights were nice to have in tandem with the optic on their rifle(s) that costs as much as an automobile. But, their scores depended on low times as well as accuracy. To take several seconds, even only a couple, to remove a failed optic, or crank the magnification down resulted in a poor score. Even worse, unless you were really, really good, if you took the time to try to find the five yard target in your twelve power scope on the high power, you stood there waving your muzzle around looking like a complete frelling idiot, until you fi-

The JP SRTS on line with the target. It is used for close shots that would be difficult to engage quickly with the primary optic.

nally found the A-zone on the (seemingly) gigantic target and got your two shots off.

This is where JP Enterprises came up with what they call the Short Range Tactical Sight. This became the first generation of back-up sight that was mounted offset to the normal line of sight, but was still at the same height and plane as the primary optic. The SRTS was (is) mounted 45 degrees to the side, and to use it you simply roll the rifle while keeping your face stationary. You maintain the cheekweld and the sights simply rolled into position, like the slides in those little picture viewers that we buy for our little kids. With a little practice this takes only a fraction of a second and allows pretty much instantaneous transition from one sighting means to another.

The JP Enterprises Short Range Tactical Sight mounted at the 45-degree angle to the primary optic. A simple roll of the shoulder brings them into line with the eye.

This concept has continued to evolve. Sometime thereafter JP added simple Picatinny mounts that were offset in the same fashion, to which were added backup sights that were normally mounted on the top of the gun. This allowed a greater sight radius for better accuracy. Other devices have since followed that are simply add on sights, both low profile, high profile, and otherwise that follow the same pattern. XS sights has a great set called the XTI that is small and has a tritium vial in the front sight. Dueck Defense's set pretty much duplicates an AR-15 A2 style front and rear sight. There are others and they all allow you to do one thing very well, and that is to transition to your backups with little effort, little time, and little movement.

Having covered all these back-up sights, it is important,

as with any accessory, that you pick the one you are comfortable using. It should be pretty clear that I think quite highly of the last option, but I'm actually in the minority. The offset sights stick out a little bit and a lot of people aren't keen on stuff sticking out to the side of the rifle. Likely the most popular option is the flip-up sights with quick detach scope mount. This set up will be found all day long on ARs and other "black" rifles. The back-up sight is here to stay, and fortunately we have many options to pick from to tickle our fancy and preference. This concept carries over to the hunt very well, and it has caught on in the tactical market too. You just need to remember to flip the flip sights up in advance, or you will not be able to use them when the instant transition is needed.

JP also offers offset Picatinny rails for mounting flip-up back-up sights. Just don't forget to flip them up before you need them.

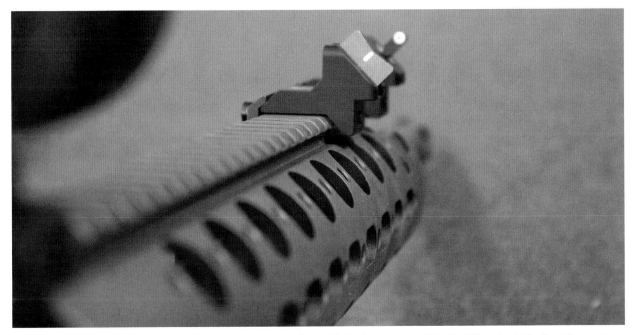

The XS Sight Systems Xpress Threat Interdiction sights are a very low profile back-up system with a big Tritium dot in the front. You can't use these if you have fat cheeks.

CHAPTER 7

LIGHTS AND LASERS

A handy accessory for any gun is a flashlight, or tactical light, particularly with HD guns. Most recorded home invasions have occurred at night when people are sleeping with the lights off, or with the lights otherwise subdued. Proper identification of the silhouette passing before you on the stairwell is essential. The light switch may not be in convenient reach and you don't want to shoot your past-curfew teenager because you mistook him/her for an intruder.

Lights have been companions for firearms since the days when the light *was* the firearm in the form of a torch, waved around by great-great grandpa Urrrrrgkklog in an attempt to keep the wolves out of his cozy cave. It simply makes sense to be able to identify the danger. When Urrrrrgkklog eventually evolved, he carried a lantern with the double-barreled shotgun as he checked on the chicken coop; he needed to see the fox to shoot it, after all.

Light is your friend and your enemy's enemy. Soldiers could be snuck upon by the enemy in the darkness, so when the soldiers got the bad feeling about this moment, or heard something suspicious, they called for starlight shells, giant flares that illuminated the night so that the enemy could be seen in their sneakiness, and shot. Darkness continues to be the friend of the criminal. Most home

Jim is ready for the pack of wild winter ostriches that are approaching his car. His Kimber Ultra with Crimson Trace laser is at the ready.

Checking the shed with a FNS-9 that has a Viridian X5L light/green laser mounted to it.

invasions, burglaries, and violent assaults occur at night or in some sort of subdued lighting for a reason. The criminal does not want to be spotted before he is ready to act.

Lights are less useful for some things than others. I'm sure some states allow deer or other game to shined at night, but not where I live. Certainly, in the darkness when you are heading to or from you deer stand, a light is useful, but the kind of tactical light we will be talking about in this chapter is not the ideal for that. That "finding your way home in the dark" thing is better handled by the cheap department store incandescent lights like a MagLite. Honestly, a flashlight is a great thing to have at any time.

In this chapter we cover the tactical light. Also known as a weaponlight when mounted on a gun, the tac light is a great non-lethal weapon all on its own. It used to be that the only choices were the models from Surefire, probably the first company to mass market the super bright high luminosity tac light. Soon there were comparable models from Streamlight, and now I can't even begin to count the

Checking the shed with a double barrel shotgun, a Citori, and blinding Nextorch Saint 3.

brands that exist to fill this market. Be aware that the majority of the tac lights on the market, cheap or expensive, are made in China, and this is what makes them affordable. The few that are made in the US are very expensive, but are said to be of extremely high quality. I have to be honest and admit that I don't know that for sure. What I do know is that the new gun owner has no business spending $400 on a palm-sized tactical light. Get a Surefire, Streamlight, or Nex-Torch to start with and if that doesn't seem adequate, then by all means move up. We'll go over a few of the more common options, and options that won't break the bank too badly.

HAND-HELD TAC LIGHTS

Perhaps I should define what "tactical light" means, for our purposes. A tactical light, whether attached to or separate from a firearm, is a device that projects a bright beam designed to over-illuminate the objective, acting supplementally as a distraction and stunning tool. Getting into luminosity and lux and candlepower or whatever each light says it is rated can be a sales trap and gimmick, as all that stuff is subjective and can be manipulated like raw statistics on dope. If you shine it in your own eyes and your reaction is the same as if you looked directly on the sun, then it's a tactical light. The extra brightness is a means to an end. The brighter the light, the better and more focused you will see the target, and the harder it will be to for he/she/it to see you clearly.

A hand-held light is more useful than a weapon-mounted light for the sheer reason that you can carry it around and whip it out without somebody yelling "GUUUUUUNNNNNNNN!!!" No, when you whip out your small, hand-held tactical light, they instead yell "Hey, that's a cute little flashli...HOLY MOSES MY EYES!!!" The nice thing is that many of the small hand-held lights also have multiple modes, so you can use the bright full power setting to impress, while using the low power setting (still every bit as bright as a dime store flashlight) as a flashlight. Ok, it's better to have both but we'll get to the mounted lights shortly.

The early models had Xenon bulbs that made them quite bright and Surefire even went to the extent of patenting reflectors and lenses that removed the bulb shadows from the beams. Then technology started humming and the vast majority now have super bright LEDs that are every bit as bright, even brighter, than the Xenon and Krypton bulbs. The LEDs don't get quite as hot as the Xenon bulbs, but they will still cook when left on for a while.

A great choice for a hand-held tac light is the ProTac series from Streamlight. You can get them for around $50 on the street, depending on the model. These lights are thin enough to fit into your back pocket next to your wallet and be perfectly comfortable there. A similar model from Surefire would be the Defender series, now discontinued, and its successors in the Fury series. Again, these are typified by being small with bright and dim modes and sometimes strobes. Factory defaults will usually be a bright/bright strobe/low with battery life on low running over 30 hours and on high around 30 to 60 minutes. All lights differ to some degree, but these I've been using for years and have been very satisfied.

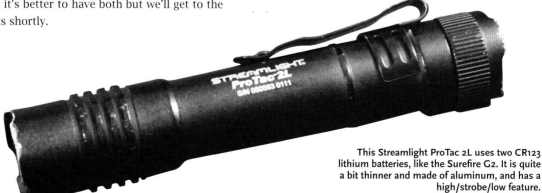

This Streamlight ProTac 2L uses two CR123 lithium batteries, like the Surefire G2. It is quite a bit thinner and made of aluminum, and has a high/strobe/low feature.

This Nextorch myTorchRC 2AA light has programmable modes and recharges through the same USB cable that is used to program it.

This style of small light is very capable of being used as a non-lethal weapon, particularly if they have the strobe feature. Strobe lights are very disorienting. Since shining a light with the intensity of Sirius A into someone's face has been shown to be an effective deterrent, it's very nice to have them in a small package that can fit into a pocket of your pants or purse. When it flashes ten to twenty times per second, it's that much more unnerving and can give you the time to either run away or draw your carry gun while the assailant is temporarily but very effectively blinded.

I want to mention a fairly recent brand of lights that have a couple very cool features. For full disclosure, I've sold a number of these lights so I'm a bit biased in this one, but they have two unique attributes that have won me over. The NexTorch brand of lights were designed with a 21st-century view in mind. Most of the NexTorch lights are fully programmable. This means that you download a free program to your computer and simply plug your light into the computer via a USB cable. The cable enters a port that is hidden under the front bezel of the light. Each light has its own number of modes, some have three others have more. The program allows each mode to be set by intensity and frequency if you are strobing that mode. For example, let's say you have three modes. You can set the first mode for 100% constant beam. The activation button acts as both a momentary on and will click to a constant on or off as well. You program the second mode for a low power beam of 5%. If the max output of the light is 200 lumens, you have just set the high power at 200 lumens and the low power at 10 lumens. You've decided to set the third mode for a strobe. You can set the strobe's intensity, let's say at 75% and its frequency, let's say 10 hz, which means you will have ten flashes per second at 75% total output. This is all easily done with sliding bars. NexTorch has many models that also are rechargeable and they will charge by the very same USB cable that you are using to program the light.

This is what you will see if you shine someone in the face. They will see nothing but blinding spotty brightness. Use this to your advantage.

The hand-held NexTorch lights are reasonably-priced and have lights that are designed as dedicated weapon lights as well. There is also a model called the Saint 3 that is astonishingly bright and is essentially a hand-held spotlight. This one would be particularly handy on a country property as it can really light up a back yard. It even comes with a sling so that you can "drop" it and use both hands for shooting if necessary. I call it the Eyebeam of God. In fact, this light makes me think of that old original Star Trek episode where the little flying pancakes stung Spock and Dr. McCoy had to shine a light as bright as the sun on Spock to kill it, temporarily blinding Spock in what has to be one of the biggest gaping plot holes in all of Star Trek. How much do you want to bet that Spock could have simply turned around and sat in the chair backwards and not been blinded, even temporarily. But then you wouldn't find out about that mega-convenient inner eyelid that Vulcans have.

If you are walking around, if you are carrying a pistol legally, then you should have a tactical light. Even if you aren't carrying, a super bright light can be a life saver and very useful tool to have on you at all times. However, if you are in the home I would advise the next option.

WEAPON LIGHTS

Many pistols, and a few revolvers, afford the option of mounting small tactical lights. It is recommended that, if you keep an HD gun, you have a tactical light that you can affix to the gun. There have been fierce arguments over whether the light is better mounted on the gun or if it should be held in the weak hand, and both sides have strong merit. In this case I prefer the mounted method. That way you don't have to remember to pick up two things. No one who is flash-blinded is going to want to stick around. But even if they do, you still have the gun it is mounted upon if it is needed. At the very least they will

The Surefire X300 weaponlight mounted on an FNS-9. It sticks out quite a bit, so you will have to clean powder residue from the top of the light.

throw their hands up in front of their face or flinch away or both, which gives you another split second to decide what to do next.

Rifles and shotguns can also mount weaponlights, most easily if they have a stretch of Picatinny rail attached to them. Of course the endless varieties of railed handguards available for AR-15s make that easy, but there are a number of clamp on, screw on, or slip on rails that can be added to just about anything.

With the light mounted on the gun, it should be placed so that it can be easily and instinctively activated with the support hand. This might require a remote switch, and a number of the lights can accept such a device, but many do not have a remote switch included, so it must be purchased separately. The point is that you should not have to fumble about trying to activate your light when you need it most. When you need it most is when you are jacked up on adrenaline, about ready to pee your pants, and you can't figure out how to disengage your gun's safety. Stress can mess you up, so most of the pistol lights have ambidextrous activation buttons so the shooter can simply extend a finger from his support hand to activate the light. Others may use a button under the trigger guard so that the middle finger of the shooting hand pulls the

The Surefire replacement Rem. 870 forend with integral tactical light.

The X300 mounted on the chin rail of a Beretta CX4 Storm carbine as the author clears the garage. He heard a strange scratching noise so he went to check it out.

trigger on the light activation. However it's done, it's to make the activation instinctive and not something that requires concentration.

Surefire has had on the market for some time a weapon light that replaces the shotgun forend furniture. The light is integrated into the front of the forend and uses a constant on switch on the left side and an instant-on button strip on the right. Both activators are perfectly placed, the thing is overmolded with a rubberized surface, and the only downside is you need to keep your support hand

away from the hump the light sits in. You'll bang your knuckles if you don't.

The pistol lights can certainly be mounted on the long guns, and frankly I rather like them for that application. The pistol lights are bright enough for any home defense use and they are and have to be very short so that they don't stick out past the muzzle of the pistol too much. So for the short, lightweight guns ideal for home defense, like Beretta CX4 carbines or Kel-Tec KSG shotguns, they are perfect. M4 style carbines will be perfect perches for this type of light as well.

However, if you really want to spend some money and have some wicked cool tactical lights, they are available and can be purchased in most outdoor sporting goods stores. But, as I said before, if you are a new gun owner, you would be best served by sticking to something under $400. Most lights are going to be much less than that, but you will find some examples of units that intuitively combine tactical lights with aiming "lasers" and that is the subject to tackle next.

LASERS

Frankly, in this author's opinion, these should only be used in conjunction with a gun that already has sights, and the laser should be set so that it is a point-shooting device, not a precision aiming device. There are a few pistols on the market that are factory supplied with lasers

The S&W Bodyguard 380 has a handy integral laser just in front of the trigger guard. This pistol is priced well under $400.

and usually they are small concealed carry style guns, like the Smith & Wesson Bodyguard 380. Lasers are imprecise when used alone, but are excellent supplements for existing iron sights, and can be extremely helpful when learning to shoot the gun, since the dot bouncing around can give great visual feedback on shooting technique.

Green lasers are less common and more expensive than red lasers, but are much easier to see, since the green wavelengths are in the center of the range of human visible light and red is at the lower end. Green lasers are great for daytime use and red for everything else. At night green lasers appear so bright that they can actually display a visible beam in addition to the terminal dot, while the red lasers can wash out in the sunlight at quite close ranges or if the user is colorblind.

There is a bit of a dispute on how a laser should be zeroed. In my opinion, the best place to mount a laser is directly below the bore of the rifle, parallel with the bore. When it is directly below, and zeroed for a particular distance, then you will only have to compensate for bullet drop, and you won't have to concern yourself with windage. If your laser is mounted below the barrel, say three inches, then all you have to do is find out how far out the bullet will be when it drops three inches. Let's say it's 50

The Viridian X5L light and laser combo. It uses a green laser that is easier to see than a red laser. The light and laser can be used in various combinations including strobes. Modes are changed by depressing both activation buttons at the same time.

yards. Anything below 50 yards will see the bullet striking high within three inches of the point of laser aim. Beyond that, the bullet will strike lower. But beyond 50 yards, you are no longer in imminent danger according to virtually any standard of self-defense in any state.

The basic Crimson trace 1911 kit. Two batteries, two shields, a legally required sticker, cleaning swabs, and two of the smallest hex wrenches you will ever see.

Military and police applications differ here; this book isn't written for them, but for the average gun owner. Laser aiming at anything on a human body between the eyebrows and groin with a maximum of three inches of vertical deviation is going to result in a hit. Now let's say your laser is mounted to the side and below the barrel, like with the excellent Crimson Trace Lasergrips. The laser is usually about one inch below the bore and a half inch to the right of the bore. If you zero the laser at ten yards, the bullet will hit the dot at that range. Up to ten yards, the bullet will strike above and to the left of the dot. Past ten yards the bullet will strike below and to the right of the dot. At twenty yards you can expect the bullet to be an inch low and a good half inch to the right of the dot. This doesn't seem like much, and it isn't but it's yet another thing to try to remember. It's much easier to simply set the laser parallel with the bore. Then you will know the bullet will always strike a half inch to the left of the dot, and either an inch high or less out to the ten yards. Past ten yards, the bullet is still a half inch to the left of the dot but will drop below the dot. Again, out to reasonable self-defense ranges you only need to know one

The Viridian X5L mounted on a Rhino revolver. You can see the green dot even in well-lit conditions.

thing: how low will it go?

Except when your sights are completely unusable, lasers are not a replacement for your sights, but a supplement. They make an excellent point-shooting aiming de-

The batteries are inserted on both sides of the grip panels. Then the two shields are placed over the batteries to act as a barrier from stuff in the magazine well. Wrap it around the front of the frame and use the original grip screws to secure it in place. There is a master power switch on the bottom of the left side panel and this model is activated by a button placed just under the trigger guard on the grip front strap.

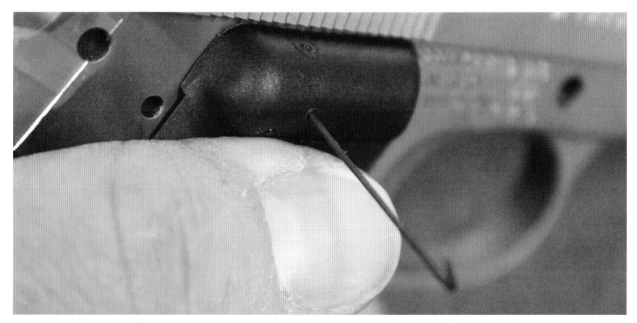

Those tiny hex wrenches are for adjusting the direction of the laser, so that it can be zeroed.

Economy model with separate, larger light and laser units. This makes the rifle decidedly front heavy, but is much lighter on the wallet.

vice if you are in a big hurry. It's easy to line up the dot with whatever needs a hole in it. Unlike regular sights, lasers have batteries that can and do expire at the worst possible moment. Laser (and light) owners would do well to replace the batteries on a regular basis, whether the batteries appear to need replacement or not.

The best answer is a combination light/laser unit like the Surefire X400, Streamlight TLR2, or Viridian X5L. You have light, laser, and gun all in a compact package, but they are spendy and can run over $500. While there are holsters that accommodate these units, most owners are unlikely to carry this type of combination for the sheer bulk of it all. They do make excellent duty and home-defense combos, so don't shy away if you can afford the price tag.

These have all been lasers designed for mounting on pistols, but that doesn't mean they can't be used on rifles. Any of the pistol lights and lasers or the combos thereof are perfectly suitable for long gun use. The compactness is a benefit. There are lights that are designed for rifle use and lasers as well, but they tend to be less compact and heavier, and also, in many circumstances, cheaper. Miniaturization is expensive, and as long as you don't mind a little more bulk, you can get lasers and tac lights more cheaply when they have not been so shrunken. For example, the Viridian X5L is a superbly easy to use and is very small besides, and it retails for $400. An alternative starts with the Nextorch T3A light kit that comes with mounting hardware and remote activation switch for a hair over $100. Combine this with the LS8100 Green Laser from AimShot that runs around $150, and you have both abilities for about $250.

"They" say that lights and especially lasers can make a good intimidation tool. Certainly, bright lights have a very tangible effect, since the first thing anyone does when a bright light is shined in their face is to either squint, shy away, or throw their hands in front of their face, usually a combination of all of the above. "They" also say that a bouncing dot on a bad guy's chest works for that purpose too (we can probably thank Hollywood for that, something good for a change) but it is also a possibility that the attempt to intimidate may fail and the trigger may have to be pulled. Crimson Trace has a great series of advertisements that you have probably seen. It shows a dude sitting in a mostly empty parking lot with his gun sitting next to him on the floor. He looks exhausted and overwhelmed, arms on his knees staring at the floor. The caption reads, "The guy with the laser won." Whether or not the laser works as an intimidation tool, it can certainly work to enhance sighting of the gun. The reason it works for that purpose so well is that when the stress and adrenaline start messing up your finely tuned body chemistry, you get tunnel vision and the ability to focus on anything but the threat diminishes. The dot is on the threat and can be recognized and utilized easier than if you try to focus on the front sight of your pistol like you would have to without the laser.

So, you will find that this particular author is in the bag when it comes to lasers on defensive firearms. If deploying the laser or light somehow makes a bad situation worse, then I suspect that nothing would have defused the bad situation in the first place, since you've already passed the point where you drew your gun (this is assuming a weapon mounted light and laser). Ultimately lights and lasers are non-lethal defensive tools and should be part of any gun owner's arsenal. Get the lights first, then the lasers. The lights are cheaper and are useful for identification, and you can uprade to the more expensive combos or laser units as you can afford to do so.

"They" (and there are all kinds of "they") have differing opinions of how to deploy a hand-held light. Do I hold it next to the gun, below the gun, behind my head out to the side, etc. There are other books that cover the semantics of the different arguments. I'm just going to say the same as I do with any other disputable concept in the gun arena. Figure out a technique that you think suits you the best, one that you can use the most effectively and comfortably. If you think that holding the light tightly between your legs and shooting your pistol upside down is the best for you, and that configuration somehow in this universe works, then by all means use it.

CHAPTER 8

SCOPES AND OPTICS

More and more rifle owners are eschewing iron sights in favor of optics. This class would include traditional hunting types of riflescopes, pistol scopes, and red dot scopes. These units usually magnify; in fact the 3-9x40mm hunting scope is so commonly used for big game hunting that it is represented in every scope manufacturer's inventory in multiple versions; but magnification is not always necessary, as seen in the red dot scopes. The big benefit to optics is that you do not have to line up two things onto the target to hit it, only one: the crosshairs (dot, chevron, or whatever the scope has).

Furthermore, magnifying optics allow you to shoot more precisely at a longer distance, and many also incorporate rangefinding abilities and corrections for wind and other factors built into the reticle. Downside: they are more expensive than iron sights and are not usually included on guns from the factory. On the occasions that they are included with the rifle as a package, the scopes are low end, basic, and cheap. Useable, but cheap. Most modern manufactured hunting rifles do not have any kind of sighting system included and are simply designed to accept an optic. Iron sights can be installed not by the

Typical traditional scope mounted on a nontraditional rifle. This .308 rifle would be completely at home in the deer stand.

A newer 30mm tubed long range Vortex riflescope with illumination and front focal plane reticle, next to the plain old standard Zeiss.

The small Bushnell TRS-25 on top of a Walther G22.

The Burris Eliminator rangefinding scope. There is a small computer in this scope's housing.

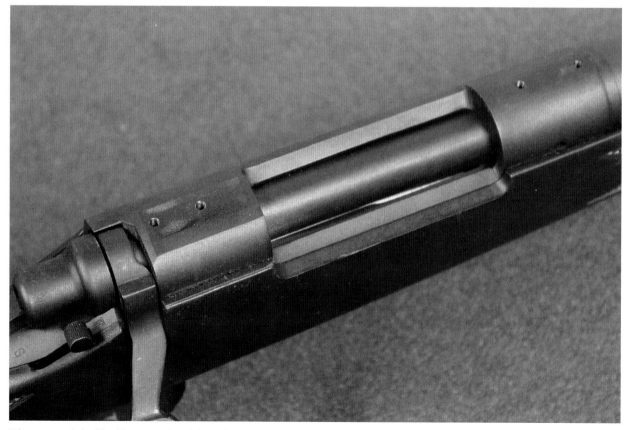

When you see holes like this on a receiver, it is just begging for an optic.

consumer, but by a gunsmith. A few shotguns will come with a scope rail and no sights; these are intended to use low power shotgun scopes. Pistols will only on rare occasions be devoid of sights in favor of optics. Rimfire rifles, like .22s will almost always have iron sights.

TRADITIONAL RIFLESCOPES

By far the most common optic used today is the traditional magnifying riflescope. The origins of this optic stretch far into the hazy past, all the way back to Robin Hood if you believe the Kevin Costner movie. Back in the day when the telescope was invented. The desire to see far away objects has ever been a quest to the human being and the telescope made it possible. Magnifying riflescopes have been used on rifles in the US at least as far back as the American Civil War, when comparatively crude devices as long as the barrels were mounted on rifles that weighed heavily, sometimes thirty pounds or more. However, riflescopes did not become a common accessory until much later, well into the 20th century.

While we still have and use fixed magnifying optics, which are pretty basic in comparison, variable scopes see the most use and are the most purchased. It is really convenient to be able to start with a wide field of view, low magnification to find the target, and then max the power out to the highest setting for precision shooting. Single power optics have made a small resurgence in the form of tactical optics such as the Trijicon ACOG, and the plain fixed multiplier scopes that are often mounted behind red dot scopes. But the variable power remains supreme.

The most common variable power riflescopes are the 3-9x40mm models. WHAT DOES THAT MEAN??? The first number is the magnification. If there is a hyphen and a second number then that scope is a variable and the two numbers divided by the hyphen are the minimum and maximum magnification possible for that optic. The "x" means "times" or magnification, and is represented by the word "by" when used in a statement, like when we talk about, say, a four by four (4x4) truck. The number after the "x" is the diameter of the objective

The WWII Japanese Arisaka Type 99, like the earlier type 38, could not mount a scope on top of the receiver, for obvious reasons.

This box indicates, in code, the capabilities of the scope within. This model is for long-range shooting with a large 30mm body and a rangefinding reticle.

lens, which is the lens at the front of the scope. Why that lens you ask? It is the primary determiner of how much light enters the scope. Theoretically, the larger the objective lens, the greater the amount of light that enters the scope tube, and the brighter the image. In practice, this is limited by the tube diameter and the anti-reflective coatings that are applied to the lenses. Furthermore the greater light transmission is not physically realized unless the magnification is much higher than most scopes are capable of displaying. Higher magnifications require thicker lenses, or larger diameter lenses, and the larger lenses stop less light.

The reason most hunting scopes have a 40mm objective is that anything bigger on an average hunting rifle gains nothing. It is in fact a negative gain because the scope will have to be mounted another half centimeter above the bore. For normal purposes, we want the line of sight as close to the bore line as possible. It makes the ballistic calculations easier. There are a lot of 50mm or larger hunting scopes, but I would stick to the same models with the smaller lenses. Hunting big game, at the range most hunters will shoot, is perfectly suited to the basic 3-9x40mm riflescope. Now, if you want higher magnification, then by all means get it. 3.5-12x40 or 50mm and 4-16x50mm are all common and are suited for longer ranges than the 3-9. Get what you want, but just be aware that you don't gain much using a larger diameter objective unless the tube is larger and your high magnification starts creeping higher than 20. Bigger scopes weigh more, cost more, and are, well, bigger.

Scopes used on tactical rifles tend to the lower powers like fixed 3x or 1-4x20mm and stuff like that. The 1x scopes are great because they are basically unpowered red dots with a crosshair, until you crank them up and then you have a four power scope, like on the Nikon M-223 1-4x. Versatile and handy, they allow precision work up to several hundred yards but will not serve for much more, since shooting stuff farther away requires the image be bigger so you can see it, much less hit it.

If you get into benchrest shooting, you will be using

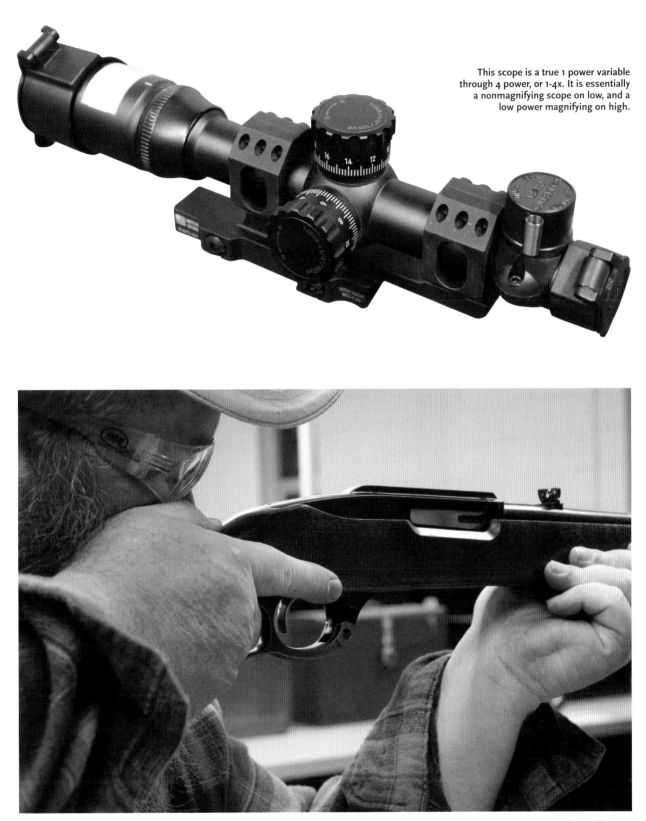

This scope is a true 1 power variable through 4 power, or 1-4x. It is essentially a nonmagnifying scope on low, and a low power magnifying on high.

Lots of guys choke way up on the stock. This can make it a little more difficult to mount scopes, as they will need to be mounted farther forward. If this is you, keep this in mind, particularly if you drop the gun off at a gunsmith. He won't account for this if he doesn't know you.

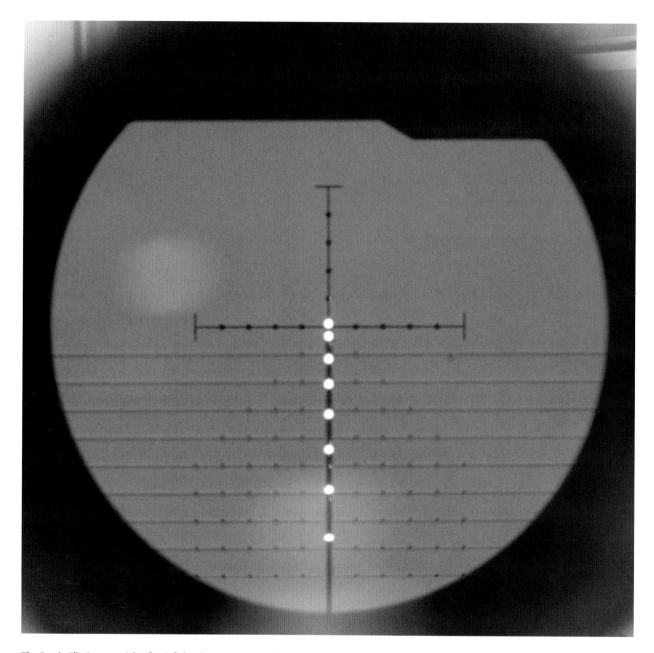

The Burris Eliminator reticle after info has been programmed into it. This is the result.

really high powered optics like 36x or higher where the tube and objective sizes really do mean something. These scopes are very long and heavy but will allow the OCD benchrester to shoot some absurdly small shot groups.

There are some new models that incorporate range-finding lasers in them. They are big, somewhat bulky and relatively heavy, though the newest version of the Burris Eliminator is lighter than it looks. This model uses a Horus Vision reticle with illuminating dots. You put the ambient atmospheric data into the scope, range the target and the scope will tell you where to aim. Pretty cool.

MOUNTING THE TRADITIONAL RIFLESCOPE

It's pretty important that the riflescope you purchase be appropriately mounted to the rifle. Since pretty much every modern centerfire hunting rifle is designed for use with a riflescope, there are on the market the means to mount them in all sorts of shapes and sizes. We'll go over just three of these types, since one is pretty unique, and the rest are mostly derivations or modifications of

Ensure the bases are installed and torqued to the correct spec.

Use a 1-inch wood dowel to lap the front ring to the front base. Secure the top strap to the ring and turn the ring a full two rotations and then align the front ring as squarely to the receiver as possible.

The rear ring can be set on the rear base, loosely between the two windage screws. Set the scope in the rings and install the top straps loosely.

Finish installing the scope rings to torque spec, then tighten the windage screws and boresight the gun. With these rings and bases, you will not likely need to lap the rings.

the second.

The Leupold/Redfield type of scope mount is separated into the base or bases, the rings, and the scope and rifle themselves. The base is the flat section that is screwed directly to the rifle's receiver. In the front base is a dovetail hole into which is placed the dovetail of the front scope ring, at a 90-degree angle to the barrel. The ring is then turned so that the ring is fully facing forward. In reality, the ring is turned all the way around several times in order to lap the ring to the scope for a tight yet smooth fit that will allow the ring to be turned slightly if necessary. The rear base or rear portion of a single piece base has two large windage screws that clamp onto the bottom of the rear scope ring. These screws are designed to set initial windage so that the full adjustability of the scope can be used if the bases' screw holes were accidentally drilled off to the side or something. The scope is mounted into the rings and the whole assembly is inserted into the front base and rotated into place onto the rear base where the screws are tightened down so that the scope is fully centered. The rifle is boresighted and fine adjustments are made to the two base screws to set the windage in the boresighter and then tightened down so they won't move.

The second pattern is the Weaver mount. Scope bases similar to the Leupold bases are screwed down to the receiver. The bases however do not use dovetails but rather use a locating cross slot. The rings clamp down around the outside of the bases, using the cross slot to accept

Level the receiver with a level. The bases should be installed to the receiver and the rings should be secured tightly to the bases.

Place the alignment rods into the rings and just snug the ring top straps to the rods. If there is lateral misalignment the rings will have to be lapped.

Lap the rings with the lapping bar and lapping compound until as much contact can be made between the bar and rings without the top straps touching the ring bottoms.

Clean up the rings and install the scope using the same level and an additional level on the scope turret. Alternately tighten the scope ring screws to spec.

cross bolts to provide the necessary compression. The cross slots also act to prevent the rings from shifting under recoil. This is arguably a more popular means of scope mounting, but the Leupold system is slightly stronger and the Weaver bases are not capable of adjusting for windage, but they are generally significantly cheaper.

Many .22 rimfire rifles have built-in rails on their receivers, but the method of attachment is like the Weaver style but without the cross bolt. The compression alone is enough to prevent movement on the low recoiling rimfire rifles. The majority of the different types of scope mounting in the gun universe use a similar or same method of attaching as the Weaver mounts. In reality, they are just slightly specialized Weaver mounts that are for most intents and purposes, interchangeable.

The one piece scope mount bases are of course stronger structurally and more rigid mounting platforms than the two piece mounts. However sometimes the one piece mount is no more ideal than the two piece and some rifles can only use two piece mounts, especially older war surplus guns. The bases are made of steel or aluminum, as are the rings and for lighter calibers and rifles the aluminum parts are perfectly acceptable. When you move to higher recoiling calibers then you might want to switch to steel mounts and rings.

The Picatinny rail is very similar to the Weaver mount. Its cross section is very close, differing only in some dimensioning. Weaver and Picatinny equipment will often be cross-compatible, but not always. The main visual and practical difference is that the cross slots on the Picatinny system are regular and identical, filling the entire rail/mount. Weaver cross slots may have only two or as many as the manufacturer desired and they do not have to be evenly spaced. The Picatinny rail, also known as the 1913

Many rimfire rifles have narrow slots machined into the top of the receiver. These rails accept rimfire scope rings.

rail was developed by .gov and is a much more versatile interface, being used just as much for other stuff like bipods, grips, lights, and lasers as for optics.

The final type of mount is really just a relocation from the standard mounting point over the receiver. The "scout" mount basically moves the optics mounting rail, usually Picatinny but Weaver is also prevalent, forward over the rear half of the barrel, using an extended eye relief, low magnification optic. This set up is often found on rifles that to not readily accept a mount

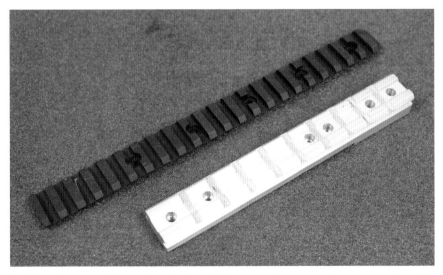

Picattinny (above) and Weaver (below) rails. Note the much larger separation between slots in the Weaver rail.

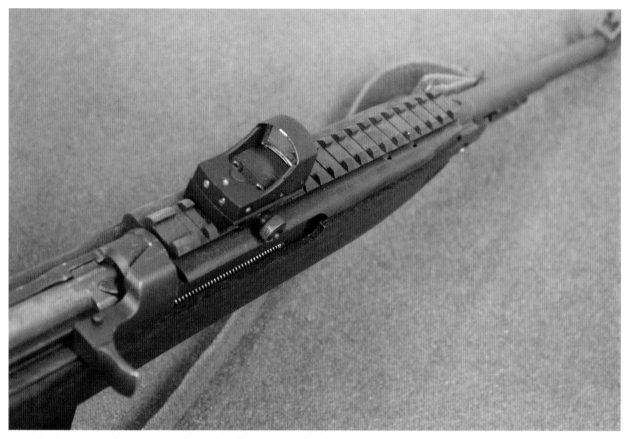

Even rifles like the M1 Carbine can have a low profile rail mount. This Ultimak scout mount replaces the standard forend wood and clamps directly to the barrel.

over the receiver, particularly military surplus rifles from a variety of sources. There are mounts for Mosin-Nagant rifles, M1 Garands and Carbines, Winchester and Marlin lever rifles, and several bolt action rifles are set up with this kind of optic platform in mind from the factory. The scout mount often is seen with a red dot type of optic, to which it too is well suited, and is a very quick-acquisition arrangement that leaves the shooter's field of view completely unobstructed.

LAPPING AND TORQUEING

It should be noted that sometimes the rings are not machined absolutely perfectly (there are tolerances after all) and the hole through one ring may not be perfectly parallel with the hole in the other. Or the ring might just be rough, and you need to clean it up. This is where the concept of ring lapping enters the fray. For the usual 1-inch rings you would use a 1-inch round bar. Place the bar in the rings and screw the topstraps of the rings down just snugly to the bar. Brownells and Wheeler engineering make these tools,

by the way. Lapping compound or other abrasive is placed on the rings and bar and the bar rotated to grind away the irregularities. WHY DO WE DO THIS??? Glad you asked. The scope tube can be easily damaged by the rings if they are not perfectly aligned or if they have not been properly machined. There are often "high" spots inside the rings that reduce contact between the rings and the scope tubes to a fraction of the whole surface area inside the ring. Lapping perfectly aligns the holes in the rings, and grinds down the high spots so that the scope can be mounted and done so without the crimping damage or tube flexing a misaligned or irregular ring would cause. The Leupold/Redfield style of rings is somewhat self-adjusting and will require lapping less commonly than the clamp on style of ring. It should also be noted that several companies ship thin tape strips with their ring sets that can be used to pad the interface between the scope tube and the ring itself.

One important thing that gun owners often do incorrectly is over-tighten scope ring screws. The top straps of the scope rings are not designed to touch the bottom to 70 inch/pounds in one pound increments. I have used it extensively and it has worked well. It's a little over a hundred bucks, but if you are the kind of guy to mount your own scopes and those of your buddies, it, or a similar offering from other suppliers, is worthwhile to purchase.

ONE-PIECE INTEGRATED SCOPE MOUNTS

Also known as tactical mounts, one-piece mounts that integrate the rings and bases into one unit are the mounts of choice for increasing numbers of shooters. Except for a few models, these are used almost exclusively with "tactical" rifles based on the AR series and others. A Picatinny top rail is required to use these mounts as they all are designed for that rail accordingly. The basic pattern is a single machined piece that incorporates both a large footprint clamping base and stems that rise to form the bottom halves of the two scope rings. The top straps of the rings are then screwed down onto the base with the scope

The lapping kit that we used on the Weaver rings earlier is shown here in its entirety. This is a very comprehensive kit for a reasonable price and can service both 1-inch and 30mm rings. It includes a FAT wrench for torqueing the screws. It is made by Wheeler Engineering.

straps of the scope ring. There should be a gap on either side. If you attempt to tighten the scope ring screws so that the straps touch the bottoms then you will crimp or otherwise damage the scope tube. There should only be sufficient torque on the rings to prevent the scope from turning or sliding. The scope, if it slides, will slide forward under the recoil of the rifle. Its mass wants it to stay put when the gun recoils so it will have a tendency to slide forward if it has the chance. Torque specs for scope rings are usually provided by the manufacturer of the rings, but they are usually in the 15-30 inch/pounds range. It doesn't require much, but high recoil rifles may require tightening to the higher end of the range. The bases themselves are similar in practice. Torque specs are often printed on the packaging. You can get torque wrenches at hardware stores, or if you want a good one to use for gun work only, I recommend the Magna Tip Adjustable Torque Handle available from Brownells. It adjusts from 10 inch/pounds

The Brownells Adjustable Torque Handle is also a great tool for getting the correct specs on screws. It's shape allows good leverage.

Traditional scope ring, and a modern heavy duty ring side by side. Note the much larger construction, longer straps, with six ring screws and heavy tightening nut.

in between.

There are major big advantages to this type of scope mount. These mounts are very rigid and usually somewhat bulky, and as a result are unlikely to break, bend, or flex, and also act as a limited armoring for the scopes themselves. Furthermore, this also allows the majority of these mounts to be removed and then remounted with negligible or no change in zero. This makes them handy for guns that need to be cleaned often (because they are shot often). There is a third, minor, advantage in that these mounts, being machined in one piece (the base anyway) and almost always to very exacting tolerances, means that you will not have to concern yourself with having to lap these ring/bases. Generally wider scope ring thicknesses also reduces the chances of crimping on the scope due to over-tightening. The thicker rings with greater surface area also means greater holding power with the same relatively low torque on the screws.

These mounts are all designed with the height necessary to bring a scope into alignment with the eyes of the average shooter when mounted on a rifle that has the barrel in line with the shoulder. This means most have been envisioned to be mounted atop of AR-15 rifles and carbines, where the axis of the scope is around 2 ½ to 3 inches above the bore. As a result, these mounts are seldom seen on traditional bolt action and other hunting rifles that have stocks that drop below the bore axis. Bolt action rifles that use the newer aluminum chassis will often use mounts like this but that's about it.

Many, actually most of these one piece mounts have quick release levers of some sort so they can be quickly and easily removed. We talked about that in the sights chapter. It's a useful but not vital to have that feature, and these levers will raise the cost of the mounts a bit. A few really good mounts will have locks on the levers, like the American Defense and Burris P.E.P.R. scope mounts for example. The lock is just a small button integrated into the lever that requires an inward push along with the outward pull on the lever itself. This particular lock is also tension adjustable for precision fitting on the particular rail that it is being mounted upon, as the overall width of the rail is not the critical fitting dimension of the Picatinny rail, and has a wider tolerance than the other angled surfaces.

Several examples of this type of mount also have the ability to mount a secondary red dot optic on top of the rings. The two most common examples are probably the AR-P.E.P.R. mount from Burris and the Flat-Top Scope Mount from JP Enterprises. A top strap with the proper

American Defense Industries scope mount. There are a number of options from this company that all utilize these adjustable, lockable throw levers.

The right side of the ADI mount showing the adjustment bolt heads. Turning these octagonal screws clockwise will tighten the tension when the lever has been closed. This is to be able to adjust to any rail that it is mounted on.

The P.E.P.R. mount from Burris is a stocky strong one piece locking lever scope mount. It comes with standard top straps and top straps that have Picatinny rails to allow the installation of a back up optic.

mounting interface, or Picatinny rail replaces the standard top strap and the micro-red dot is mounted on this top strap. In a similar way to the see through scope mounts, the shooter can then make a small adjustment of his head, raising it slightly to make use of the secondary optic in very short order. While you do lose the cheek weld doing this, most of the micro-red dot optics like the Fast-Fire III and JPoint that pair with these mounts are parallax corrected so that your dot does not have to be in

A small JPoint mounted on the top strap of the JP Enterprises Flat Top Scope Mount to use as a secondary optic.

the center of the picture for you to hit the target. A little shaking or displacement will not cause the shot to suffer.

Mounts of this type still should not be hulked when it comes to the screw torqueing. The torque specs on most of these mounts are going to be in the same range as the scope base ring screws on more conventional hardware.

MODERN TACTICAL-TYPE RIFLESCOPES

We just discussed how there are a number of one-piece scope mounts designed to be mounted on flat-top Picatinny rail-equipped rifles, like AR-15s, SIG556s and others. We should not neglect to address those particular optics housed in such mounts as they are an entire study in ballistic technology, optics technology, and ergonomic technology all wrapped into one long extended experiment.

Many tactical riflescopes resemble their more mundane brethren in appearance, but deviate when it comes to the components and materials therein. Very few hunting riflescopes for example, have first focal plane reticles. The reticle is the crosshair, but rarely in these scopes is it anything like the traditional crosshair. Modern optics have reticles placed on one of two planes, the first, or you guessed it, the second. When placed on the second focal plane, the reticle is fixed in size. No matter which magnification your variable scope is set to, the reticle will always be the same size in when looking through the scope. With first or front focal plane reticles, the reticle will zoom with the zoom in magnification. This is what happens with a first focal plane reticle.

Let's say you are aiming at some piece of crap truck on your back yard and the door is exactly as tall as the lines on your traditional duplex crosshair where they get thicker, a little ways out from the intersection. On this scope, if you zoom in from 3x to 9x the truck will get bigger and now the door handle will fill the same image area, but the door now fills the entire picture. This is a second plane scope. Instead of duplex lines, you might have dots or hashes that run all the way up and down, left and right from the intersection. As before, the truck door fills the area in the center of the scope, one hash above to one hash below the intersection. Now zoom it up to max, in this case from 6x to 24x. Not only does the truck door expand to fill the picture because of the zoom, but the crosshairs and reticle grow with it at the exact same ratio.

Any scope with any sort of deviation in the reticle that allows an imaginary line to be drawn between two points can be used for determining range, whether it was really designed to do that or not. However, on a second focal plane reticle it will only be possible at one specific magnification, unless you want to have to memorize a whole bunch of formulae. Some guys like to do that, so let loose dudes, let loose. For the rest of us we can get a scope with a front or first focal plane reticle that allows us to range at any magnification, since the distance between the two points will always be x at 100 yards, or 200 yards, or whatever you determine it to be.

There's a reason that this feature is rare in the hunting scope market and common in the tactical market. Hunters simply don't need the feature, and it costs more to make a scope with a first plane than a second plane reticle. The vast majority of rifle hunting occurs under 200 yards where this capability is unnecessary, and impact points are regularly within four or five inches of the original zero. In reality this is practically point blank, and most recreational big game hunters are kind of cheap. That's not a put-down. There's no reason to spend a huge amount of money on an optic just to bag a deer or two every fall, unless you have more money than you know what to spend it on. The reason the long range shooters, tactical competition shooters, or real life shooters need these scopes is that they will often have to engage targets at completely unknown distances, distances so far out that they have to have the scope maxed out to even see the target. You might think it's easy-peasy to hit a 12-inch white painted steel target, but it's not when that steel target is 684 yards away in a 15mph crosswind. Notice the yardage. I gave you a freebie. You're lucky if the situation even tells you where the target is much less the exact yardage. You can get into some real challenging shooting and I heartily encourage new shooters to try out some long range competition shooting if they have the chance. It can be very discouraging at first, because I will tell you right now that you will miss that 684 yard 12-inch target on that first shot unless you are really, really lucky. But with some practice, knowledge of the science, and a halfway good gun you can achieve some pretty good practical long range marksmanship. But traditional riflescopes won't cut it and you will have to buy one of the more expensive and more capable tactical scopes.

As well, reticle illumination is much more common in tactical riflescopes than in traditional models. It isn't completely absent, as it is very handy in the dusk and dawn times of hunting. But since all the other cool features are in the tac scopes, there is no point in leaving out illumination, and a much higher percentage of tac scopes will have illumination. Be warned that like on la-

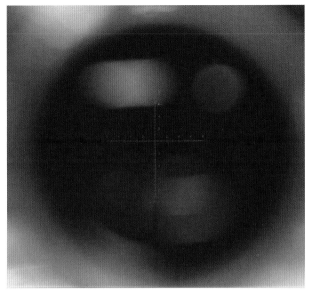

Illuminated reticles dimly light up so you can see the reticle in reduced lighting situations.

sers and lights, the batteries will be exhausted at just the wrong time, so change them frequently whether they need the change or not.

RED DOTS

Now we enter a category as vast and varied as the traditional riflescope. The original idea behind the red dot scope was to have a single illuminated aiming point, sort of like a crosshairs in a riflescope, but at zero magnification, with a wide field of view. There are a lot of different sized dots, different colored dots (don't have to be red, but most are, and the originals were), not dots at all but circles, triangles, whatever, powered and unpowered, small and large.

The basic theoretical red dot sight will be encapsulated in a smallish housing roughly 30-50 mm in diameter and three or four inches long. And black. Black is still the new black. A diode inside the back of the housing shines

The battery housing on an illuminated reticle scope. The common CR2032 button battery is used here.

A simple red dot is the reticle on most red dot sights. It will have an intensity dial to adjust to the ambient light.

a beam forward that reflects off the front lens assembly back through the rear lens into the shooter's ocular sensory apparatus. Adjustments are present to move that dot around the inside of the optic so that you can adjust the point of impact. There is generally no magnification. The dot covers a certain sized circle at 100 yards. 4 MOA dots are common that cover a four inch circle at that range. In a way, the dot size can allow some basic rough ranging ability, but the dot size can be variable and often is of different sizes for different tasks. Larger dots are better at short ranges where precision is secondary to speed, and smaller dots, as small as 1 MOA or less, are used past 100 yards with good precision. Intensity settings on the theoretical red dot scope are user adjustable so that you can set it high for bright sunlight or quite low for those times when you are protecting your home in the dead of night. This theoretical model will also have a clamp mounting system integral to the housing so that it can be slapped down on a Picatinny or Weaver mounting rail. The theoretical model, since it is basic is also cheap and can be found for under $50. There are all kinds of models available.

Let's expand out from there. You can go up to the $100 range and find something with a little more in the way

This is a basic entry level red dot sight, perfectly at home on this .22. This one was made by BSA, but similar models are available from numerous optics companies.

A Bushnell Trophy red dot scope. It has the ability to change reticle shapes. Some models are switchable from red to green.

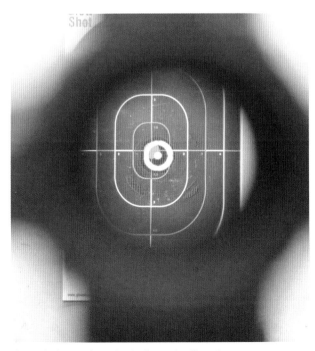

The circle dot reticle setting in the Bushnell Trophy.

The cross hair setting for the Bushnell Trophy reticle.

of flexibility. A Bushnell scope has the ability to switch between red and green colors, as well as four different reticle shapes, a small dot, a big dot, a circle with a dot inside it like a donut with a pinprick hole, and a crosshair. All these different shapes are quickly chosen by means of a small dial on the left side of the optic body. The downside is the traditional Weaver style rings that come with the scope may not be of the proper height that you need and you will have to purchase rings of a more suitable height. Up to this point, the battery life of these red dots mentioned is in the dozens of hours, using a watch battery as a power source, usually a CR2032 button. This battery is common (get it at any department store) and inexpensive.

One of many variations of the red dot sights made by Aimpoint.

The EoTech Holosight uses a circle dot reticle. It uses holographic technology rather than a red diode.

A red dot optic of which the origin is unknown. It was a "buy a rifle get a free sight" kind of optic. The box says nothing of brand name or origin, but it works rather well, with four different reticle settings.

The next tier of red dots gets expensive. This is because we are entering into the tactical realm of this particular universe. Tactical, competition, and military/LEO shooters have a much more demanding agenda with red dots, just like with riflescopes. Likely the most well-known red dot optic at this level is the Aimpoint. This is the small scope seen on many rifles carried by our military and is known there as the M68 Close Combat Optic. This model is based on the Aimpoint CompM2 red dot scope. In use it is much like the theoretical baseline model but with some under-the-surface enhancements. Battery life has been extended to the tens of thousands of hours. You can leave these things on at full power for well over a year. The housings are reinforced and overall, the durability of the Aimpoint red dots is an order of magnitude above the previous tier of red dot optics. The CompM2 is pretty much obsolete now and they are a couple generations past it as of the time of this writing. Aimpoint also makes low magnification red dots in their line as well, in a nod to traditional hunting scopes.

A different but still common alternative to the Aimpoint has been the EoTech Holosight. First of all it's not round. It's more squarish and boxy. If you are into squarish and boxy then boy, is the Holosight for you. Rather than using a red diode, the Holosight uses a "laser." I only point that out simply to point that out and be a know-it-all. It doesn't really matter in the grand scheme of things. The effect is the same in that you have a dot, or in this case a circle dot that appears to project onto the target but never leaves the confines of the optic body. Rather than using dials to adjust intensity, it has buttons either on the rear or the side of the housing that activate and adjust up and down accordingly. The fun part about this model is that is uses the common AA battery, or the becoming common CR123 battery. Formerly used solely in cameras, the CR123 is regularly used in optics and tactical lights so that it is much more common. This is unlike the 1/3N battery that earlier Aimpoints used and you had to dig up online or at Radio Shack. There are a host of Holosight models (same with Aimpoint) that you can

This little red dot from Sightmark is a simple yet well-put-together model sitting on a CX4 Storm carbine.

choose from, based on requirements and cost. This tier of red dots ranges from $300 to over $600. Fortunately most now come with integral Picatinny mounts from the factory, so you don't have to pay extra for mounting hardware.

Micro-red dots are also increasingly common, and as the name would suggest, are quite small. These include the JP JPoint, Burris FastFire, Docter Optics red dot, Trijicon RMR, and others. They are small, very lightweight, use button batteries and last a long time, and often are constantly on, with no on/off switch, using a light sensor to self-regulate brightness. Prices come within a wide range.

The final (at least for now) tier of red dots is rarely red and there are only a few models to choose from. Most of these are passively powered, either by the great firebox in the sky or by radioactivity and usually by both. We've already mentioned in a previous chapter the amazing existence of Tritium and its usefulness in making self-illuminating gun sights. Models like the Trijicon Tri-power and the Meprolight optics use Tritium to make a visible reticle in subdued light and use fiberoptic technology to illuminate during the rest of the time, and they do so in a way that self regulates to ambient conditions. In a way, what goes in comes out again in a perfectly visible, perfectly intense reticle. Meprolight calls it an Electro-optical sight, but the idea is that you don't have to do anything to the sight. You don't have to turn it on. You don't have to play with settings. Nothing. But this convenience comes at a higher price tag.

It's pretty clear that red dot sights are in a very real manner similar to the traditional magnifying optics in one crucial aspect: price. You get what you pay for. If you only want to spend $100 you will get a unit that is somewhat bulky or has relatively short battery life, works well, but is made in the PRC. If you want to spend $300 or more, you will get a more streamlined or lightweight unit, that has battery life measured in the hundreds or thousands of hours, works really well, and is made in the USA, Japan, Israel, Germany, or Sweden, with a lifetime warrantee.

BACK TO BORESIGHTING

There is a little thing called boresighting that must be done to a freshly mounted optic. "Why?" you ask? Well, I'll tell you. If you just slap the bases onto the gun's receiver, then slap the rings down on the bases, and then slap the scope down into the rings, go to the range and try it out at fifty or a hundred yards, there's a good chance that you will wind up wasting a good box of ammo trying to sight the scope in. Boresighting got its name from the idea that you set up (or down) the gun so it won't move and then you look down the barrel bore from the back end. Pick something to look at. Maybe it's the door knob on the other side of the room. Perhaps it's the headlight on your beat up Chevy at the end of the driveway. Then you look down the scope and adjust it so that the cross hairs are on the same point as the item you centered down the barrel.

It's most important to get the left/right correct. The vertical alignment can and will be off a little. With some

The Meprolight optics are completely passive. Mount it and concern yourself not of batteries, nor switches.

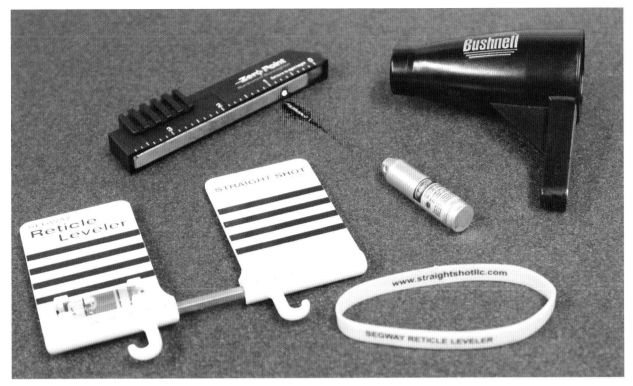

Small laser boresighter that looks like a cartridge (fits in chamber and beams down barrel) is small and silver. The Leupold optical boresighter is skinnier than its contemporary from Bushnell. The Segway reticle leveler is a must have tool.

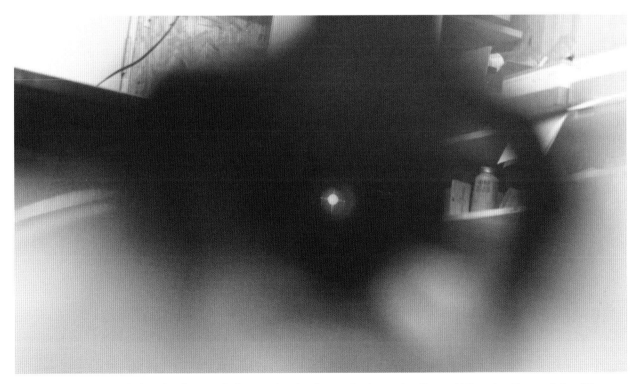

A literal boresight. Down the barrel at the target bullseye. Otherwise, fuzzy and uninteresting. You would then place the crosshairs of the scope on the same spot.

The arc on the lower left of the target is the laser transmitted through the barrel. It is slightly out of alignment, hence the arc rather than a dot. The reticle would be placed on the "dot."

boresight to the center of the circle. If you can do this whole process at the range at a certain distance, like 25 to 100 yards, then this will be a perfect boresight, and you just compensate a few clicks for the bullet drop. For example, a .223 bullet will drop about one inch at 100 yards, so set the scope's vertical adjustment so that you are aiming through the scope an inch or so below the dot that is projected at 100 yards. Of course the point of boresighting is simply to get the shots on the average paper target, say a 12x12-inch square. If the shots are on target, then you can easily adjust the crosshairs to move the point of impact.

The most commonly used means of boresighting are the various models of optical collimators. You can get them so they clamp to a barrel mandrel that slides down the muzzle end of the barrel. These are usually an inch and a half to two inches above the barrel. The other models are those that use a rare earth magnet to affix the unit to the muzzle. I prefer these models myself because you can then vary the height according to the height over bore of the scope. Some guys will say that doesn't really matter, but I disagree. I want the vertical and the horizontal as close as possible, and if the boresighter isn't high enough, you won't even be able to use it. These magnetic models work with standard and stainless steel just as well. Most are passive, using only ambient backlighting to light the collimator, but the very compact Leupold model has an

experience, and a little knowledge of ballistics, you can get the vertical boresighting down so well that the rifle will shoot vertically within an inch of where you bore-sighted it, and right on horizontally. This is, with the average hunting rifle, zeroed from the shop, for all intents and purposes. "So," you ask, "how exactly do you do it?" I've already told you the old fashioned way, but that is less precise than using a purpose built collimator. Another way, similar to the old fashioned, original look down the barrel method is to use a laser insert, either in the chamber, or in the muzzle to project a laser beam from the barrel onto the wall, or even better, a grid or target on the wall. The scope is then adjusted so that the reticle centers on the projected dot.

There is a possible weak point in the laser boresighting method. The laser may not be perfectly aligned in its housing. With a chamber model, if the dot is visible to any degree, use it. With muzzle variants, particularly the under forty dollar models, rotate the laser in the muzzle a full 360 degrees. If it light scribes a circle on the wall,

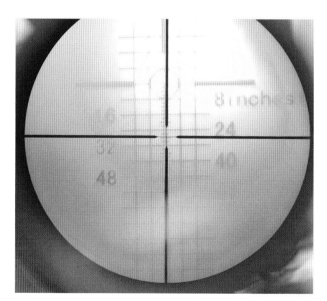

This is a view through a scope into a traditional optical boresighter, in this case the Leupold Zero Point. The slight angular offset indicates that the reticle or the boresighter or both are not level. It also indicates that the scope is aiming quite low which would result in a very high point of impact at 100 yards.

The Zero Point unit affixed to the muzzle. Note the scale on the side of it.

internal power source as well. You will want to make sure that the magnetic models are centered left to right on the end of the barrel.

Possibly the most frustrating aspect of mounting a scope is getting the reticles level to the gun. Some rings when you torque them will cause the scope to rotate slightly (or a lot) so you have to take that into account. I've found that just barely snugging one set of one ring and then doing the same to the other ring will fully immobilize the scope, allowing the other two pairs to be tightened normally, followed by the first two pairs. This is assuming that each ring has four strap screws. I can tell you that most of the rings you might purchase from sporting goods stores that are mounted on traditional rifles will do this to you. Very few of the rings from one piece scope mounts for Picatinny rails will. Then alternate screws side by side and diagonally to tighten.

An arbor mounted optical boresighter set up in a Mini-14 rifle. It is not adjustable for height without an extension.

A level mounted on the turret of a scope for boresighting purposes.

The reason we want the scope to be level is that when we make corrections, particularly at ranges greater than say, 200 yards, we want those corrections to be accurately reflected in the shots. Let's exaggerate and give an example. Let's say our scope is canted by ten degrees to the left or counterclockwise, and when you shoot for zero, the first shot is three inches directly to the right of the bullseye. You adjust the windage to account for those three inches, and you shoot again. Congratulations! Instead of making a hole right smack in the center, you just made another hole one quarter inch to the right of the center and an inch low. The adjustments will not work correctly and precisely if they are not level to the gun and the gun is not level to the ground. When you are mounting a scope, you can only account for the scope to gun arrangement, so we try to level the reticle to a flat on the gun, say the flat on the top of the receiver, or the scope rail before the rings are mounted, or something on that order. Then, the scope is leveled so that the reticle, or the horizontal crosshair line, is level to the gun. You can

do this often enough by using bubble levels, utilizing the scope adjustment turrets. Be it known that I have boresighted a lot of scopes and some of the reticles are not square with the flats on the turrets. Remove the caps and use the turrets themselves.

Here is a little leveling tip. The vast majority of scopes are not properly leveled. When the reticle is perfectly leveled to the gun, it will not look level to your eye. This is caused by the compound angle your eye and face is displaying when you are cheek to stock and looking down the scope tube. It's an optical delusion. If you are a righty, you will be looking up and to the left with your right eye and this will make the reticle appear to be slightly rotated to the counterclockwise. If you then mount the rifle on the other side with a left handed hold and look through with your left eye, the reticle will then look ever so slightly misaligned clockwise. Most people, including some gunsmiths, will align the reticle so that it looks perfectly squared when they have the rifle mounted, and because of this optical illusion, is actually slightly rotated clock-

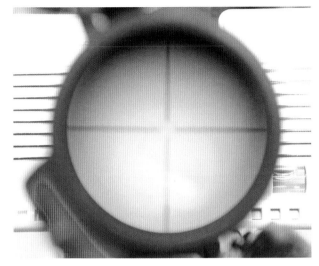

The Segway reticle leveler at work. The scope is canted to the right.

This 5-yard shot is a little close, a bit of a joke, but you need to start short, like at 25, to check that you actually boresighted well enough to hit the paper. A shot that is four inches off at 25 yards and on the paper will be 16 inches off at 100 yards and off the paper. You will have no idea where it went.

wise (if you are a righty). So if the crosshairs looks ever so slightly rotated counterclockwise with your right eye, but is the reverse when using your left eye, you are right on.

To compensate for or just remove the possibility of scope reticle misalignment, you can use the Segway Reticle Leveler available from Brownells. This is a wonderful product that will allow you to square that reticle off based on the reticle itself and the scope mounting rail which is screwed to or integral with the receiver.

Looking the scope and through the collimator you will see a grid that represents a target at 100 yards, gridded off usually into two inch demarcations. To do it really quick and easy, use your scope turrets to move the crosshair intersection to match the same intersection in the boresighter. To compensate slightly for bullet drop to get the closest possible boresight to zero, then set the scope crosshairs to subtend the boresighter grid two inches lower than the center intersection. This is a bit of a generalization, but making that little adjustment has gained me some very happy customers who were very satisfied with having to shoot only two rounds to establish their hunting zeroes.

Finally, when boresighting is completed, the gun needs to be shot first at 25 to 50 yards to ensure that the shot is somewhere on the paper. Then go out to 100 or whatever you want for your zero. If you start at 100 or farther out, and your boresight was a dismal failure, you may not even be on the paper. I always tell customers to start at short range for a couple shots then move out to their desired zero range.

OPTIC IDIOSYNCRACIES
Eye relief

Through all of this you need to make sure you have the scope set properly for distance from your eye. We've all (well, in my admittedly limited circle of friends) seen people with the cuts on their eyebrow from the scope's ocular bell hitting their mugs on recoil. This means the scope was too close to their face and/or they were not holding the stock firmly against their shoulders when they made the shot. It's one of those things that's incredibly amusing when it doesn't happen to you or your daughter. Scopes with magnification have a limited "eye-box" in which your shooting eye must be placed in order to see the full field of view in the scope tube. If you are not in the eye-box you will see a hazy black ring flipping around the periphery of a too small image, or the scope will gray out entirely, par-

The white lines indicate the focal distance of the current scope magnification. Higher mags will shorten the distance, and lower mags tend to lengthen it. This range makes up the length of the "eyebox" in which you can functionally use the riflescope.

ticularly on high magnifications. The bigger the eye-box is, the better, as it makes the scope a little more forgiving during use. Anyway, the scope needs to be mounted so that your eye is in the middle of the box when you are cheek welded to the stock. The box will sometimes vary in size based on what power a variable power scope is set to, so setting the scope to the middle or highest magnification is the best idea. The box will be biggest on the lowest magnification setting.

Unfortunately on many, well most, long action bolt action rifles (chambered in .30-06, .300 Win. Mag., .270 Win, etc.; we're talking big long cartridges here), you will not be able to mount the scope far enough to the rear. Optics mount manufacturers have addressed this by making extended scope bases and rings. For example, most Leupold front receiver bases have the dovetail hole in between the two mounting screws, but the extended base moves the hole behind the two screws, offsetting the dovetail hole a full inch to the rear. Extended rings either have a sharp slant offset to them or, like on the Leupold rings have

an extension at the very bottom. These can be reversed of course, so that the scope is mounted further forward. Then your concern is whether your set up fits the scope, as you only have a couple inches behind or in front of the turret housing to place the scope rings.

This conundrum is less prevalent in the short action rifles (.308, .243, .300 WSM, etc.) whose front receiver ring is much further to the rear because of the shorter receiver. On AR-15s, it's just the opposite, where most of the one piece scope mounts have a very sharp forward offset to place the rear of the scope just above the charging handle or pistol grip. This is especially true for the guys who choke up on the stocks so that their noses are boogering up the charging handle. Man, that is so not cool for your neck, or my rifle, dude.

Parallax

Without getting into too much boring detail, parallax is the effect of the crosshairs moving off the point of impact when your eye moves out of the centerline of the scope,

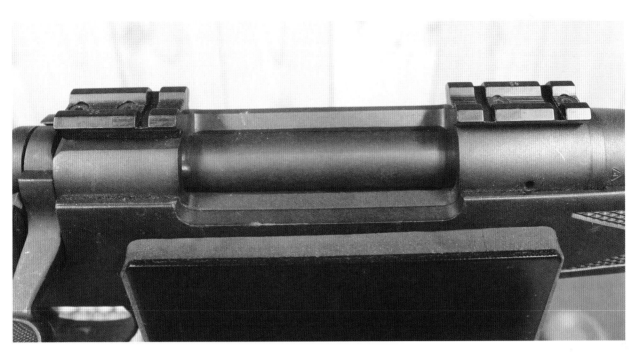

These Weaver mounts offer a choice of mounting points. Extension rings will make this flexibility even greater.

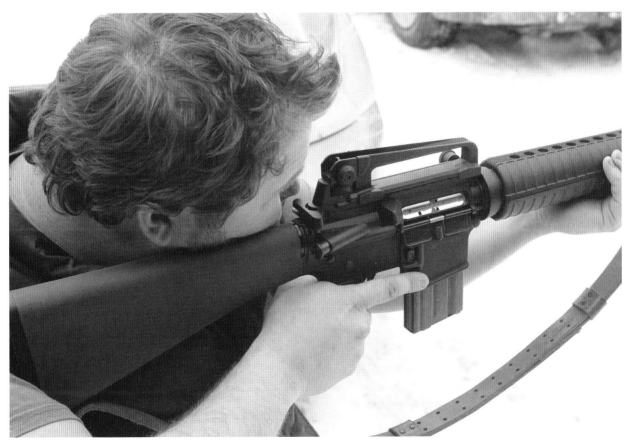

Nose to charging handle. Common.

This Leupold varmint scope has a side parallax adjustment.

The diopter adjustment on the ocular end of the riflescope. The + and – gives it away.

or the scope axis (the image is essentially not on the same focal plane as the reticle. Most commercial scopes are parallax corrected at 100 yards. Other scopes have manual parallax adjustments and many shooters consider this knob to be more of a focus ring, and it sort of is, since you set it by focusing your eye on the image and then turning the knob so that the reticle also is focused onto the image plane at which you are looking. This is the knob or dial that has measurements from like, 50 yards to infinity. If this is set correctly, you can be off center in the scope and still hit the target at the given yardage. Better yet, maintain a good cheek weld and keep your eye in line with the scope axis. The more expensive red dots are also parallax free or corrected, the cheaper ones generally are not. So, in a nutshell, parallax is very much an important property of optics to be aware of, but you can minimize or eliminate any bad effects by keeping your eye placement correct.

ONE-INCH VS. 30MM TUBES

It used to be that the only size scope tube was a one-inch diameter tube with larger bells on either end. In the last ten to twenty years the 30mm tube has become very common. The larger tube allows greater internal light transmission, allowing larger objective lenses to be more effective, theoretically more internal adjustment range, and a few other minor enhancements. For the average big game hunter, there is little benefit to a larger tube, other than the privilege of paying more money for it. For tactical and competition shooters there is an advantage, and it is to these markets that most of the larger tubed scopes are directed. In fact there are now, 34mm, 35mm, and even larger coming out. Depending on what kind of shooting you are doing, you can make good use of a larger tube, but for the new shooter that isn't competing, save your money and get the standard one-inch diameter tube models.

Incidentally, there really isn't the same standardization when it comes to red dot optics, since most of them have mounts integrated into their housings anyway. Also, historically, ¾-inch and 7/8-inch tubes used to be common, and you will still find such sizes for rimfire and airgun mounting.

DIOPTER ADJUSTMENT

There is a little focus ring on magnifying scopes on the ocular lens at the very rear of the scope to help you adjust the scope to your crummy eyesight. When looking at a distant object through the scope (with parallax adjustment set accordingly, if you have it), turn the diopter ring until the image is perfectly clear. There will be a lock ring. Lock that crap down and leave it there forever. It is also poor etiquette to then use someone's scope and mess up their diopter adjustment, so don't do it. These adjustments will be obvious and marked with a "0" + and – something.

CHAPTER 9

SLINGS AND BIPODS

If you have a long gun you will probably want a sling. It's just convenient to carry a rifle over your shoulder over distance rather than in your hand. Slings can also offer additional stability when firing. There are three main types of slings available: single point, two point, and three point. Traditional slings that attach at the front and back of the rifle are considered to be two point slings. Single point slings are basically a loop that wraps over one's torso with an extension that clips to the rifle, generally on the buttstock or on the receiver where the stock attaches. Three point slings are a hybrid of the single and two point styles, where a loop goes around the body with an exten-

sion to the gun. However, this extension then splits to attach to the rifle front and back like the two point sling. Unless you are a real fighting man, then you will likely be best served by a standard, traditional, two point sling.

A good sling will usually run over thirty bucks and can hit over a Franklin if you get really picky. Still nothing can replace freeing up your hands by hanging the gun on your body. So let's look at a few specific slings that you might want to buy.

TRADITIONAL SLINGS

There are so many types of this sling that it would be

Pulling this strap on the Viking Tactics sling tightens the rifle to your chest.

Pulling on the buckle tab loosens the sling so the rifle can be used on either shoulder without removing the sling.

The author with a heavily padded wide sling...on a Ruger 10/22.

An unpadded nylon or leather adjustable sling may be all you need. The pads on padded slings can get in the way sometimes.

literally impossible to cover all of them. They run from a piece of string tied around the barrel and stock to a multi-component, heavily padded, fully one hand adjustable quick release super sling. Slings will take up at least a quarter aisle in a sporting goods store like Gander Mountain or Cabelas and as a result choosing can sometimes be intimidating. So how about we look at it by application. Let's take it as a default for now that every long gun should have a sling, because at some point you are going to want to not carry it in your hand.

If you are the kind of guy or gal who likes to stake out a good spot to set up a stand or blind in order for the deer or whatever to come to you, then you aren't going to need a very complicated sling. A basic non-padded simple rifle sling will be a great choice. Since you will likely only be using it to carry your rifle from your car or ATV to the stand

and back again, and maybe for stabilization while shooting, then that's all you need, particularly if your rifle or shotgun is relatively light weight, which is almost always the case with a big game rifle in America.

If on the other hand, you are carrying around a much heavier gun, or if you are going to have an extended foot trip like you might find when hunting something in some of the western states, then a wider more padded sling would be ideal. The larger and heavier magnum chambered rifles that are the usual choice for that kind of hunting would do well to have a nice squishy recoil pad and a nice wide, padded adjustable sling. Padded and wide distributes the weight. Adjustable allows you to quickly use it to help stabilize your aim and then comfortably return it to your shoulder, and enables its use whether you are wearing a thick jacket or thin windbreaker.

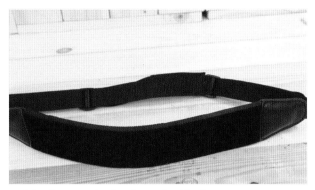

Squishy sling, stretchy sling, is comfortable sling.

SINGLE POINT SLING

Single point slings have one purpose: to keep the firearm positioned across the front of the body so that it can be raised and fired quickly. A single point sling will have one attachment point on the gun, and this usually is placed on the buttstock, either at the upper rear corner at the heel, or at the intersection of the stock and the receiver, sort of in the middle of the gun. Because of this placement, the long gun in question can be raised from the carry position quickly and can even be transitioned to either shoulder with little effort. When the shooter is finished, he can lower the gun so that it literally dangles in front of his chest.

Traditionally, the rather short sling goes from the gun to a loop that the shooter places so that the loop crosses diagonally over one shoulder and under the other. Here is where there is a rather notable downside. The rifle tends to want to hang in such a manner as to make a male shooter appreciate the benefits of the internal placement of the reproductive organs of the female shooter. Single point slung guns are often slung with one hand on the gun to control the bounce and sway to avoid some singularly male discomfort. This sort of mitigates the advantages of having a sling, since the point is to keep your hands free to protect your face when you trip and fall, and it tends to make the gun feel a little heavier because you are often resting one hand on it to keep the whole set up from sterilizing you. The extra hand weight can be felt, particularly if you are just looping the sling about your neck.

THREE POINT SLING

The three point sling started out with tactical applications but has proven to be of usefulness in other areas as well. It's really just a refinement of the normal two point sling. People used to, and still do, carry their rifles equipped

A Blackhawk single point sling mounted to a SIG551A1. Here the stock is folded and the gun is hanging comfortably in front of the body.

The 551's stock is now extended and the rifle shouldered. The sling stays out of the way and will take up the slack when the rifle is lowered.

The Lauer Custom Weaponry three point sling is fully adjustable and has a release buckle so you can get it off quickly.

with a traditional two point sling by looping the sling over their neck and hanging the rifle across their chests, or alternatively, by making the sling really long and carrying it cross shouldered but with the gun in front of them, rather than behind them. The point is to be able to make use of the load bearing nature of the sling yet be able to quickly aim and fire the rifle without having to unsling first. The three point sling makes this possible, but in a more comfortable fashion.

These slings are usually set up in a way that there is a sling attachment point up toward the muzzle and an attachment point back toward or on the stock. These points are almost always at the heel of the stock and the forward end of the handguard or forend, not on the bottom but rather on the support hand side of the forend. This placement keeps the gun relatively upright when slung preventing discomfort that might be caused by magazines extended below the gun that would be caused if the sling attachment points were in the traditional bottom arrangement.

The nice thing about the three point set up is that it is almost as versatile as the single point sling as far as shoulder transitions and quick sighting from rest, but is not as uncomfortable to the masculine mentality, since it tends to cause the rifle to hang slightly to the weak side, or is cinched up so tightly to the chest that it does not hang below the waist. Most three point slings have quick using adjustments to them so that shoulder transitions are easier or so that the sling can be converted to be used as a two point sling. The thing that typifies three point slings is the habit of connecting the front and rear attachment points on the gun and then both points to the loop or whatever is retaining the whole assembly to the shooter's body. This forms a triangle, and hence the "three point" moniker.

SLING ATTACHMENTS
The means by which a sling is attached is a short subject that should be discussed as well. There are some very useful advantages to some of the modern methods of sling attachment of which many traditional hunters and shoot-

The M1 Carbine sling is held in at the back by the body of the gun's oiler.

ers, and new shooters are likely not aware.

The traditional way to attach a sling to a rifle was to have a sling loop affixed to the barrel or forend and another loop affixed to the stock. Both points were on the bottom of the gun so that the sling was generally out of the way when the rifle was fired. This was the situation until more modern guns, particularly those with long magazines, started becoming popular. Slings then started moving to the left side of the rifle, most often using the same kind of steel wire loops that used to be placed on the stock bottoms. There were some notable variations such as the sling setup on the M1 Carbine from WWII onward. The front loop was placed on the left side and the rear loop did not exist. A small oiler bottle was used to retain the sling, with the sling wrapped around the bottle and the bottle snapped into a thin cutout on the stock.

I'm not sure when, but it was certainly post WWII, when "quick detach" sling swivels and independent sling studs became common. A domed stud with a cross hole in it is screwed into the wood or plastic of the stock and

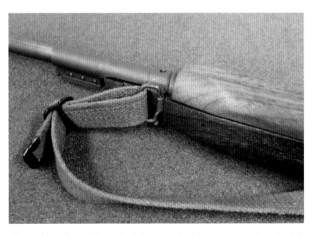

The carbine front sling swivel is a standard loop mounted to the left side. The fully side mounted sling set up is much more user friendly than when they are on the bottom.

forend. The cross hole accepts the swivel assembly itself by means of a peg attached to the swivel. These swivels have a cap of sorts that is lifted from the peg and turned

The quick detach dome stud has become the industry standard sling swivel attachment, and the associated swivels the standard on slings.

out of the way so the peg can enter the dome stud. The cap is then rotated back over the peg and spring tension holds it in place. Other models have a screw mechanism on the cap that when screwed tight locks the cap in place. This arrangement allowed the sling to be removed with relative speed and ease when necessary or desired. If the sling gets in your way in the deer stand, you can take it off and then later in the morning when you get hungry you can put it back on and tromp back to the house for an omelet and toe warming.

Now we get into the really cool stuff. The aforementioned loops and "quick release" sling swivels work exceptionally well and are common and cheap to boot. But here we truly examine the quick release concept in its current form.

Somebody figured that the "quick release" wasn't quick enough. You can remove those slings in a few seconds per swivel, maybe ten seconds each, with your gloves off. But what if you could detach each swivel in less than one second a piece with thick gloves on? I'd buy that for a dollar. Or ten. The newer "quick release" swivels do just that. While somewhat heavier, these units utilize an integral stud that uses ball bearings and a lock that is inserted into a steel or aluminum receptacle with a slot in it. This is just like a quick release coupler on an air compressor hose. The ball bearings are unlocked by means of a large button on the face of the swivel. Just push the stud into the hole or press the button and pull on the sling to remove it. In fact, this system is so effective that many guns, particularly aftermarket stocks and forends (mostly for ARs), are made with the receptacles in them to begin with, and the fad is catching on with other platforms. You can buy the swivel and receptacle sets from Brownells that can be attached to just about any gun. You simply drill out the holes to the proper depth and diameter and use an epoxy or Brownells Acraglas to glue them into the stock or forend.

The quick release sling uses a push button in the middle to unlock and remove it. It has four ball bearings that extend into a groove in the small housing that is affixed to the stock. Many MSR forend tubes have the receptacles built into them.

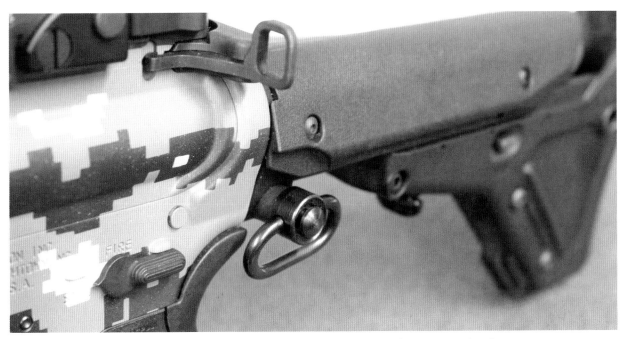

This MagPul UBR stock has two QR receptacles on either side, one each at the receiver interface and one each at the rear.

The QR usage is generally much higher in the AR-15 crowd than the general population of gun owners. This ratio will even out eventually as the QR type of swivel arrangement is extremely versatile and useful. It is however, not as cosmetically appealing as some of the older sling loop patterns that have been around for a number of decades. For example, a QR set up will not look appropriate on a high grade Browning A-Bolt, but would be completely in place on a synthetic stocked new-type bolt gun like a Savage Axis. Furthermore, the swivels also rotate, and this will increase the likelihood of them scratching nice wooden stocks of the kind that people don't generally want scratched. On the other hand the traditional sling is much less useful and convenient on any black rifle than the QR type of swivel.

There are other sling attachment options that exist but they are nowhere near as common as the ones I just covered. The only other one of note I will discuss in the next section.

SLINGING UP FOR STABILITY

Whatever your preference for sling type or attachment type, it should be stressed that almost any rifle and most shotguns are going to benefit from the attachment of a sling, purely for the ease and utility of carrying it around. Home defense guns would be the exception where I would expect a sling to get in the way. This kind of rifle or shotgun should be short and handy and you aren't going to be toting it about much. Furthermore, the sling could snag on some item in your house just when you don't need that kind of headache. So if you have a rifle or shotgun for the home defense purpose, I'd recommend leaving the sling off.

However, the sling has another use. Slings have long been used to add stability to a standing or sitting/kneeling shooting position. By wrapping the sling around the support arm, tension can be placed into the shooter/rifle combination that helps to settle the hold down a bit. There are several ways to do this, but what you are ultimately doing is to attach your elbow to your body via the sling, giving the support arm more support of its own. I want the reader to understand however, that you can easily flex the barrel or the entire gun doing this. There is a very good reason that free floating the barrel to a large degree with a large gap between the barrel and handguard or forend is necessary.

When some guys sling up, they pull the forend or handguard, or tragically the barrel, an appreciable frac-

tion of an inch out of line, through the sheer flexing of the part. This is why, on a gun from which you desire repeatable consistent accuracy, you DO NOT attach the sling to the barrel, and why you MUST free float the barrel and see that the sling attachment point is on the handguard or forend.

There are a number of sling attachment points that affix to the barrel or the front sight tower of an AR-15, many of which use a Picatinny rail, and the sling loop is attached to that Pic rail. It's quite practical as long as you don't want to hit your target when you are slung up. If you must use one of these, be sure you shoot enough to get a good idea of what the point of impact shift difference will be between the slung up shots and the non-slung up shots.

In competitions that allow sling usage when shooting, the most obvious being the Service Rifle type of match, the handguards are free floated with the sling swivel attached to the lower front end of the handguard tube, moved from the rear sight tower/gas block. The reason this is done is that service rifle guys sling up so tight that it would very definitely change their points of impact. The downside is that the human body is not a CNC machine and cannot reliably exert the same amount of tension every time. Even if you could, your point of impact would change significantly when you shot the same gun without slinging up.

As you see, the free floating handguard or forend has a real purpose, to improve accuracy by removing stress from the barrel, particularly from the forces exerted upon the gun by the use of a sling. I have had customers call in asking why their gun shoots dead nuts on the bags at the range, but when they shoot from the shoulder the shots are grouping much less well and are six inches to the left. It's because they were slinging up on the rifle tightly enough to shift the group over and were doing it inconsistently enough that he groups were opening up like a shotgun pattern.

The moral of the story is this: Adding a sling to your rifle or shotgun is a great idea in most situations, and the best way to mount it is to do so in a way that minimizes interaction with the barrel in order to maintain precision in shooting.

BIPODS AND OTHER STABILIZERS

There are a lot of people that like to shoot from the bench or from prone, or like to have something to help stabilize their rifles when they are shooting them in the field. When shooting from the bench, whether competitively or just for sighting the rifle in, you are going to want something

This is one way to sling up on a rifle. The support arm wraps around the sling once to reduce the slack and exert tension on the sling.

This is another way to sling up. Rather than wrapping the sling, the support hand is brought to the rear and the sling tensions across the chest.

The X7 bags are really innovative. Four small bags are filled with filler and can be held inside the large bags or used as bunny ears alone. The bags can be stacked, connected, and combined in a number of ways.

on which to rest at least the front of the rifle's forend to reduce the movement prior to firing as much as possible. So, I suppose it will work better to cover bags and rests before bipods, even though the section is titled "Bipods and other stabilizers."

Shooting rests and bags

A popular accessory for shooting at the range is a set of range bags. In a nutshell, these are bags filled with a fine media and used to rest the rifle when on a shooting bench. The usual filler material is sand, but I've seen people use all kinds of stuff like kitty litter, salt, and rice, but none of that stuff works as well as sand. There are synthetic materials designed as bag filler that are pretty lightweight and work quite well as a bag filler. Anyway, most rests or bags come empty and you fill them up when you get home.

These bags usually have a common design, called rabbit ears. They only look like rabbit ears from the front and back. From the sides they look like a bag with sand in it. Why have the "rabbit ears" on the top of the bag? Well,

Traditional bunny ear rear bag.

Grasshopper, I shall tell you. Rabbit ears in the front give the rifle a perch from which it will not fly. The forend is placed between the ears and stays there, plus the soft

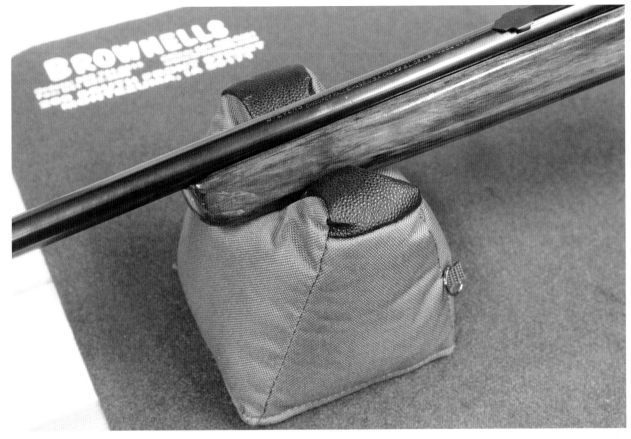

The front bunny ear bag that acts as a forearm rest.

leather that most bags are made from will allow some flex and shape changing in the bag to allow for the small adjustments to the rifle that the shooter will make. The rear bag has ears for a similar reason. It differs in that the shooter will squeeze the ears together to raise the stock, or release the hold slightly to lower the stock and thus raise the point of impact. The point is to make adjustments in very small increments since you are trying to establish a very precise aiming point. Pulling or pushing to either side slightly will also allow lateral adjustment.

Most shooting rests are used for the same purpose but by different means. What I mean by "shooting rest" is a mechanical assembly that does not compose rest bags (though they are often times used together and complement each other). These usually take the form of an adjustable assemblage of plastic and metal that duplicate the utilities of the range rabbit ears. Sometimes you can strap the gun down into the assembly, but you are kicking yourself in the butt if you strap down on top of or even touching the gun's barrel. The good units have a sliding subassembly that allows the shooter to perfectly position

Hyskore sells inert filler to use instead of sand in rest bags. It has a pretty good weight, but is not as heavy as sand. It appears to be a granulated rubberized material.

the rear section the optimal distance from the front rest for the shape and size of the rifle. Some rests even have what amount to micrometer adjustments to the front or rear (or BOTH!) rests so that minute corrections can be made in lieu of a rabbit eared bag.

The Hyskore Cleaning and Sighting Rest can be used for maintenance and shooting for just about any long gun.

The rests tend to be expensive to very expensive and the bags are often very affordable. I've been impressed with the combination of reasonable price and quality with some company's products, such as Hyskore and Caldwell. The Sinclair International products from Brownells are a great example of the higher end stuff with all the cool adjustments and features you would expect from a premium product. A great place to start, if you have no shooting accessory like this, is to simply go to your local sporting goods store and purchase a basic set of front and rear rabbit ear bags. Go home, fill them with granular sand and try them out on the back forty or the range. They will come in real handy when you are trying to get a four or five hundred yard zero sighted in.

BIPODS AND MONOPODS

Okay, now we can get to the bipods. A bipod is a device that you attach to the front of your rifle and has two legs by which you prop the rifle up above the surface of the bench or the ground. Nowadays, bipods fall into two broad categories and their uses are mutually exclusive, depending on what type of shooting you are doing. The guys who do bench rest and other super precise disciplines will spend a good deal of money on some really nice bipods, like the KLM Colossus that literally is wide enough to span two benches side by side. Okay, I made that up. But the recent bench rest bipods have a very large footprint and are quite heavy to allow for stability. Since new shooters are not going to be going in that direction, or are not likely to, that's all we'll say about that style of bipod here.

The second and much more common style of bipod is the small, lightweight, folding type that attaches via a Picatinny rail or sling attachment dome stud on the bottom of a handguard or rifle forend. I'd strongly encourage purchasing a bipod for use on a field rifle. The cheaper versions like the Rock Mount from Shooter's Ridge will do well for an amateur shooter. This model is closely modeled upon the Harris series of bipods but is made of thinner and lighter material. If you are not going to subject your gear to a beating, the Rock Mount is a good choice.

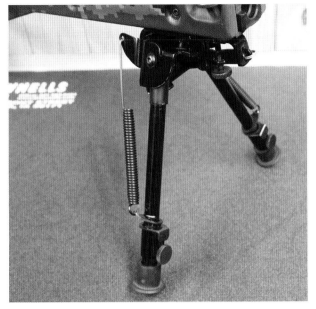

The Rock Mount bipod from Shooter's Choice is an entry level, inexpensive bipod modelled on the Harris bipod. The legs extend and will also fold under spring tension. Here it is shown extended.

The Versapod has a quick release mechanism for convenience. The legs are pinched together and raised. When extended, there is some degree of pivot ability as well as yaw.

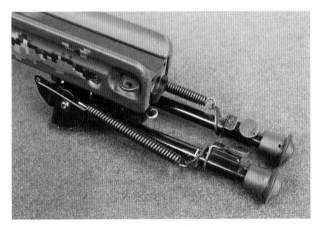

The Rock Mount bipod in the folded configuration.

The Versapod in the folded position. Note the QR sling swivel on the hand stop/base.

If you want a much better resilience, go with the original Harris. These bipods typify this genre of front rest. The two legs use a spring to hold them in either the folded or extended positions. Folded, they point to the front, extended they point down. I should point out that folded forward is the correct position and this is addressed in the sidebar. Futhermore all these folding bipods also have telescoping legs so you can adjust to some degree how far above the ground the rifle will be.

In the last couple years there have been a string of excellent folding bipod designs that have unfolded (ha!) in the market. The Versapod is a cool example that has a spud that inserts into a housing that attaches to the sling stud and serves as a handy hand stop. It has quick detach abilities so you can pull it off quickly when you are bagging the gun back up for transport. The Bobro bipod has an innovative locking mechanism that allows the shooter to open and close with little manipulation but will not do so without intent, by accident. Naturally, these more complex and featured units will cost more but the benefits are many to those who do a lot of outdoor shooting, whether it be hunting or competition.

Bipods with folding legs are designed so that the legs fold forward. When the legs are down, they have limited overtravel movement to the rear, and then they stop. This is to allow the shooter to push the rifle forward slightly to fix the feet into the ground and put steadying tension on the bipod. If they legs fold to the rear, you will lose this important steady base function, which also helps to compensate for felt recoil.

The shooting sticks are very stiff and allow a stable shooting platform.

Monopods can make up for the absence of a rear bag. This CTK Precision monopod is unfortunately no longer in production. It will extend and twist lock, and also has a secondary extension that unscrews and locks with a lock ring.

It's hard to overstate the utility of a bipod. Even if you are not prone or bench-ridden a bipod can be used on a fence post or rock and since most of them pivot or have independently adjustable legs to some extent you can still obtain a level shooting position even if the ground is uneven in the extreme.

Monopods are uncommon. Monopods can still rock about where bipods do not, requiring the shooter to steady the monopod. However, this can be done easily since the monopod itself is supporting the rifle and the shooter only need stabilize the monopod. Monopods can also be found that attach to the buttstock and act to replace the rear bench bag bunny ears. Since it can be a chore to carry around a heavy rear bag when you are walking around, an adjustable monopod can be very useful for rear stock support when shooting in the field.

Shooting sticks can take several forms but is essentially a hand held temporary bipod. The idea is similar to the long monopod/walking sticks that some guys use. You simply carry the sticks until you need them and then set them on the ground like a pair of chopsticks and set the rifle in the crotch of the joint. You might even find a shooting stick set that has three legs.

Fortunately the ability to stabilize a rifle for shooting is a science that has been well developed. Between bipods and their cousins and slings, the ability to carry and use a rifle or shotgun for an extensive time in the field has been and will continue to be adequately addressed. Funny though, there are a few pistols that have sling swivels on them because of their size. Pistols based on rifles, such as AR, AK, and SIG rifles, tend to have sling attachments as well.

Shooting sticks are like tent rods, collapsible and with a belt frog.

CHAPTER 10

TRIGGERS AND FIRE CONTROL

FBI records suggest that Americans purchase guns in the millions every year, particularly in the last five or six years. Every one of those guns has a barrel, a receiver, a stock or pistol grip, and a trigger. Except for the first item which will come next chapter, we've covered the rest. This time it's the trigger, or the fire control assembly in general that we will examine. Needless to say, the fire control is the most important part of the firearm as it is composed of the parts that make the gun "go off" and also of the parts that keep it from "going off." Preventing the gun from firing when it isn't supposed to is just as important, or more so, than getting it to shoot in the first place.

So there's always been a balance to maintain. Triggers that come on factory guns are generally poor in quality of feel, but as a result tend to be of the sort that requires a more concerted effort to pull and which will be far less likely to fire because of a drop, for example, than a highly tuned minimal engagement trigger that "breaks like glass." This same poor pulling trigger will however have a detrimental effect on accuracy. If it hops, skips,

An old-style Remington 700 trigger with a bit of rust, awaiting replacement

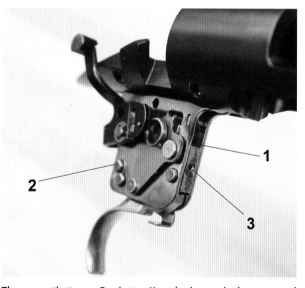

The new anti-attorney Remington X-mark trigger. 1 is the over travel screw, which you cannot adjust. 2 is the sear engagement screw that you cannot adjust without effort. 3 is the weight screw which is user adjustable.

and jumps before it releases, this causes shifts in aim and results in wider groups and just plain reduced precision. While these yucky triggers are perfectly suitable for plinking, basic target shooting, and close range hunting, they are not desirable for anything else, including self-defense.

Some guns, almost entirely bolt action rifles, do have triggers that can be adjusted to the user's taste. This type of trigger has evolved significantly since the early models back in the 1950s and '60s, or I should say, devolved. The early adjustable triggers worked very well and could give excellent-feeling trigger pulls, but the insane movement towards more and more litigation in this country has prompted manufacturer's to attempt to lawyer-proof the guns, which means triggers that are nowhere near as flexible as they used to be. In most cases now, you have to go to an aftermarket trigger manufacturer like Timney or Jard to get a trigger that you can fully adjust for sear engagement, a trait that many triggers have had lawyer-proofed out of them. Even if there is such an adjustment there, it is often taped or glued over with a statement to the effect that even looking at this screw will void the warrantee, like a giant sword of Damocles hanging overhead.

The truth is that a clean-breaking trigger of medium to low pull weight is a godsend for any firearm. Mushy triggers never quite break the same every time, and attempting to pull them in as slow and controlled a fashion as possible in order to get the best results only promotes frustration. A further truth is that few people, and this includes the majority of gun owners, have any idea what a good trigger is *supposed* to feel like, since the lawyer proofing has been going on for generations.

Before we go any further a statement must be made so that you are informed: Modifying your firearm in any way from the factory specification will void any warrantee which the manufacturer may offer on the firearm, especially and specifically when it has anything to do with the fire control. This is lawyer-proofing at its finest. Everyone does this, just be aware of it when you do. Because the only dude who leaves his guns alone is already dead.

A BRIEF HISTORY OF TRIGGERS

A brief history lesson of modern triggers is indicated here just to get a little perspective and understanding. The traditional bolt action rifle, upon which every modern bolt action rifle is based in some part, is the Mauser, specifically the models 95 through 98. The early triggers for these guns and their immediate descendants and competitors used what is known as a "direct action trigger" – a very long trigger hung beneath the receiver which used leverage to move the sear. The problem was that that leverage still required a very long trigger stem. The long stem required a very long trigger pull. What you then had was a long sometimes smooth trigger that was hardly what we today would consider "good."

Here is a very good analogy: Most everyone has used a manual water pump, at the grandparents' farm, or at the park. Why do you suppose there is such a long arm on the pump? Ob-

Old Mauser style direct action trigger from an Arisaka rifle. Pulls were long and heavy.

viously, a shorter arm would require more effort to pump the water. The arm is there to provide the leverage to operate a pump that requires a great deal of force. The downside is that you are pumping up and down literally the full height of your body, if you are a kid. The direct action trigger in the Mausers, and Springfields, and Arisakas and others operated with the same concept.

It was after WWII that the Mauser descendants like the Weatherbys and Winchesters, followed by the Remingtons and Savages, began to replace the old direct action trigger with a trigger assembly that allowed a much more refined interaction between the trigger, sear, and firing pin. This quickly led to the entire fire control assembly being contained inside a hous-

A Cooper trigger with a Void Warrantee if you look at this screw sticker over the sear engagement screw.

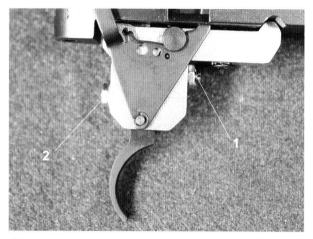

The Howa 1500 trigger. 1 is the weight adjustment with lock nut. 2 is the sear engagement with lock nut. Overtravel is fixed.

ing retained by a screw or a pin or two to the receiver, and this has been the formula ever since in regards to a bolt action trigger. Epitomizing this design is the original Remington 700 trigger, the Howa/Weatherby triggers, and virtually every available aftermarket trigger for bolt actions in the world.

Repeating rifles (other than bolt action rifles) have also evolved but not as much. The triggers on lever action guns tend to be changed very little from original examples back in the mid 1800s. Other than having some manual safeties or hammer blocks, transfer bars and that sort of thing added they are only a little different in form and function.

Pump-action guns and semi-automatics (which are little more than pumps that pump themselves) have to add parts to keep them from firing automatically when they cycle. Some pump shotguns back in the early to mid-20th century (I won't say which ones) would fire when you pumped the gun if you kept the trigger back. You could just hold the trigger and keep pumping. There are some potential safety issues in this, so that kind of thing is no longer done. Semis and pumps must have an apparatus that disengages the trigger until the bolt has been closed and the trigger has been released and thereby, the entire system reset.

Furthermore, the vast majority of semi-auto rifles and pumps use some version of a couple of trigger designs made by John Browning, or modification thereof. Basically, with minor modifications, we are still using the same fire control mechanisms as the very first semi-auto rifles made. Just with better metallurgy.

FIRE CONTROL AND WHAT IT INCLUDES

The "fire control" encompasses the parts that make the gun fire and the parts that keep the gun from firing. You can consider the trigger, sear, and hammer or striker if it has no hammer (and associated springs and such) as the things that make it fire. You can also consider the disconnector, manual safeties, firing pin safeties, and other assorted interlocks as the things that keep the gun from firing, though those may not necessarily be part of the fire control group. It should be noted that any of these parts can fail or break, so the admonition to keep your shaky Red Bull addled finger off the trigger until the instant you are ready to fire should be re-stressed.

The primary component of the fire control system is the shooter's behavior and brain.

Let's get into some specifics. What goes into the mechanics of a trigger, and why would you want to improve it?

Sear engagement

This is the amount of distance the sear travels before it releases the hammer or striker. This distance as it is being moved is often called "take-up" or "pre-travel." The longer this take-up is the poorer the quality of pull (exception: two stage trigger). The quality of the surface finish of the two parts is also of importance. A smooth surface feels better than a rougher surface. The average factory AR-15 trigger has a very long sear engagement and a rough one to boot. Sear engagement can be minimized to the point that the pre-travel is mostly eliminated which brings a

This hole is common on trigger housings allowing for the examination of the sear engagement.

The set screw poking out the back of this Volquartsen 10/22 trigger is for setting overtravel. Above that is the trigger return spring plunger.

Overtravel

Overtravel is the distance the trigger still moves after the sear has released the hammer, or if you want to think of it in this way, after the trigger breaks. A minimal amount is desired. The more overtravel you have the more the opportunity for that motion in concert with your finger to cause movement in the gun, right when the firing is occurring and the bullet is moving down the barrel. Consider it this way. When you throw a baseball to someone, you have to follow through with your throwing arm, or when you golf you have to have follow through with your club or the shot gets screwed up. Minimal overtravel helps your follow through to be smooth. Too little overtravel, i.e. none at all, will result in the gun not firing at all.

"glass breaking" feel, which is good, up to the point where the sear engagement will not hold reliably or at all, which is bad. A trigger that breaks cleanly at the same place and with the same effort every time, which does not break when it is jarred, is a good trigger that displays the best adjusted sear engagement.

Trigger pull weight

This is merely the amount of force required to pull the trigger, in the US measured in pounds and ounces. Depending on the gun, this weight can be altered by compressing the trigger weight spring (bolt actions), or changing the hammer spring (most semi-autos).

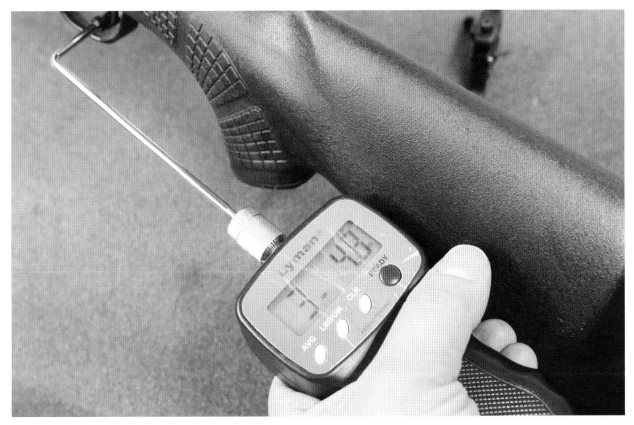

Checking the weight of the trigger with a Lyman electronic trigger pull gauge.

WHAT ARE THE PARTS?

Trigger – That thing you pull to make the gun go off. On real guns it's a lever in the bottom of the gun. On TV it's often a button on top of the gun. Stupid dumb Next Generation screwed up Star Trek that way too.

Hammer – The thing that hits the firing pin with force to set off the primer that sets off the powder in the case to send the bullet a-flyin'.

Sear – The thing that connects the trigger to the hammer. It is often just a part of the trigger piece itself, like on an AR, or a completely separate piece, like on a Remington 700.

Connector – Some guns have things that connect the trigger to the sear because of distance (Saiga shotguns) or the need for better leverage, or to use as a better, smoother, surface to engage the sear (Remington 700).

Disconnector – The most important part of a pump or semi-auto. The disconnector is the part that disengages the trigger so that the gun will not fire again until the trigger has been reset and pulled a second time. If this part breaks the gun could fire in an uncontrolled fashion, or refuse to fire at all.

Manual safety – This would be a safety device that blocks the movement of the hammer, trigger, or sear to prevent firing, that can be engaged or disengaged at will. Most firearms, though many do not, have one of these manual safeties. Examples would be the thumb and grip safeties on the 1911 pistol (thumb safety blocks sear, grip blocks trigger) or the safety switch on most bolt action rifles, which generally blocks the trigger or sear movement. Mauser safeties and those of some other bolt rifles completely disengage the firing pin from the sear by lifting it off. This would also include most safeties on lever action rifles like Marlins and Winchesters which prevent the hammer from impacting the firing pin.

Associated hardware – Every assembly needs stuff to hold it together like pins and screws, and to make the things move, like springs.

TRIGGER TYPE
Single-stage

The trigger's full weight is broken on trigger release with no intentional division into multiple stages. These triggers have short pulls with short resets, with all of the trigger weight being engaged and pulled against in one short action. The aftermarket triggers in this category have very nice trigger pulls, short, crisp, and with short resets. It should be mentioned that some training is recommended when using a high end single stage trigger. It is very common for someone who is not used to a trigger like this to finger bounce the trigger, making it look as if the gun malfunctioned and fired two rounds instead of one. It wasn't the trigger's fault that you pulled the super nice trigger twice.

Two-stage

This refers to a trigger that intentionally incorporates a long trigger pull that comprises the first stage, derived from the term "staging the trigger," or pulling it to a certain point after which it will break. The advantage is that you can load some, most, or very little of the total trigger pull weight to that first stage, depending on your preference. If you want a five pound trigger, but want the break to feel like two pounds, you set the trigger up so that the first stage, which is essentially a long sear engagement takes up three pounds of the total five pounds. Since you are already pulling the trigger most of the way, breaking the trigger for the remaining two pounds makes the entire trigger seem like a two pound trigger with a short, crisp break, like would be found on a single stage trigger. These triggers are often considered inherently safer, because of the long sear engagement, where well-tuned aftermarket single stage triggers generally have very short sear engagements.

Let's look at some examples of specific firearms and why you would want to upgrade your trigger or fire control assembly. Each example is an effort to personalize the firearm to the owner's own specific desires. This is not to say that the original parts are in any way defective. Indeed, we've already mentioned the lawyer-proofing that has become a necessity in today's gun industry.

REMINGTON 700 TRIGGER

The original 700 trigger was a very good example of a quality factory trigger. However, after several frivolous lawsuits and a major main stream media hit-job on the gun, Remington had to discontinue shipping that trigger and replaced it with the X-Mark trigger. I'm sorry to say that this model is not as user adjustable as the original and has been intentionally designed to make it difficult to adjust, in the form of adhesives and set screws with the sockets ground off. While you could adjust overtravel, it is set to a good place, and this is the screw that is ground off and glued so you can't adjust it. The sear engagement screw is buried and glued. Only the weight adjustment is

The old Remington trigger on the left and the new Timney trigger on the right. 1 is the overtravel screw, 2 is the sear engagement, and 3 is the pull weight. Both triggers have the same adjustments in the same locations. They are adjusted in the same order.

user changeable and this, nicely, from the outside, without having to remove the stock. Fortunately there are options for replacement.

What we are going to do is replace a factory 700 trigger, in this case a perfectly serviceable original, with a Timney model. Timney Triggers makes a wide variety of trigger upgrades for a great many rifles and shotguns, including guns you would not expect, like AKs and Mosin-Nagants. There is an assortment of triggers for Remington 700 rifles alone. Like the Remington trigger assembly, the Timney is housed inside a housing that contains the whole package, including safety arm. However, unlike the Remington model which is a bunch of parts pinned between two halves of a shell, the Timney unit is composed of a machined block into which the parts are housed. While there was in this case, nothing wrong with the old trigger, the gun it was hung under was mated to an Accuracy International Chassis System and the curve of the trigger

shoe did not sit low enough to shoot as comfortably as I would prefer. This particular Timney unit has a straight trigger shoe that hangs a little lower and further to the rear.

This is a perfect example of personalization. I am replacing the original, intact trigger with a very similar model from an aftermarket source that better suits my preference and the current form of the gun in question. As this rifle is a competition rifle the new trigger is set to its minimum, 1.5 pounds. Personally, I don't like super light triggers, and this low a weight should never be used for a hunting rifle or on a semi-automatic. It is, however, light enough with a crisp break that it is an asset when shooting at long ranges.

To install it, you press out the two trigger housing pins, the front one all the way, the back one most of the way (to hold in the bolt stop arm), pull the original trigger out, put the new trigger in the old one's place, and push

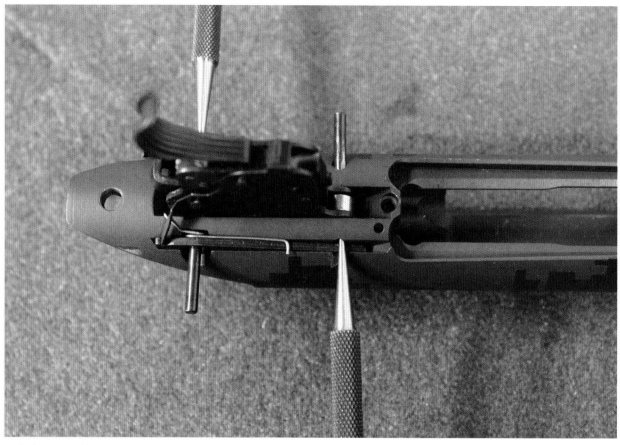

Push the pins out like this to easily remove the old trigger.

the pins back in. Reinsert or close the bolt, and proceed to adjust the settings accordingly.

As a general rule, you should set the overtravel screw on a trigger first, then the sear engagement if necessary, then the pull weight. If there is insufficient overtravel, the sear engagement cannot be set anyway. Since the sear engagement has an effect on the trigger pull weight it should be set before you start fiddling with the weight adjustment screw. Now, there are exceptions to this, but it is a good rule of thumb when it comes to adjusting trigger screws. When the trigger is fully set, make sure the screws will not back out of place from vibration. If this requires the addition of thread locking compound then so be it. Use low to medium strength, so that you can, with a little heat, get the screws out again, if necessary. Then make sure the manual safety works and that it blocks movement so that the trigger cannot be pulled when engaged, and so that the firing pin does not release when the safety is disengaged.

The new Timney trigger is flat shoed and very similar to the trigger it replaces. However, it is a true housing rather than a plate sandwich like the Rem trigger and has a safety that works differently inside.

A Nowlin trigger pull upgrade kit that includes everything but the trigger. The trigger itself has little to do with the pull, but the pull is rather determined by the interactions of the sear, disconnector, hammer, hammer spring, and sear spring.

1911 PISTOL TRIGGER

The 1911 comes in so many flavors, sizes, and with so many aftermarket parts that it is impossible to go over them all. The funny thing about most of the aftermarket trigger pull kits that are available for the 1911 is that few, if any, of them actually have triggers in them. The 1911 trigger is merely a means to move the sear. So these kits will contain the other parts like the sear, disconnector, hammer and hammer spring but not the trigger, and usually not the thumb safety either.

The science behind the 1911 trigger and making it nicer seems to have been settled. A number of fixtures have been designed to work on the fire control parts of the 1911 alone, certainly more than any other gun. The 1911 has shown itself to be not only an excellent combat and defensive pistol, but also a superb base upon which to build a competition pistol. Theoretically, the drop-in parts are going to feel better than the run of the mill parts that most major manufacturer's use, certainly better than

the lower end models and the parts that are on the original pistols from way back when. However, those parts will likely require just a hair of tweaking, not much, but a hair.

It's not my desire to get to deeply into the tweaking, but suffice it to say that with the drop in kits the sear/hammer interface will usually be pretty good. You will have to fit the thumb safety to the sear. There should be no sear movement with the safety on, and many of these nicer sears will be slightly oversized so that you can then fit the safety projection to the sear. When on "SAFE" this projection should sit right behind the sear with only a few thousandths of an inch of clearance, but there should be just that little bit. There should not be touching or the sear will be cammed against the hammer. You don't want that.

A fine balance must also be maintained between the trigger and sear tension. The multi-leaf sear spring also tensions the disconnector and the grip safety. The Clark Custom four leaf sear spring also has a separate leaf that

The thumb safety will always have to be checked and usually modified to fit the new sear. A very small amount of material would be removed at this point to adjust to the new oversized sear body.

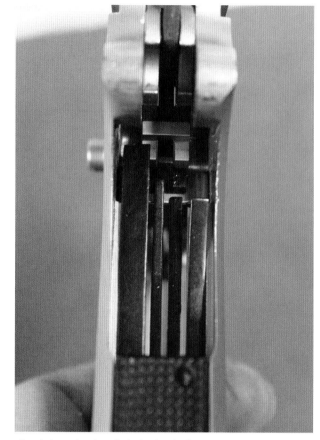

The Clarke spring installed. The first leaf on the left tensions the sear. The next one tensions the disconnector, the third tensions the trigger only, and the fourth tensions the grip safety.

The Clarke Custom four leaf sear spring which allows independent modification of the trigger reset, without fiddling with the sear or disconnector leaves. On the left is the standard three leaf sear spring.

regulates the trigger reset and is a very nice, inexpensive upgrade. Normally if you lighten the sear tension too much, you can compromise the reset, making it sluggish, slow, and light. The separate trigger return leaf allows you to set a vigorous trigger reset without it affecting the trigger pull more than a small amount, or having to make the actual trigger pull too heavy.

This isn't to say that you can't get a new trigger, just that they rarely come with the upgrade kits, but independently. Most have overtravel adjustment screws in them. These set screws are turned by using a small hex wrench stuck into the front of the trigger, and this screw then bears against the magazine catch to stop the trigger movement.

There are entire books dedicated to the 1911 specifically, some from Gun Digest, and I would direct the reader to those for more specific details on fitting these parts to a 1911. The Gun Digest book *Gunsmithing Pistols and Revolvers* book is a great place to start.

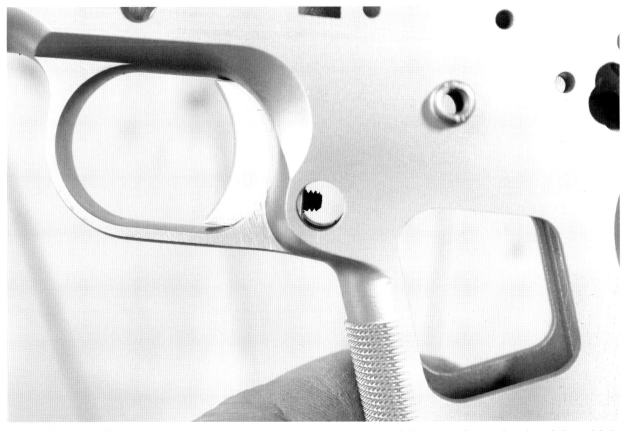

Over travel is regulated by a set screw in the trigger shoe that bears against the magazine catch. You can see the screw here through the catch hole.

AR-15 TRIGGER

Like the 1911, or even more so, is the AR series of rifles represented in the aftermarket. If the 1911 is America's pistol, then the AR-15 is America's rifle.

We'll start with the easy way. If you want a good trigger upgrade to your AR, that is virtually effortless and will be a major step up in trigger pull quality, then you can purchase one of a host of modular trigger units. All you do is remove the pistol grip so that you can get the safety out. Push out your hammer and trigger pins and remove first your hammer, then the safety, then the trigger and disconnector. Drop the "drop-in" modular trigger into the receiver and put the trigger and hammer pins back into their holes, or if the kit came with its own pins, install those pins instead. Slide the safety back into the receiver and reinstall the pistol grip. You are done. Except for adjusting the pull weight with a set screw, which only one or two modular triggers allow, you have finished the install. The modular triggers are easy and cost about the same to a bit more than most non-modular upgrades. The down-

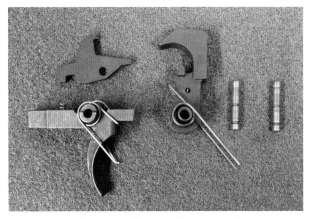

This is the standard trigger, hammer, disconnector of an AR-15 that comes in most factory rifles.

side is they are generally come-as-they-are and you can't do anything to adjust them. This is very intentional since most are excrutiatingly made to tight tolerances that the manufacturers can't have you messing about with.

There are a number of modular triggers on the market. Take out the crummy factory stuff, drop in the new trigger module, and put the pins in. These units generally provide a much improved trigger pull quality.

A JP Enterprises Match trigger with speed hammer. These are usually available with anti-walk pins as well.

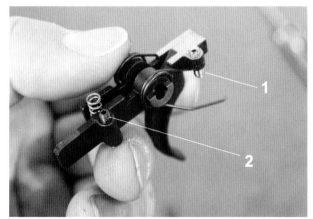

The JP match trigger. 1 is the overtravel screw and 2 is the sear engagement screw. This trigger has been copied and gives a high quality single stage trigger pull.

The Geissele High Speed Match Trigger. This fully adjustable two stage trigger is very popular and is designed for National Match competition use.

The less easy way, but with an even better result is to use one of the drop in trigger kits. Two great examples are the JP Enterprises Triggers, and the Geissele Automatics triggers. The JP kit is a single stage model with adjustable overtravel, sear engagement, and to some degree, the disconnector. With the trigger and hammer installed, the overtravel screw is set with high strength thread locking compound, like Loctite 271 or 263, then the sear engagement is set with the same thread locker. Then the disconnector is set so that its timing with the hammer is correct (buy the kit and see the instructions; not going to explain it here) with the same thread locker. The JP kit comes with a replacement adjustable safety that can then be set to be perfectly fitted to the trigger with minimal clearance and maximum safety. These adjustments are meant to be adjusted to optimal and then left alone, hence the high strength thread locker. Trigger pull weight is determined by the hammer and trigger return spring, and can be swapped out as desired for different weight springs.

The Geissele unit, a two stage model is installed very much like the JP kit, first the trigger then the hammer. As with the JP kit, it may be necessary to first remove the safety, but it depends on the receiver. Some will require it, others may allow the trigger to slide under the safety without having to remove it. Like the JP unit, it comes with its own replacement trigger and hammer pins. However, the adjustments on the Geissele trigger are not permanent and can be adjusted at any time. The overtravel, second stage engagement, and second stage weight can all be adjusted by screws.

Both of these triggers are very popular in the competitive market and both are very reliable and durable, long lasting trigger kits. Yet again, it really depends on your particular preference. There are single stage guys and there are two stage guys and nary will the two ever agree. I'm leaving out a great number of other models. They range in design from upgraded traditional factory model to way in the outfield redesigns that bear no resemblance to the rest.

RUGER 10/22

The 10/22 is one of the most commonly owned .22 rimfire rifles. It also has voluminous aftermarket support mostly in the form of barrels, stocks, and trigger assemblies. In a similar fashion to the AR, you can purchase "modular" trigger units that replace all the fire control parts, but in this case, the entire trigger guard unit and its attendant parts are removed and then replaced as an assembly. Units such as this are available from Jard, Timney, Volquartsen and others. Individual parts are provided by the same companies, but when the housing is available as an assembly, that is the best option. You will have to really like your 10/22 though since most of these upgrade kits approach or exceed the value of the unmodified rifle. Just the parts can run about half the rifle's value. I'm not trying to discourage buying the parts, I'm simply saying that with any accessory excursion, you will be spending money. To get good performance you will have to put down good money. You can make a 10/22 REALLY nice with these upgrades.

1 is the overtravel adjustment. 2 is the second stage pull weight, and 3 is the second stage engagement. First stage pull weight is determined by the hammer spring.

The 10/22 uses a trigger housing containing all the fire control components. There are upgrade kits that replace the individual components or the entire housing completely.

The Ruger 10/22 rifle is an extremely popular semi-automatic .22 rifle that retails for $200.

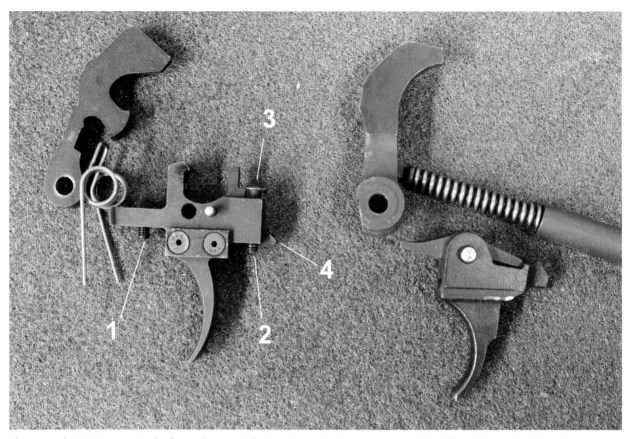

The new Jard FAL trigger next to the factory fire control that it replaces. The designs are completely different, but are both based on Browning designs, as are most triggers in existence. 1 is the overtravel screw, 2 is the sear engagement screw, 3 is the disconnector engagement screw, and 4 is the safety adjustment screw. They should be adjusted in the same order.

FN-FAL

I wanted to mention this one because to my knowledge there is only one enhanced offering for this rifle. You can get American made replacement original fire control parts to satisfy regulations from several sources. DS Arms is the most obvious place since they still manufacture the FAL rifle here in the U.S. In fact DS Arms and Entreprise Arms are about the only clear places to get brand new parts for these rifles.

The fire control I mentioned a few seconds ago is a match quality assembly from Jard Triggers. The original trigger arrangement of the FAL is ripped from the M1 Carbine and is virtually identical to that rifle's, but of course that rifle's trigger set up (and incidentally, the Ruger 10/22) was in turn ripped from the Winchester Model of 1905, designed by John Browning. You are going to find that most things in the rifle world will ultimately go back to Paul Mauser and John Browning. The Jard trigger deviates from the 1905 Browning design and instead goes to the other prominent Browning design largely seen first on the Auto-5 shotgun. This is commonly referred to as a "double hook" trigger. If you've seen triggers from an AK, M1 Garand, Auto-5, Benelli, or AR (two stage models) then you've seen one of these double hook triggers. The sear and disconnector are both attached to the trigger, the sear rigidly, and the disconnector sometimes so and other times is pivoting. The sear hook faces the rear, and the disconnector hook faces forward. The hammer has a projection that engages both the sear and disconnector.

This type of trigger can be single or two stage and the Jard unit is the former. I can't even begin to describe how much better the trigger pull is when you install the Jard unit over the original, and it is definitely one of the greatest improvements over an original trigger I have seen, and is a recommended upgrade if you have an FAL. So far they are only available from the manufacturer. However, the pull weight on this trigger can be quite light so care must be made not to finger bounce double the trigger.

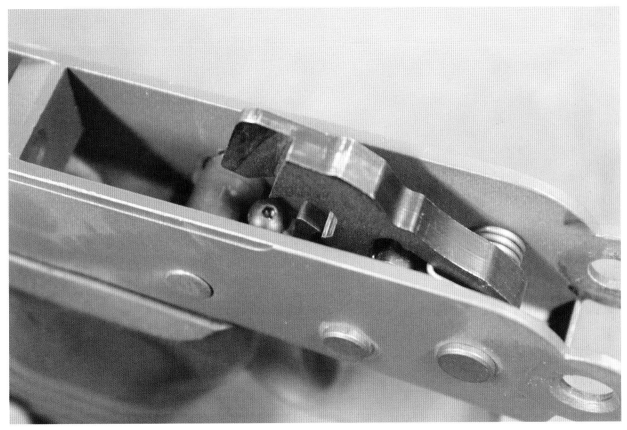

The Jard unit installed in the trigger housing of an Argentine FAL rifle build.

And make sure you set and then use thread locker on the screws as they will back out if you don't.

TRIGGER WEIGHTS AND APPLICATIONS

I'm not going to spend a lot of time on this and will just throw out some educated opinions on what constitutes an appropriate trigger weight on guns used for certain applications. I will state these in terms of minimums, since I've yet to meet anyone who really wanted to have a heavier trigger. Actually, that's not true. People who don't trust themselves to not pull the trigger on a gun without a manual safety when they are stressed out (this is a very reasonable rationale) often want a nice heavy trigger on their carry guns, but they still want a super slick quality feel to it. Glock owners are famous for this, particularly when the owner is a municipality like, say, New York City, where the department wanted insanely heavy triggers because the officers could not apparently be trusted to decaffeinate enough to not shoot people by accident. So Glock

complied and offered 8- and 12-pound trigger upgrades, called "New York triggers." Yuck. Okay, here we go. These numbers are my rule of thumb, and of course there will be exceptions, but those of you doing this stuff to your own guns should stick to the rule.

Pistols
- Recreational – 4 pounds
- Hunting – 4 pounds
- Carry gun, 1911 – 3-4 pounds
- Carry gun, Glock and other striker fired pistols – 5-6 pounds
- Carry gun, revolver – whatever the heck it started with
- Duty gun – whatever the heck it started with
- Competition, amateur – 3 pounds
- Competition, experienced – 1-2 pounds
- Competition, master – who cares/whatever you want, dude.

Rifles

- Recreational – 3-4 pounds
- Hunting – 3 pounds
- Carry gun – Really? I mean, really?
- Duty gun – 5-6 pounds
- Competition, amateur – 3-4 pounds
- Competition, experienced – 3-4 pounds
- Competition, master – who cares/whatever you want, dude.

Shotguns

- Recreational – 4-5 pounds
- Hunting – 4-5 pounds
- Carry gun – Uh, no.
- Duty gun – Are there any duty shotguns anymore? 5-6 pounds.
- Competition, amateur – 4 pounds
- Competition, experienced – 8 pounds. These guys have no muzzle discipline. At all.
- Competition, master – who cares/whatever you want dude.

I know I'm going to take lots of flak on this little section, but I've seen way too many people let off "accidental discharges" because they either had poor brain/trigger finger interfaces, waved their trap gun around like a ballerina with a ribbon stick, or had their triggers way too light for the application. Light trigger pulls require a good amount of practice to get used to. If you are a deer hunter and you come to me wanting a one-pound trigger I'm going to say no, and tell you that you are just going to get someone hurt when you drop it out of your stand. He'll say no he won't, I don't know what I'm talking about. I will then tell him don't let the door hit your butt on the way out. If someone comes in with a carry gun that has a trigger pull of ten pounds and ask for two pounds, I'm going to say "how about four?" When a guy who shoots a couple dozen matches a year ambles in asking me to drop his STI 2011 down to a pound, I'll say, "sure."

People have got to realize that the application matters and experience does also. Anything beyond swapping parts as I've mentioned in this chapter should be left to a gunsmith. If the trigger pull on the new stuff you dropped in is still gritty or jumpy, then don't worry, you didn't waste your money. But the gunsmith will have a much better understanding of how these things interact and he or she will be able to eke the most out of the parts in question.

CHAPTER 11

Traditionally, the changing of barrels on firearms has been a gunsmith-only job. Reasonably expensive tools are necessary for most cases and a thorough knowledge of the intricacies involved in the process is handy. The truth is that anyone can take a pipe wrench to a barrel and get it off, or get a new one on in the same fashion with the same tools, but the result is far from ideal. The surface finish will be ruined and there will be deep impressions from the wrench teeth in the surface of the barrel or receiver. To change a barrel on most bolt action rifles (Savages are notable exceptions) you need an action wrench specific to the receiver you are trying to remove, a barrel vise with the proper sized bushing to clamp the barrel (a hydraulic press is the preferred method), and a breaker bar to extend the reach and leverage of the action wrench's handle. This is still a gunsmith project. Most bolt action rifles, lever action rifles, and revolvers will still fall into this category.

There are increasing numbers of guns, mostly of European make, that are designed to have interchangeable barrels. Those rifles come with the instructions to do that. The CZ 455 is a great example. As are several of the Blaser rifles.

However, the great percentage of semi-auto pistols

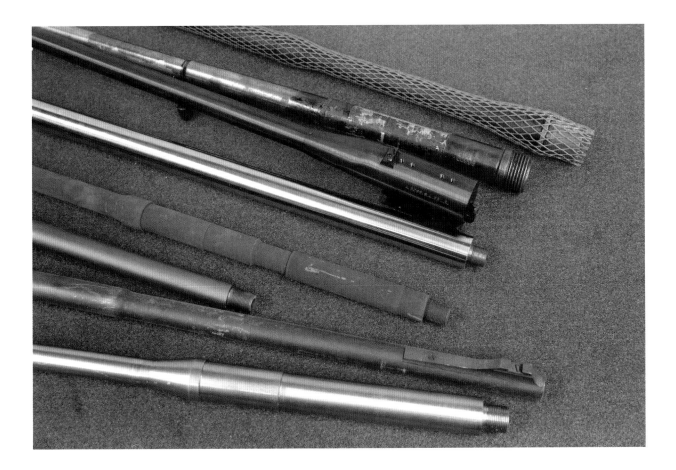

Changing barrels often requires action and barrel wrenches. Don't get into this unless you want to buy the tools.

tend to have drop in barrels that need little to no fitting at all. Glocks are a perfect example of this, with aftermarket barrels available from a number of sources. The pistols that need fitting tend to be the ones with the Browning style link mechanism on the bottom of the barrel. Those will always need minor fitting in the lug areas, but usually not much and it is still a project that can be done by the average gun owner with a little patience and reference to available sources in books and online.

Shotguns almost always have barrels that can be removed and reinstalled at will, and therefore will almost always have a selection of barrels available for it. Let's look at the Remington 870. Generally it will ship from the factory with one barrel, a standard smoothbore barrel of 26 inches that is most suitable for bird hunting and sporting clays. However you can easily buy a slug barrel for this gun which is still smoothbore, but is 20 inches long and has rifle sights mounted on it instead of the standard bead. This barrel is used for mainly deer hunting using rifled slugs (slugs that have grooves on them, since the bore has no rifling). Next, you can buy a rifled slug barrel that

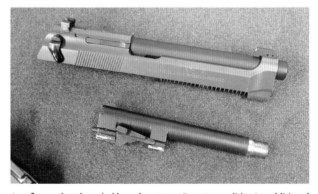

An aftermarket threaded barrel next to a Beretta 92 slide. An additional locking block and pin needed to be procured to place in the rear lug of the barrel.

has rifling in it, no sights, but has a cantilevered scope rail that extends from the chamber area of the barrel back and over the receiver, so that you can mount a traditional rifle type scope, though most users will get one of the low powered shotgun hunting scopes. Finally, you can get a "tactical" barrel that will be 18.5 inches long, smoothbore,

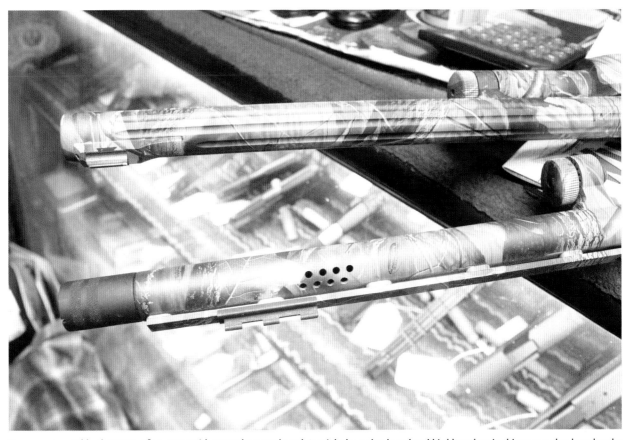

Some guns, notably shotguns, often come with more than one barrel. It might be a slug barrel and bird barrel, or in this case a slug barrel and a turkey barrel.

with no choke tube in it, just having a straight cylinder bore. This barrel is mounted onto the gun, maybe with an aftermarket magazine tube extension and placed in the closet, just in case the zombies have an outbreak. Most popular shotguns, be they pump or semi-auto, will have a similar selection of options to replace the original barrel if the owner so desires.

Certain rifles will also have user changeable barrels, or I should say semi-changeable barrels. You still have to have a couple specialty tools in order to do such a thing, but these tools or wrenches will run less than $100. The two most obvious and present examples are the Savage bolt action rifles (and others that copy this innovation), and the AR series of guns. Both types use a barrel nut to tighten the barrel to the receiver, but in different methods. We'll go over each in turn. About the only super easy barrel change in a rifle is the Ruger 10/22. Two screws and a clamp. That's it. And that's all I'm going to say about it. It's way too easy.

First we'll examine the whole barrel thing - what it is, why is it the way it is, why length or twist or velocity has meaning and impact in your life, and a few other little things.

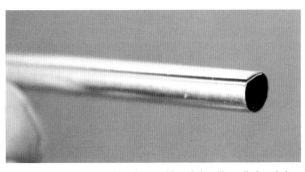

Early barrels were made like this acid brush handle, rolled and then forged. The handle is not forged, by the way.

THE BARREL

Early barrels, like on most matchlock and flintlock muskets, started out as a sheet of iron that was then pounded into a radius bottomed slot to curve it back upon itself. Then a mandrel, or rod of harder material was inserted and the sheet was hammered down onto that mandrel to create the bore. In the process, the edges of the sheet were hammer welded back onto each other to form the full barrel wall. The mandrel was used to ensure uniformity,

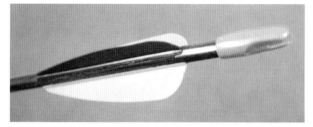

Arrow fletching or feathers are designed to spin the arrow and use drag to keep the tail behind the tip.

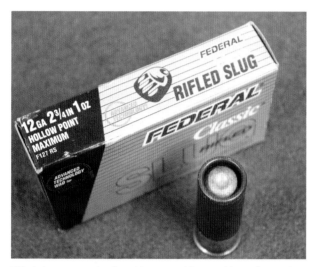

Rifled slugs are used to hunt big game with smoothbore shotgun barrels. They are inferior to standard slugs fired through rifled barrels.

straightness, and smoothness in the barrel. As technology improved, barrels began to be drilled out and later rifling was added.

Firing a bullet down a smoothbore will result in a bullet that, because of air resistance and imperfections and voids and such in the bullet, will not fly perfectly straight. After only a few yards, the bullet will usually veer off. Bullets need some kind of stabilization. There's a reason that they used to line up a thousand musketeers to shoot at the other thousand man line of musketeers twenty yards away. If they all fired together, they might hit something. It's the same concept with arrows. Why do arrows have feathers or fletching? Everybody knows why. To keep the arrow going in a straight line, to keep the tail directly behind the tip. Have you seen what happens to an arrow as the archer releases it? It compresses, flexes, and bends out of shape as the tip tries to catch up to the tail which is instantly going much faster than it is. The fletching, through the use of the air resistance, keeps the tail of the

arrow behind the tip, when the arrow really just wants to flip backwards from the stresses. Furthermore, that fletching is not perfectly straight, but has a slight helical pattern to it, which causes the arrow to spin as it flies through the air. This spinning is what causes the arrow to stabilize, fly true, and hit the target that the shooter was aiming for. Without the helical fletching, you would not be able to hit something past a few dozen yards with an arrow.

Some brilliant dude figured out that you could stabilize a bullet the same way in order to make it hit a target much further away than a bullet fired from a smooth bore could do. Of course you could put the helical "fletching" on the bullet, and that is what we do today with rifled shotgun slugs, but the better way is to put the helix in the bore itself. Then, the bullets can be simpler and cheaper to make and the helix can then bite into the bullet and form a good gas seal, maximizing the velocity and the spin stabilization. That's how we came up with "rifling" in a barrel and this technology remains today and probably forever.

BORE, LANDS, AND GROOVES

Rifling is divided into lands and grooves. The grooves are the valleys and form the outer diameter of the two diameters present inside a barrel. The lands form the inner diameter and are actually the remnant of the originally drilled bore. For example, a .308 Winchester rifle shoots bullets that are .308" in diameter. The barrel blank is initially drilled out to .300 inch, or eight thousandths of an inch smaller than the bullet, forming the barrel bore. Then somebody comes along and forms the grooves, buy forcing a tool down the barrel to either cut the grooves (cut and broach rifling) or swage pressing the grooves (button rifling). The grooves are cut to a diameter of .308 inch, the bullet size, and are generally much larger in surface area than the lands. When the bullet is fired through the barrel, the lands impress their shapes into the bullet and the bullet is then forced to follow the path of the lands and grooves down the barrel. When the bullet emerges from the muzzle, it is spinning just as fast as it was when it was in the barrel, and will continue to until it hits something downrange. It is important to note, that despite what you might have seen on the internet or heard from your drill sergeant, modern bullets do not expand into the rifling. The rifling compresses the bullet.

Modern rifled barrels are made by taking a steel rod, drilling a hole through it, and then cutting or swaging the

The deep rifling in a rifled shotgun barrel. "A" indicates the grooves and "B" indicates the lands.

A hammer forged barrel like this Glock barrel will sport rifling lands that are not square. The Glock rifling appears to be a shallow round ridge. Other hammer forged barrels may look polygonal.

The standard cut rifling in an FNS-9 barrel. The intersections between the lands and grooves are sharp and square.

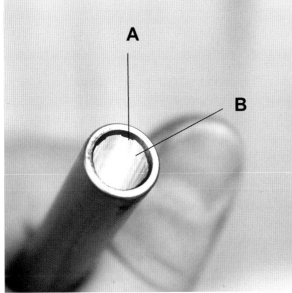

The shallow rifling in a pistol barrel. "A" indicates the lands, and "B" indicates the grooves. The land to groove ratio in this pistol is about 1:1. In most rifles, the ratio is more like 1:4 or higher.

rifling grooves into it. The exception is in hammer forged barrels which are still formed by hammering over a mandrel, however, the "rifling" is in negative form on the mandrel, and its shape is usually significantly different than rifling that is cut or swaged into the bore.

BARREL LENGTH AND TWIST OF RIFLING

Most folks believe that the longer the barrel, the more accurate it will be. That used to be true, and now it's only

These bullets require a fast twist of 1:7 to 1:10. In slower twist barrels like 1:12, the bullet will not stabilize.

If you get into reloading, you will want to watch your twist rates a little more closely than the average joe. You can really put a bummer on the whole reload.

half true. The accuracy of a rifle is much more dependent on the twist of the rifling (in relation to the bullet and its velocity) and the relative thickness of the barrel than it does the absolute length.

Depending on the manufacturer, a .308 Win. barrel may commonly have rifling that is anywhere from one twist in 12 inches to one twist in seven or eight inches, the average being one in 10 or 11 inches. What I mean by rifling twist or barrel twist is that the rifling will rotate a full 360o in the stated amount of inches. A 1:11 twist barrel will have rifling that makes a full rotation every 11 inches. So a 24-inch barrel, allowing for two inches of unrifled chamber, will spin a bullet twice over the remaining 22 inches of barrel length before the bullet leaves the muzzle. This will sufficiently stabilize most bullets fired from .308 barrels, those in the 110 to 170 grain range. If you want to shoot heavier bullets, you would want to get a faster twist barrel, say 1:10, which is also very common. Generally, and there are very few exceptions, heavier bullets are longer bullets. Longer bullets require a faster rifling twist to fully stabilize for the best accuracy. Therefore, a 180 grain .308 bullet will require a faster twist barrel than a 110 grain .308 bullet for best results.

The bullet is accelerating as it goes down the barrel and continues to do so until it leaves the muzzle. The longer the barrel is (within reason) the faster the bullet will be going when it leaves the muzzle. In a direct relationship to rifling, the faster the bullet is going, the faster the bullet will be spinning as it leaves the muzzle. A bullet that leaves the muzzle at 2000 feet per second will be spinning half as fast as a bullet leaving the same barrel at 4000 feet per second. Is this making sense? So the longer the barrel, the faster the spin, the better the bullet is stabilized, the more theoretically accurate that bullet and rifle combination will be. So longer barrels will theoretically be a little more accurate because the bullet will be travelling a few hundred feet per second faster and spinning slightly faster. In reality, with modern bullets and barrels, little effect is seen, except at quite long ranges. On older blackpowder guns, where the rifling was much slower and the bullets much more massive, the effect was certainly tangible.

Just like the arrow flexes when the archer released it, the barrel flexes because of the stresses imparted by the bullet traveling down the bore and the attendant recoil impulse. The barrel, in effect, vibrates. Thinner barrels really flex, and it is really amusing to watch a thin barreled gun, like an AK, in slow motion. The barrel whips around like you wouldn't believe. Most rifles designed for long range accuracy will sport a very thick barrel. This extra thickness is intended to make the barrel stiffer so the flex and vibration will have a minimized impact. The ideal barrel will be as thick as it is long, and will be long enough

The thick barrel on top is more accurate than the thin barrel below. It also happens to be a faster twist to shoot very heavy .22 rimfire bullets.

so that all the powder will be just barely fully consumed. This would result in a .308 barrel approximately 28-30 inches long and just as thick. Hardly practical. So we do what we can.

SWAPPING BARRELS ON THE THINGS YOU CAN SWAP THEM ON

So you see the mechanics of the barrel. Now how do we go about the practical application? Let's say you have a Savage Model 10 chambered in .308. You want use this deer gun but you want to be able to shoot 220 grain bullets from it, but the barrel you have doesn't do it very well. Let's also say you have a 1:11 twist barrel on that. If you want a new barrel, you don't just go online and order the first one you see. The problem may be a crummily made barrel, sure. It's more likely you simply don't have an adequately fast twist. 220 grain bullets are going to need a 1:10 or better twist to properly stabilize for best results. You are gaining nothing by buying a 1:12 twist barrel then are you?

Let's say that Model 10 was initially chambered in .223 Rem. and you like to shoot prairie dogs with it. You have been using 40 grain pinched nuclear warheads. The barrel is a 1:12 twist. This shoots those little death hornets like they were laser beams, but you've shot 20,000 rounds through the gun and the laser beam is not so precise anymore, and you want to rebarrel. You are going to want a barrel that duplicates the current barrel, just newer. What you do not want to do is purchase a barrel that has a 1:7 twist barrel that is designed to shoot 77 grain bullets. If you mount that barrel to your Model 10 action, and then go to the range you will be (rather coolly) disappointed. You will pull the trigger and see a diffuse gray puff of smoke when you fire. That puff of smoke is the super-fast twist spin-disintegrating that light-weight, thin-skinned 45 grain bullet. It literally flies apart as it leaves the barrel. And no, no part of the bullet will reach the target.

So, obviously you have to be picky when it comes to barrel replacement, so that the barrel fits the task you need. If you are a generalist, as most shooters and gun owners are, then pick something in the middle. There's no shame in asking a gunsmith what barrel you should get as a replacement, though it would then be good form to then have him install it, or at least buy the barrel from the gunsmith if you are going to install it yourself. Working on your own guns is something I encourage. It helps you learn how the gun works, what its little idiosyncracies and preferences are, and allows you to be more aware of how to fix things that are wrong, broken, or just not quite right. You aren't going to be able to do everything; that's what gunsmiths are for.

CHANGING A GLOCK BARREL

Field strip the slide like you normally would. Put new barrel in. Put gun back together. Function check that the barrel locks up and the slide fully closes. Take slide back off again. Check headspace, should be in the GO range. Check headspace with the extractor in by slipping the gauge up under the extractor and then by finger closing the barrel into the slide. If the barrel hood (chamber area) does not rise so that it is flush with the top of the slide, then the gauge did not pass. The GO gauge should fully seat in the chamber and the barrel should be flush with the slide. NOGO gauge should prevent barrel from rising to flush. If GO, reassemble gun and have fun. If GO doesn't drop, or if NOGO, return the barrel or go see a gunsmith.

CHANGING AN AR BARREL

 AR barrels are even easier, provided you have the tools. We'll assume that you are removing a 1:9 twist barrel and replacing it with an off the shelf 1:8 twist barrel. You are switching because you want to shoot 77 grain Sierra MatchKing bullets that don't stabilize in the 1:9 twist original barrel. You will need an AR-15 armorer's wrench, headspace gauges, and some form of receiver block. As far as a receiver block goes, there are several choices, two of which have been around for some time, and one that approaches the whole thing a little differently.

The first thing you should do is check that the chamber headspace is okay by removing the extractor from the bolt, and using the headspace gauges while the new barrel is still outside of the receiver. You can leave the ejector in the bolt face alone. Insert the GO gauge. If the bolt will turn fully in the extension with no effort, or by effort of your fingers only, things are good. Insert the NOGO gauge and do the same thing. If it turns, guess what? It's still okay. The ideal headspace for reliability in an AR is GO

plus .002 inch, which is the same thing as NOGO minus .001 inch. The gun is still safe to shoot even if the headspace goes a couple thousandths into the NOGO range, so don't freak out if the bolt closes on NOGO. Then insert a FIELD gauge. If the bolt closes and turns on the FIELD gauge, then you can go ahead and freak out. You need a new bolt and/or bolt barrel combination. This is very rare, as AR bolts and barrels are all made to a spec that tends to make the vast, vast majority of barrels and bolts compatible to measure in the GO range. The minimum headspace of GO plus zero is not recommended for the AR or for any self-loading firearm. If the bolt does not turn with the GO gauge inserted, then the chamber headspace is too short, and can be fixed by reaming the chamber a couple/three thousandths with a finish chamber reamer. Your gunsmith can do this. When you are done with this task, then reinstall the extractor to the bolt.

If you forgot to do this before you installed the barrel, reassemble the carrier assembly without the extractor, and gently push the bolt closed onto the gauges. The carrier will fully close on the GO gauge and there will be significant space between the carrier front and the receiver if the gauge does not drop.

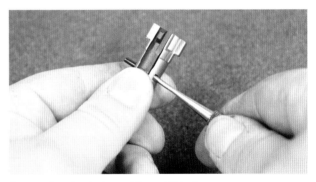

Remove the extractor by pushing out this pin.

Headspace should be determined, if possible, before the barrel is installed.

The GO gauge is in the chamber and the carrier is fully closed.

The NOGO gauge is in the chamber and the carrier is not fully closed.

The Brownells/Prairie River receiver vise block with flat top AR upper receiver.

The traditional types come in two flavors. The clamshell and the insert. The clamshell was originally designed for the upper receivers with the integral carry handle. It literally opens up like a book and wraps around the upper receiver (flat top receivers work too) and is then clamped tightly in a vise. A plastic bolt replacing insert is included to fill the gap, so to speak, and prevent the receiver from being crushed.

The second type is a literal insert, where a plastic block is inserted from the bottom of the receiver and two pins hold the receiver down, using the front pivot pin and rear takedown pin holes. Very simple, and then the block is clamped in the vise. This block and the first clamshell block are fine if you don't have to torque too much on the barrel nut. The clamshell lacks somewhat in rigidity and the block can flex, and the insert places a great deal of stress on the pin loops of the upper receiver, and suffers from the same lack of rigidity as the clamshell. Again, these models work well as long as you don't really have to crank on the barrel nut.

The third is an interesting concept. Rather than use a plastic insert or wraparound shell, JP Enterprises simply made replacement vise jaw pads that are cut out for the Picatinny to rail on one pad and both AR-15 and AR-15 front pivot lugs on the other pad, allowing the user to work on both small and large frame rifles. The receiver is held on its side with the jaws engaging the top and the bottom of the receiver, holding the receiver directly in the middle of the clamping force. The pads are soft anodized aluminum that will not mar the receiver. At this point, you simply loosen the barrel nut and take the barrel out. There is no need to insert a filler block into the receiver as the clamping force is being exerted along the receiver walls, rather than against the rounded radius on either side of the receiver.

The armorer's wrench is vital to this role. It has teeth or pins that interact with the teeth on the barrel nut. On standard barrel nuts, the nut itself is protected by a cover which holds the handguard halves in place. This cover should be pulled to the rear and the handguard pieces

The JP Enterprises Vise clamps perfectly fit the Picatinny rail of the flat top upper on one side and the front pivot pin lug on the other. It works for small and large frame ARs and is rock solid.

A standard AR barrel nut shown without the delta spring ring. The teeth fit into the slots in the wrench.

A factory upper carbine length 5.56 barrel is about to be replaced with a Ballistic Advantage 5.45x39mm Russian barrel.

removed. Use a magic marker to mark the tooth gap that the gas block went through into the receiver. The wrench can then engage the barrel nut and be loosened. (The gas tube and gas block must have been removed prior to this operation). The nut can then be removed off the front of the barrel and the barrel pulled out of the upper receiver. It's possible that heat may be necessarily applied to the receiver, as some companies think it's pretty cool to Loctite their barrels into their receivers. I do not concur, but it is a simple process to burn off the thread locker with propane heat and then pull out the barrel. If the barrel needs to be tapped out because it still is too tight, then a cleaning rod guide designed for ARs can be inserted and tapped upon to drive the barrel out.

Insert the new barrel. Reinstall the barrel nut to the same place and torque that it was before, using the tooth gap that you previously marked. This torque should be somewhere between 30 and 100 foot/pounds. If you aren't using the same nut, then you will have to consider that. Put the gas block back on, making sure the gas tube goes into the receiver straight, reinstall the handguard halves and enjoy.

Marking the current top.

Removing the nut.

Pulling the old barrel out.

Inserting the new barrel. This Ballistic Advantage barrel is fully Nitrided inside and out, and has an extension that is plated with Nickel-Boron Nitride. 5.45 tends to be somewhat corrosive and these barrel treatments will help deal with that.

THE IMPORTANCE OF THE MUZZLE CROWN

As briefly mentioned in the cleaning chapter, the uniformity of the muzzle crown is paramount. Any burr, ding, or gouge on the crown will immediately cause accuracy to suffer. Suppose you have shot sooooooo many rounds that the crown has built up a thick coat if residue on the barrel face. This is called a false crown. As long as that crown doesn't chip, remains uniform all the way around, you will be fine. But after you shot the 21,843rd round your accuracy went to heck in a fruit basket. That 21,843rd round actually chipped off a segment of that false crown.

By the way, this only happens on barrels that have muzzle brakes, compensators, and flash hiders on them. You can sped literally hours trying to get the rest of the gunk off with solvent or you can easily take a brass punch and simply chip the rest off. Be careful that you do not touch the rifling. Press down firmly at the outer edge of the false crown and it should just chip away. When the false crown is gone, clean the crown with a Q-tip and solvent.

Let's say that there is damage to your crown, like when you accidentally dropped your rifle out of the tree stand and it fell muzzle first onto the rock at the bottom

Dirty muzzle with false crown present.

Starting to remove the false crown.

The false crown has been completely removed. Only a dental pick was used (away from the crown/bore interface) and Q-tips with solvent.

This barrel crown has two heavy dings in it. It will have to be reamed, and possibly even cut and recrowned.

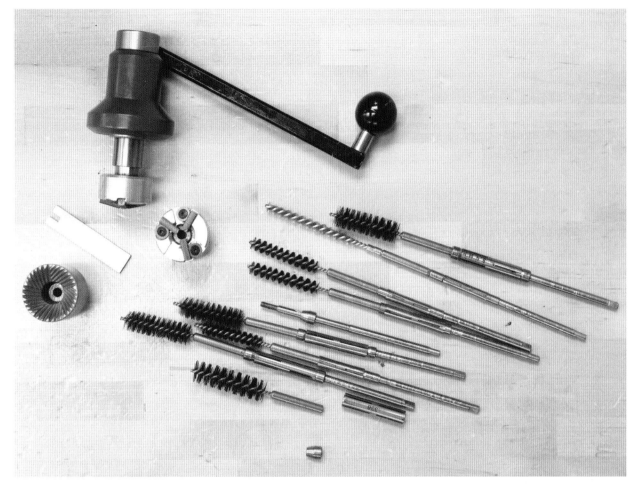

Dave Manson Precision Reamers has a hand crowning tool. It is expensive, but it will make a good crown in the absence of a lathe.

of the tree. You are going to have to take this to a gunsmith to fix. He is going to have a muzzle crowning kit that costs around $400 and he will fix up that muzzle for you. Your gun will be a good 1/16th inch shorter than before, but that's simply the way it has to be. Don't drop your gun out of the tree stand.

Okay, how about this? You want to make your barrel shorter by two inches. You can do what a lot of guys do and just take a hacksaw to it and then filing the muzzle flat. This works okay with shotguns, which are naturally imprecise anyway, but not much with a rifle or pistol. You might still hacksaw the tip off, but you will still need a

crowning set to get the crown back to shootable condition.

As much as I'd like to tell you that you can just go ahead and do it, I can't. The specialty tools here are completely necessary, and the knowledge to use them too. You'd be nutty to buy $400 dollars of tools to fix a little bang up on the barrel of a rifle that probably only cost you $500 in the first place. If it's a Savage or AR, you could buy a new barrel and the tools to install it for probably $200. Just take a ruined crown to a gunsmith and pay him the 50 or 60 bucks to fix it. Please remember that there are minimum legal barrel lengths. Rifles must have a barrel greater than

Hacksaw. Tacticooling shotguns since 1850.

A1 style AR-15 muzzle device, a flash hider. If you don't like it...

16 inches. Shotguns must have a barrel in excess of 18 inches. Go with 16 ¼ and 18 ½ respectively. Be sure to measure twice and cut once.

OTHER BARREL STUFF

Unfortunately, most barrel work requires expensive equipment. If you want a muzzle attachment, like a flash hider, muzzle brake, or sound suppressor, you will have to have the muzzle threaded. You need a lathe. Take it to the gunsmith.

You want to rechamber from 7mm-08 to .308. You can't. Unless you get a new barrel.

You want to rechamber from .308 to .30-06. You can, but you can't without a longer receiver. So I guess you can't.

You want to go from .270 Win. to .270 Ackley Improved. You need reamer and gauges. Take it to the gunsmith.

You want to add iron sights to the plain barrel. Okay, you could do that. You will need high strength solder, flux, MAPP gas at the least, some way to fixture the barreled action, and oh yeah, you'll need to refinish the entire gun because the process of soldering the front sight to the barrel will mess up the finish good. At this point, unless you are going to paint the gun, you should have just taken it to the gunsmith.

Replacing sights with different sight inserts? Go ahead and do it.

In the end, your options for accessorizing your barrels are fairly limited without a gunsmith shop full of tools. There is no problem doing stuff that

...then get one of these. In the middle is a JP Recoil Eliminator. Starting from the left is a JP TRE-9 9mm compensator, a JP Benny Cooley Tactical compensator, an Vltor flash hider, a Vais stainless steel .308 muzzle brake, an aluminum rimfire brake by Vais, and a YHM Phantom flash hider.

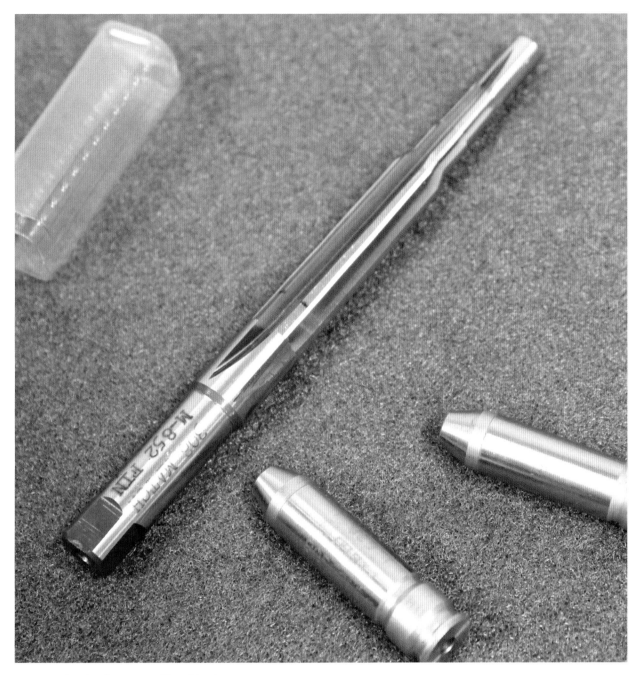

Manson M-852 chamber reamer with .308 headspace gauges.

most people do to barrels such as a spray on finish (next chapter), basic maintenance, certain swaps, and the most common thing – putting on a different muzzle attachment.

Keep in mind that if you shorten your barrel, or have it shortened by someone else, you will sacrifice some muzzle velocity in the form of 100-200 feet per second or more per inch. Shorter guns are definitely handier and lighter and better balanced, but is the trade-off worth it? Thinner barrels will generally be less accurate than thicker barrels because of less rigidity. Is the reduction of a few ounces worth a group opening up on paper, a loss of precision?

Only you can answer that question.

CHANGING A SAVAGE BARREL

Savage bolt action barrels are easy to change and it can easily be done by a non-gunsmith. You will need a bench vise with padded jaws or aluminum bushings that have been bored out to the size of the barrel's diameter at the chamber area. You can make these from a block of aluminum pretty easily or buy them from Brownells, along with the bench mounted barrel vise. You will also need headspace gauges for the caliber you are changing, let's say .223 Rem. to carry on the previous analogy. A Savage barrel nut wrench will also be necessary. That's about it for tools. You will want some anti-seize grease to put on the barrel threads but you can get that from an auto supply shop or you can use the choke tube lube you apply to your shotgun choke tube threads. Any of these things can be purchased from Brownells or MidwayUSA.

Use the vise and blocks to tightly secure the barrel. You will have to slide the wrench onto the barrel first. Then you gently and firmly loosen the barrel nut. It should not require a great deal of effort as this nut does not have to be heavily torqued in place. When the nut has been loosened, then unscrew the receiver from the barrel. It should be noted that the bolt should be in place in the receiver when you are breaking the nut loose, but it should be removed before you unscrew the receiver from the barrel.

Set the receiver and recoil lug down on the bench and remove the barrel nut. Take the old barrel out of the vise, and put the new barrel in the vise in the original's place. Put the wrench over the barrel. Then screw on the barrel nut. Place the recoil lug over the threads and then screw the receiver on most of the way.

Remove the extractor from the bolt before you put the bolt into the receiver and close the bolt down. Gently turn the receiver onto the barrel until it stops, then back it out a full turn. Insert the "GO" headspace gauge into the chamber. Close the bolt over headspace gauge and then tighten the receiver/barrel until it stops and feels like it is starting to snug. Lightly hand tighten the barrel nut against the receiver to lock the parts together. Open the bolt and remove the "GO" gauge, replacing it with the "NOGO" gauge.

The goal is to be able to close the bolt on the GO gauge, but not on the NOGO gauge. At this point, the NOGO gauge should not allow the bolt to close entirely. If that's the case, then take the bolt and gauge out and tighten down the barrel nut to the receiver with an "oomph." You don't need to crank on it. An oomph is enough. Reinstall the bolt and the gauges to double check that the GO and NOGO fit or do not fit respectively. Reinstall the extractor into the bolt and you should be done.

This is a quick and easy barrel replacement that anyone can do. It's possible that any writing on the barrel may not be "on the top" or exactly where it should be. If that's the case, then you will have to take the thing to a gunsmith to have him do it. If you care. Having the writing offset isn't that big a deal, more cosmetic. A lot of Savage replacement barrels will have no stamping on them for this reason, leaving it up to you to stamp the barrel after installation. You are legally required to stamp the barrel with the chambering.

CHAPTER 12

REFINISHING AT HOME

It used to be that if your firearm's finish was scratched, damaged, scuffed beyond your ability to endure, or you just didn't like it, you could have your local friendly gunsmith refinish the thing. You can still do that.

Or…you could do it yourself. You aren't going to be able to blue your gun at home. That still requires multiple very hot tanks and is a very expensive operation to do to just one gun. And it takes a while. And it's very expensive. You could parkerize, or phosphate your guns at home. All you really need is a stainless steel kettle, and thermometer, and some parkerizing solution. You simply heat the solution and keep it just below boiling, dip the parts for a few minutes and then rinse them off with cold water for a few minutes. Dunk the parts in oil and you are done. In most cases, the used solution can then be put into a sealed container and used again. Lauer Custom Weaponry has a kit to do just this. It comes with a dilutable container of parkerizing solution and a bottle of post-treatment

The Lauer Custom Weaponry zinc parkerizing kit. Parkerizing can be done on a standard kitchen oventop.

My daughter's T/C Hotshot. She really wanted purple hearts on pink background.

When you paint it, the paint actually intercalates into the pores and forms a better bond than if the surface finish was not there and you were just painting untreated metal. So for the internet zombies out there who like to blast off the parking and anodizing before you apply the spray on coat...stop it. It doesn't help.

In the last twenty years, we have in a way, gone full circle. Back in the day, guns used to be painted all the time with enamels (and often still are, DuraBake is an enamel) because it was easier and cheaper than blueing. Now we sort of do the same thing for two reasons.

The first reason is the same as before. To rust proof the gun and make it more resistant to environmental assaults. Steel can't rust if the oxygen and water can't get to it. Blueing is simply a controlled form of rust, begun and stopped at certain points so that it looks pretty and provides something of a protective finish. But that finish compares not to the modern spray on finishes. Whether it is DuraCoat, Cerakote, KG Guncote, Alumahyde, or whatever, the spray on finishes completely protect the metal from corrosion, and depending on the product, from a number of solvents and acids as well.

These coatings also vary in hardness, scratch and abrasion resistance, flexibility, and ease of application. So I'm going to go over in a fair amount of detail the two most commonly used gun industry specific spray on coatings, DuraCoat and Cerakote.

The second reason is purely cosmetic. Remember that this book is about personalizing and taking care of your guns. You want them to be unique and different from the other guy's. You may not consciously recognize this but it is indeed there. These coatings will allow the final touch, the icing, to be put on the cake to make it entirely yours. Yeah, Bob across the street might have the exact same model gun, down to the scope and rings, but his isn't purple and gray camouflaged. Is it?! These products come in so many colors it makes your head spin, and even then you can still mix those to make colors that don't come from the factory. In fact, I do a lot of this kind of refinishing as part of my business and at least a quarter of the paint jobs are done with special mixing involved. I do what I want.

If you want a flat green gun, entirely, down to the last pin, you can do that. If you want a Saddam Hussein Gold colored AK, you can do that. If you want purple hearts on a pink stock, you can do that. If you want a funky camo pattern, or a real camo pattern, you can do that.

Both of them...

solution, essentially a thin light weight water displacing oil. Your wife also needs to not be home when you do this. And don't use the kettle to cook with afterwards, either.

It turns out that parkerizing, especially the zinc phosphate variety, is the best surface treatment for the spray on finishes that we well be going over in this chapter. Anodizing on aluminum is also excellent as a substrate surface finish. This is because both are chemically bonded to the part, and are essentially a transformed outer skin. This skin is also quite porous, especially the parkerizing.

A MagPul OD Green AR. The upper and lower receivers along with the handguard are painted.

Both DuraCoat and Cerakote require essentially the same preparation to the metal parts. Get it out of your head that you can get a good result by painting the gun in assembly. You can't. If you want to Krylon-Kamo your gun in assembly then you go right ahead and to it. These are not that product and they require a full disassembly of the gun, followed by a complete degreasing of the parts that you are going to be painting.

For example. An AR needs to be completely take apart, down to the last pin, spring, and screw. Let's say you are only painting the handguard and the two receivers, and leaving the rest of the gun alone. These parts should be ideally immersed into some kind of degreaser, and at the very least hosed down with it, if you don't have enough for a bath. It should be left in the degreaser for at least several minutes. Good degreasers would be lacquer thinner or acetone. LCW (DuraCoat) offers a solvent called TruStrip that works real well. This stuff comes in containers and in aerosol cans.

When removed from the degreaser, let it evaporate

An immersion degreaser bucket is better than sprays. Dunk. Leave it. Swish it. Pull it and let the solvent evaporate.

If an immersion degreaser is not practical, then you can spray degrease with something like LCW's Trustrip.

from the parts. If you want anything masked, like receiver threads or the inside of the upper, then now is the time to do so. You may then want to preheat the part to see if more oil sweats out of the pores of the metal. If nothing happens then you are ready to paint. If oil seeps out, then repeat the degreasing procedure as necessary.

Most companies tell you to hang the parts by wire, but I hate doing that. It's clumsy and uncontrolled. An AR-15 upper receiver bore is one inch in diameter. Get a wood dowel that is one inch by 12-18 inches long. Run it all the way through the receiver so that one end sticks out the back of the receiver about an inch. Wrap masking tape around the receiver threads at the front where the barrel nut screws on, so that the tape is also wrapping the wooden dowel. You now have a very useful fixture that is easy to use, fully supports the part and when it is painted,

can simply be held in a bench vise until the paint is cured. If you are baking the part then you may have to hang it after all, or you could take a small piece of two-by-four board and drill a one-inch diameter hole in it and insert the fixture dowel into the hole like a peg. This can then be moved in and out of the oven, assuming the oven is tall enough. It may be necessary to shorten the dowel.

The lower receiver can be held in a similar fashion. Wrap enough tape around a one-inch dowel so that you can screw the taped end into the threads at the rear of the lower receiver. You don't need to get paint on these threads any more than the threads of the upper receiver, and no one will know the difference later.

Both DuraCoat and Cerakote are best applied with an HVLP gun. Most of you don't have one, nor will you want to buy a nice one, so you can get by with a good airbrush. It'll just take longer to paint the gun. Both products are binary, consisting of the base pigment and a hardener that is added just before the application of the product. Ratios are different but that is a semantic we don't need to cover. It is fun to note though, that more hardener makes a more glossy appearance in the coating when done, and less hardener makes a flatter appearance.

The pigment and the hardener are mixed in the airbrush jar and then applied to the parts. They will go on fairly wet looking if you are doing it right, but not too wet as you don't want to have to deal with runs. A good plan is to put on multiple thin coats. Enough coats are necessary to fully cover the original color of the work piece and give a solid uniform color to all the pieces of the gun. Both companies say that you want a coating that is a half thousandth to a full thousandth of an inch thick. Well if you are like me, you have no way of determining exactly what that is by eye. Just paint it fully and uniformly. It should look like the solid color you painted on, with no black or whatever showing through, but should not have that thick, soft, "painted on" appearance.

When application is complete, you can drop the residual paint in the wastebasket. It will dry and the solvents will evaporate. There is a limit to this. Don't dump a jar full of paint in the trash. But a tablespoon or two is okay. The airbrush can be disassembled and cleaned with acetone or lacquer thinner. It also doesn't hurt to spray the solvent through the brush for a second of two to make cleaning the nozzle easier.

Needless to say, you should have sufficient ventilation for a project like this. Don't do it in your basement. Do it in the garage, with both the front and back doors open. Wear

This is the way most application is done. It's clumsy, but it works.

The same concept of fixturing is used on the lower receiver. Use the design to your benefit. In this case, a ¼-28 bolt was glued to a ½-inch wood dowel. The bolt is screwed into the pistol grip screw hole.

The better way to apply surface treatments. Fixture it up. No matter the shape of the part, there is usually a way to fixture it.

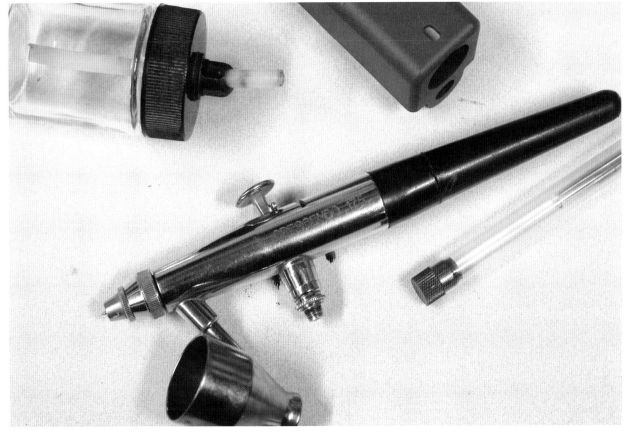

Badge Crescendo 175 airbrush. Not too expensive, but a very good airbrush kit.

A spray booth is a good thing to contain the overspray. This booth has two very good exhaust fans to evacuate the air.

If you decide to start painting guns you can get carried away in a hurry. Just warning you.

a respirator, and if you have a spray booth, even better.

DURACOAT

DuraCoat is the easier of the two to apply for several reasons. First is that you don't have to bake it. Standard DuraCoat will cure over a period of time at room temperature. After only a few minutes you can handle it. Do not f-ing play with it or reassemble it for at least a month. The cure time is fairly long, but it does cure, and it continues to harden for quite some time. If you can manage leaving it alone for a year, it will be extremely durable and tough, however the protection is still excellent after that first month. Put it in a closet and leave it there.

Secondly, the air from the airbrush or HVLP will flash off a great deal of solvent, so you can make an application pass, followed by a pass with just air, and keep doing this until the part is completely painted. If you do this in a slow and controlled fashion you need not stop, just fill in the spaces and uniform the thing with slow alternating passes of DuraCoat and air. You can do the same thing by putting it in an oven on low temperature, if you have a bunch of stuff to paint and want to make more efficient use of time. This property also makes it the easiest to create a camo pattern with. You can pump out a camouflaged

rifle in very short order with DuraCoat.

Third, DuraCoat is very tolerant of residual oils that you didn't quite get off. Also, and I found this out first-hand, if your air compressor is spitting oil or water out with the air, because your tank and filters hadn't been emptied in a while, you will see little fisheyes on the part. Just leave them alone until the stuff has flashed off. Let it sit for ten or twenty minutes. Then take a rag, or Q-tip and wipe it off. The DuraCoat literally will get under the oil spot or water. Wiping it will leave a slight blemish that you can then fix with a new coat.

Fourth, if you mess something up, like putting a finger print on the part, just to see if you could, you can just let the part flash off for ten or twenty minutes and then sand off the stupid fingerprint you left on the part and repaint over the fix. This cannot be done with any of the other products since you would have to finish the baking cure first. DuraCoat is very fixable. It is also very flexible and will deform with the part if the part is dented, rather than chipping, as long as you thoroughly degreased the part.

DuraCoat can be obtained in standard form and also in a form called SL that includes PTFE (Teflon) in the mix. This gives it some self-lubricating properties and greater point impact and abrasion resistance.

DuraCoat can be purchased in different sized containers, including paint cans. It is mixed with a hardener and sprayed.

CERAKOTE

Cerakote is very hard. It has ceramic particles in its matrix and this, when cured, forms a very abrasion resistant coating. Cerakote tends to go on thinner than DuraCoat, but with a denser deposition. It will look wet, but will flash off if you put it in the oven for a few minutes. The oven must be hot. Normal baking temp is 250 degrees F for two hours, though a slow, low heat cure can also be used for woods and plastics. You can, if you are good, apply Cerakote in one coat and bake it, but you have to be really good and have a good eye and good finger and hand/eye coordination with the airbrush. I still recommend applying a thin coat, baking it for five or ten minutes to flash off the shine, and then putting another coat on it, making sure that everything is uniformly covered.

Do not, under any circumstances, touch the painted part with anything whatsoever. It will look dry after ten or fifteen minutes in the oven but, it. Is. Not. You will then have to wait till the stuff is cured, and hope you can make a touch up. NIC Industries, the manufacturer of Cerakote, says not to even do that. Strip the paint and start over. If you got a dust mote or something, wait till the Cerakote is cured and out of the oven and cooled off. You will be able to flick that crap off the part, with likely little or no blemish remaining.

Cerakote's greatest advantage is abrasion resistance, and this makes it ideal for handguns that will see lots of holster wear. The down side to Cerakote is that it is the most expensive of the do-it-yourself spray on applications. For the most part this, and its hardness properties, has made it much more popular as an OEM finish for gun manufacturers, than for home application. Still a small 4-ounce bottle will paint three or four pistols and for 35 bucks, that ain't bad either.

Like DuraCoat, Cerakote is available in various sizes, with a significant savings per ounce in the larger size jars.

AEROSOL PRODUCTS

There are other quality spray on products that work well if you don't have an airbrush. Brownells has a great assortment. They offer Teflon/Moly paint, Alumahyde, DuraBake, and Gun-Kote, as well as the standard DuraCoat and Cerakote. All are superb finishes, some are baked and some are not, so you can use them on just about anything.

The aerosols generally require some preheating. You can do this in an oven or with a heat gun, like you would use when stripping paint. Do not use open flame like from a blowtorch or propane torch to preheat as they will leave residue and ash on the parts. The cans all have fanning nozzles so that you can easily make wide coverage passes, and if a nozzle clogs up, you can buy them by the dozen from Brownells as well. If you want to camouflage the gun with some funky pattern you saw online or on your father's brother's nephew's cousin's former roommate's gun, you can get stencils to do so.

We will conclude this book with sickeningly self-gratifying pictures of firearms that the author has refinished using some of these products. Have a nice day and make your gun your own!

Aerosols work well too but require baking and/or preheating. LCW makes DuraBake, an enamel, and Brownells offers their Teflon/Moly spray on coat. Both make a very good finish that requires no cure time.

Patterns can be added to guns by a good free-hand ability or by the use of stencils.

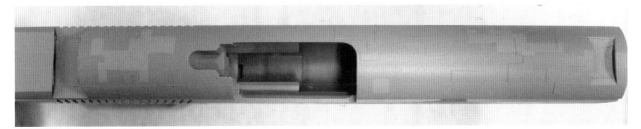

This slide has some stencils still on it, after two colors.

A piston upper using a JP tube and Adams Arms Piston upgrade. Cerakote Burned Bronze color.

AR home build with Spikes Tactical Havok flare launcher in Urban camo.

Long range competition rifle in AICS chassis. The plastics on these chassis are really greasy and require a great deal of preparation.

A SIGSAUER P239 with navy camo.

SIGSAUER 1911-22. The original paint on this gun was not impervious to gun solvent and required a different application later. It is now covered in OD Green DuraBake.

A DPMS free float tube with Tungsten Gray Cerakote.

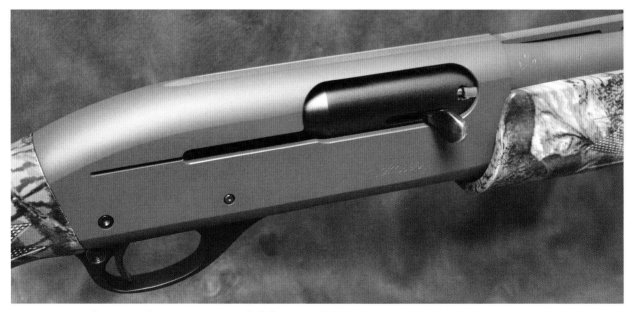

A Remington 1100 that is painted OD green Duracoat. The bolt is Matte Black DuraCoat.

APPENDIX 1

BUILDING YOUR OWN, LEGALLY

In a nutshell, if you want to build a semi-automatic firearm that would otherwise be illegal to import, you can't. Well, you can, but the penalties are stiff. However, you can build a firearm that is substantially manufactured or entirely in the US that might resemble a firearm prohibited from importation. This is commonly referred to as the 922(r) rule. For example, I cannot import or contruct from imported parts an AK-47, even if it is just a semi-automatic and not a machinegun. However, I can build one from US made parts. Furthermore, I can use some foreign manufactured parts as long as those parts don't exceed a certain quantity. That quantity is 10. No more than 10 foreign made parts can be included on that gun. Those parts are on a list of 20 specified items. These are major components, not screws or pins or crap like that. The AK series of rifles contains 16 of those parts. As long as I use at least six US made parts from that list (better safe than sorry, use more) I can build that AK. Why does this matter in a book on accessorizing?

If you decide to switch out that handguard, it might have to be US made or you may no longer be in compliance. If you want to use surplus imported magazines, you better have the necessary parts count in the gun itself or the use of the magazine (three parts) could put you over the ten maximum. Newer gun owners probably won't run into this issue until they become gun nuts like me, but there are a great many gun nuts like me that don't even know about this part of the US Code, or don't care. You need to. It's an easy law to follow and honestly, the US parts are frequently so much superior to the originals that it is hard to even comprehend making use of the old stuff anyway when better options are around to replace it.

Here is the list. Remember, there can be no more than ten of these parts that were made outside of the US on your foreign-inspired semi-auto firearm. You will run into guns on which you will simply not be able to legally install a muzzle brake (common upgrade).

1. Frames, receivers, receiver castings, forgings or stampings
2. Barrels
3. Barrel extensions
4. Mounting blocks or trunions
5. Muzzle attachments
6. Bolts
7. Bolt Carriers
8. Operating rods
9. Gas pistons
10. Trigger housings
11. Triggers
12. Hammers
13. Sears
14. Disconnectors
15. Buttstocks
16. Pistol Grips
17. Forearms, handguards
18. Magazine bodies
19. Magazine followers
20. Magazine floorplates

APPENDIX 2

PARTS RESOURCES

Virtually everything that was used in this book can be purchased from Brownells. Also, many local stores will carry at least some of the items that were examined in the previous chapters. I strongly recommend that you seek these things from your local establishments before looking elsewhere, simply because that is the polite and courteous, locally supportive thing to do. However, I list here a number of great online sources, should you not have access to a local shop, or yours is unable to fulfill your requests. This list is far from exhaustive...

Brownells...www.brownells.com
MidwayUSA..www.midwayusa.com
SWFA..www.riflescopes.com
Optics Planet ....www.opticsplanet.com
JP Enterprises..www.jprifles.com
Lauer Custom Weaponry (DuraCoat)..www.lauerweaponry.com
NIC Industries (Cerakote) ....www.cerakoteguncoatings.com
Timney Triggers..www.timneytriggers.com
Jard Triggers ....www.jardtriggers.com
Browning Arms Company...www.browning.com
Remington ....www.remington.com
Gun Digest Books ....www.gundigest.com

ENTER TO WIN

NEW PRIZES BEING ADDED ALL THE TIME!

HIGH CALIBER
SWEEPSTAKES

www.GunDigest.com

ENTER ONLINE TO WIN! CHECK BACK OFTEN!

NO PURCHASE NECESSARY TO ENTER OR WIN
Open only to legal residents of the United States and the District of Columbia age 18 years or older.
However, because of state regulations, this sweepstakes is not open to residents of Rhode Island.
All firearm transfers will be conducted in strict compliance with all applicable federal, state and local laws.
Limit: One online entry per person.